Militant Jihadism
Today and Tomorrow

CURRENT ISSUES IN ISLAM

Editiorial Board

Baderin, Mashood, *SOAS, University of London*
Fadil, Nadia, *KU Leuven*
Goddeeris, Idesbald, *KU Leuven*
Hashemi, Nader, *University of Denver*
Leman, Johan, *GCIS, emeritus, KU Leuven*
Nicaise, Ides, *KU Leuven*
Pang, Ching Lin, *University of Antwerp, and KU Leuven*
Platti, Emilio, *emeritus, KU Leuven*
Tayob, Abdulkader, *University of Cape Town*
Stallaert, Christiane, *University of Antwerp, and KU Leuven*
Toğuşlu, Erkan, *GCIS, KU Leuven*
Zemni, Sami, *Universiteit Gent*

Militant Jihadism

Today and Tomorrow

Edited by

Serafettin Pektas & Johan Leman

LEUVEN UNIVERSITY PRESS

Published with the support of the
KU Leuven Fund for Fair Open Access

Published in 2019 by Leuven University Press / Presses Universitaires de Louvain / Universitaire Pers Leuven. Minderbroedersstraat 4, B-3000 Leuven (Belgium).

Selection and editorial matter © Serafettin Pektas & Johan Leman, 2019
Individual chapters © The respective authors, 2019

This book is published under a Creative Commons Attribution Non-Commercial Non-Derivative 4.0 Licence.

The license allows you to share, copy, distribute and transmit the work for personal and non-Commercial use providing author and publisher attribution is clearly stated. Attribution should include the following information:

Pektas, S and Leman J. 2019. *Militant Jihadism: Today and Tomorrow*. Leuven, Leuven University Press. (CC BY-NC-ND 4.0)

Further details about Creative Commons licenses are available at http://creativecommons.org/licenses/

ISBN 978 94 6270 199 1 (Paperback)
ISBN 978 94 6166 302 3 (ePDF)
ISBN 978 94 6166 303 0 (ePUB)
https://doi.org/10.11116/9789461663023

D / 2019/ 1869 /39
NUR: 741

Layout: Coco Bookmedia
Cover design: Paul Verrept

Contents

Note on translation and transliteration   7

Introduction   9
Johan Leman & Serafettin Pektas

1. Salafism, Jihadism and Radicalisation: Between A Common Doctrinal Heritage and The Logics of Empowerment   19
   Mohamed-Ali Adraoui

2. The Libyan Jihadist Outlook: Origins, Evolutions and Future Scenarios   41
   Arturo Varvelli

3. The "Unreturned": Dealing with the Foreign Fighters and Their Families who Remain in Syria and Iraq   59
   Nadim Houry

4. Cyber Jihadism: Today and Tomorrow   83
   Laith Alkhouri

5. The Role of Women in Post-IS Jihadist Transformation and in Countering Extremism   101
   Anita Perešin

6. The More Things Change, The More They Stay the Same: The Post-Caliphate Jihadist *Modus Operandi* in Europe   123
   Teun van Dongen

7.	Jihadists in Belgian Prisons *Johan Leman*	141
8.	Urban Terrorist Sanctuaries in Europe: The Case of Molenbeek *Adolfo Gatti*	151
9.	Migrant Smuggling Networks and Jihadist Terrorism *Johan Leman & Stef Janssens*	177
10.	Prospects for Counter-Theology against Militant Jihadism *Serafettin Pektas*	187
	Concluding Considerations *Johan Leman & Serafettin Pektas*	217
	About the Authors	229

Note on Translation and Transliteration

The chapters in this volume examine cases from different countries; they hence include sources from different languages. Non-English sources are translated by the authors themselves if not otherwise stated. This volume is written to address a general audience and not only experts; therefore Arabic words are transliterated without diacritics. The Arabic names of people, who are/were citizens or resident in Europe, are not transliterated but instead left as they appear in the official documents of the country in question. Similarly, some Arabic names of cities and places are left as they appear in English.

Introduction

Johan Leman and Serafettin Pektas

In Western Europe, most countries have been deeply affected by the recent surge in militant jihadism and have been the scene of various terrorist attacks. Every single violent incident, irrespective of the size of its impact, has received broad media attention and reignited and intensified the debate on Islam, among both non-Muslims and Muslims.

In the UK, intelligence services estimate that the UK is still home to 23,000 jihadist extremists, among whom 3,000 are judged to pose a threat and 20,000 to be a "residual risk". At least 850 left the UK for Syria and Iraq (O'Neill et al., 2017). In France, UCLAT (The Unit of Coordination in the Fight Against Terrorism) informs us that there are 11,400 jihadist extremists, among whom 25% are women and 16% minors; 1,800 left for Syria (Dell'Oro, 2015). Also other Western European countries, such as Belgium, Spain, Germany, have a considerable number of jihadist terrorists and sympathisers among their nationals.

But even on continents and in societies where one would least expect it, jihadism may be present. In Latin America, a very small country like Trinidad and Tobago, home to only 1,3000,000 inhabitants, saw more than 100 young citizens leave for Syria (Graham-Harrison and Surtees, 2018). Jihadism encompasses a very complex amalgam of people and is itself the result of a myriad of motivations and situations. However, we should remain aware that even if these figures are at first view quite high, we are speaking about 1.6 billion Muslims worldwide (Lipka, 2015:2) and active jihadist extremists among them represent a very small percentage.

At the moment that we are writing this Introduction, there is clearly a territorial decline of the so-called Caliphate of the "Islamic State" (IS). But it does not necessarily herald the defeat of either the militant Islamist organisations or the ideology they represent. Both remain present in Iraq and Syria. Many experts (e.g. Orsini, 2018) and observers (e.g. Europol, 2018) highlight that in what seems to be becoming the post-IS period, various militant groups will remain involved in violent attacks and continue to be a threat to global security. IS jihadism is, for instance, currently active in the northern Sinai, in Libya, in West Africa, in South Asia, and al-Qaeda jihadism controls parts of Somalia.

Many observers suggest that a transformation is likely to happen. The character, place and strategy of transnational Islamic violent extremism will change, yet not disappear in the next few years. Jihadists will try to employ enhanced and updated tactics in implementing their strategies of organisation, operation, mobilisation and recruitment. Rather than mass mobilisation in a particular territory, they will probably prioritise network building in different countries in order to control small networks of dedicated affiliates from Europe to South Asia. Concurrently, new kinds of ideals, symbols, theological sources, mobilisation, communication techniques and recruitment practices will be generated and put forward. The evolution of global militant Islamism since the Soviet-Afghan war of the 1980s indicates that jihadist groups are deliberate in maintaining a rational and long-term struggle. They are not driven by a sense of urgency and are thus able to constantly modernise themselves and adapt to changing conditions. One may therefore expect them to follow a similar rational and adaptive *modus operandi* in the future. We should, however, note that today's globalised world is fundamentally different from that of the 1980s. To understand how jihadism is renewing itself today, it is thus critical to consider the dynamics of globalisation. More concretely this means that among the unfolding jihadist strategies, we will probably witness increasing glocalisation, a more widespread use of cyber tools, and an enhanced exploitation of migration moves.

This book will explore various parameters of the prospective transformation of jihadist militancy. Its focus will accordingly be on the future of militant jihadism and not on its history or past developments, areas of inquiry dominating current research. The book aims to find answers to such questions as the following: what is next after IS? How will the jihadist landscape change, particularly in and around Europe, both in rural and urban settings? What does the case of Libya – arguably the most probable candidate for a new jihadist centre after Syria and Iraq – tell us about how the jihadist networks will be reshaped? How about those who are stuck or detained in conflict zones and those who are "unreturned"? How will jihadism work, particularly in cyber space? What will be the role of women both in jihadist circles and in countering violent extremism? What are the challenges and opportunities with regard to the "returned foreign fighters" in Europe? What are the challenges regarding the role prisons in the West play with respect to radicalisation and de-radicalisation? How will jihadism try to organise itself physically in Europe? How may it finance itself? Given that theology does matter in Islamic extremism, what would be the (new) elements to exploit from Islamic theology in reorganising the jihadist movement? How would the Muslim critiques of jihadist ideology affect Islamist militancy? What would their counter-theological strategies look like?

In answering these questions, the first three chapters look outside Europe. The first chapter is more conceptual. Mohamed-Ali Adraoui reflects on the common doctrinal heritage between Salafism and Jihadism and observes an increasing conceptual and strategic divergence between the two. He argues that the latter also evolves from a conversion-processed gradual jihadism into an instant jihadism. Some five years ago, it was an aggressive *takfiri* (excommunicatory) branch of Salafism that pushed some people to violent jihadism. This is currently changing. One no longer needs the ideological support to turn to violence. Adraoui develops the idea that jihadism as the ideologisation of Salafism has shifted to an instant aversion to society. The observations made by therapists and counsellors throughout European prisons support this notion, as chapter seven will expose.

The fact that this volume opens with a chapter on Islam does not mean that we propose to examine the future developments in jihadism with a frame that is principally biased or only understandable by religion. Militant jihadism is the result of a conglomerate of religious, geopolitical, societal, social and personal factors. The impact of religion cannot be denied. We are, however, conscious that geopolitical causes are perhaps more important than religious ones. Religion gives a typical coloration and complementary motivation to young jihadists to take action. It is our conviction that the future developments of the geopolitical tensions around Europe will be crucial for the evolution of jihadism in the West. This is why the second chapter in the volume is dedicated to a political and geopolitical analysis.

We already know that some former IS members are at large in desert areas of Syria and Iraq. There are signals that in Iraq, particularly in the Basra region, jihadism is again gaining influence. Some jihadist leaders left for Afghanistan, others went to North and West Africa, South or South-East Asia, or the Caucasus. In these respective regions they join active jihadist fighters among the locals. Furthermore, some Central Asian countries already provide fertile grounds for local IS cells. For instance, among 8,717 jihadists who are believed to have left former Soviet Republics for the Levant over the last few years, 1,500 are from Uzbekistan only (Barrett, 2017:11).

Libya is of particular significance at this point, and in Chapter 2 Arturo Varvelli explains how jihadist networks develop in that country. Libya has recently been a critical destination for the jihadist militants escaping from Iraq and Syria. It has, in fact, always been an attractive country both for al-Qaeda and for IS. Its attraction is not without reason: the availability of lucrative natural resources, isolated areas suitable for training camps, the lack of effective state and governmental authority, opportunities for migrant smuggling and its strategic position vis-à-vis Europe. Due to its "failing state" structure, it is a "safe haven" for insiders and a "blind spot" for outsiders. Some regions in Libya will probably remain like that for some time, even if creating a new common government were at one point to succeed. In the light of these and other (geo) political dynamics, Varvelli provides an analysis of the most recent situation of militant jihadism in Libya and makes projections for the future.

The geopolitical context for the future of violent jihadism evidently cannot be limited to Libya. Both al-Qaeda and IS are clearly searching for new possible countries where the dream of a new caliphate may be realised. Also other potential candidate regions would have effectively illustrated how the geopolitical framing may complement the religious one. Nevertheless, the case of Libya is relatively less studied and poses a more imminent threat to Europe over the medium term. Furthermore, Syria and Iraq, which will still be critical for future jihadism in Europe, are not absent from our analysis. The third chapter by Nadim Houry discusses the situation in Syria and Iraq, focusing on the "unreturned" foreign fighters and their families who remain there.

Nadim Houry refers to sources that estimate that around 40,000 to 41,490 foreigners have come to Syria and Iraq over the recent years (75% men, 13% women and 12% children), of whom 7,000 died on the battlefield and 7,366 returned to their country of provenance, while 5,400 others are currently detained by Kurdish forces or by Turkey in Syria and about 7,500 are in Iraqi prisons. Among these are approximately 5,300 residents of the European Union who left to join jihadists in the region and are accompanied by around 1,000 children. They were outnumbered, however, by locals. In 2015, IS had some 125,000 soldiers at its disposal, of whom around 80,000 were locals and around 45,000 were foreigners. In July 2017, General Raymond Thomas, head of the US Special Operations, said he thought that 60,000 to 70,000 IS followers were killed during the international campaign against IS, among whom 7,000 were foreigners. These figures suggest that in Syria some 20,000 foreign IS sympathisers (men, women or children) are still alive next to the local IS sympathisers. Some 1,400 of them are estimated to be the children of jihadists there. There may be a total potential of around 50,000 jihadist fighters still present in Iraq. These figures are obviously approximate, yet their lack of precision is no cause for them to be neglected. Nadim Houry frequently visits the region and is locally working with many of these former foreign fighters and their family members in the camps or prisons there. He is personally well aware of the current situation. In the third chapter, he gives a detailed analysis of the "unreturned" jihadist fighters and their families in Iraq and Northern Syria. He particularly calls attention to the challenges from the human rights perspective and reflects on what may become their future considering that these challenges potentially pose another set of threats to the stability of the region as well as to the whole world.

After these reflections on the dynamics that take place around Europe, the next three chapters in our volume discuss global trends that directly affect Europe. Laith Alkhouri analyses the jihadist use of cyberspace and projects what is to be expected concerning future cyber jihadism, while Anita Perešin examines the role of women in post-IS jihadist transformation. Teun van Dongen, on the other hand, explores the possible future careers of (returned) foreign fighters and shares his observations with respect to the future jihadist *modus operandi* in Europe.

Cyber security expert Laith Alkhouri, who on a daily basis follows the probable developments of cyber technology in the hands of jihadism, presents his findings in Chapter 4. In his view, one should not overestimate the personal capacities of the jihadists in creating new cyber tools. He does, however, warn that they may increase their cyber skills through hiring more professional non-jihadist cybercriminals and hackers or buying their know-how. Jihadist leadership has clearly understood that the future of jihadism will depend a lot on their use of the most leading-edge technology that allows them to outpace the experts and intelligence people following them. One may expect them to be most interested by the use of drones and the development of communication strategies that facilitate the exchange of digital messages in the most clandestine way possible. There are also signals that they may be preoccupied by producing simple biological weapons whose production can be learned by social media. A recent Europol report (2018) identifies so-called "lone wolves", online propaganda, improvised explosive devices and weapons that do not require much preparation as the most likely future sources of jihadist threats. All are related to cyber technology in one way or another. Alkhouri (and partly van Dongen) reflects on how jihadism may take advantage of the cyber technology for jihadist terrorist purposes.

Militant jihadism has often manifested itself as a male business, yet the presence of women proves to be no less important. IS's women's section *al-Khansa'* is in that sense an example. The women this section consisted of took on a policing role within IS's "Caliphate", controlling how women dressed or if they had permission to walk on the streets. Nevertheless, after the defeat in Raqqa, another possibility for a new role seems to have emerged. Instead of being used for surveillance, this time the role of jihadist women is more directly associated with the world of the fighters. This leads to important debates among jihadists about the position of women: whether or not the new more active roles for women can be accepted in the traditional conservative views hitherto endorsed by the jihadists on the role of women in Islam. The question of women jihadists also poses new questions for the authorities in Europe, especially about the future role of returning members of *al-Khansa'*. In Chapter 5, Anita Perešin analyses this complex issue. She develops the idea of a possible feminisation of jihad, and what may even be the role of women in raising their children as future jihadists. Perešin, on the other hand, examines the possible and critical contribution of women in countering jihadist terrorism.

In Chapter 6, Teun van Dongen discusses what may become the *modus operandi* of future jihadist terrorist attacks in Europe. His analysis takes the "returnees" as a starting point and explores the possible career paths of foreign fighters after the territorial decline of the IS Caliphate. The debates on "lone wolves" and cyber possibilities are also part of his reflections. He suggests that in pondering upon the future jihadist *modus operandi* in Europe it is better to develop more realistic assessments rather than assume that the worst case scenario is the most plausible one.

We are aware that a good analysis of whether (and how) Emni is still functioning would have been interesting in the context of this study. Emni was the IS's intelligence unit and derived its name from the Arabic "*amn*" which means "trust," "security," and "safety." Anne Speckhard and Ahmet Yayla (2017) published a study which still remains, to the best of our knowledge, the only scholarly work on its functioning. This study was undertaken before the fall of Raqqa. In a recent personal communication, Yayla wrote us: "I know how the Emni operates and how it would be one of their prime goals to have their members or cells established in EU; however, at this moment I am not aware of any active cells in EU." As we wanted in this volume to make future projections based on concrete facts and evidence rather than speculation, we decided not to include this topic. From another personal communication, we learned that there might already be at least one such cell in a south-eastern European country. Due to the sensitive character of this intelligence information, it is difficult to write extensively on it. If it is really an Emni cell, then we may expect that its first function will most probably be to smuggle jihadists into Europe, given the geographic position of the country in question.

The next two chapters focus, in the form of case studies, on particular institutional practices in Belgium. They are quite representative of what may happen in the West in general. While Chapter 7 investigates the relationship between life in prison and jihadisation, Chapter 8 looks at life in some neighbourhoods that, at a certain moment, were discovered to have been "safe havens" for terrorists.

In Chapter 7, Johan Leman explores the relationship between Belgian prisons and jihadism. His exploration is based on personal interviews he held with two therapists and psychologists working with radicalised prisoners and with a director of a Belgian prison holding jihadists. In Chapter 8, Adolfo Gatti examines what happened in Molenbeek in the 2002-2016 period and traces the evolution of the idea of "terrorist sanctuary." Some of the cruelest attacks in recent years in Europe (e.g. Paris in November 2015, Brussels in March 2016, Barcelona in August 2017) were prepared in some specific European urban settings which are "blind spots" for the outsiders and "safe havens" for the insiders. Gatti refers to them as "terrorist urban sanctuaries" and attempts to answer whether we will in the future see such other possible "sanctuaries" in liberal democratic European countries.

In Chapter 9, Johan Leman and Stef Janssens scrutinise how "migrant smuggling" may be related to jihadist terrorism. It is obvious that pursuing terrorist jihadism requires money and in all likelihood jihadists may be producing financial capital via criminal money. Along with other financial sources, such as bank reserves, weapons and arts trafficking, Leman and Janssens discuss the possible use of migrant smuggling by jihadists as a financial source. Their discussion is based on some Belgian judicial files where human trafficking is somehow related to the support of jihadism. Warning that migrant smuggling is a wider phenomenon in Europe and its victims should be recognised, they yet point out that jihadists may most probably be using this illegal channel as a possible financial source. The files they discuss reveal the possibility of migrant smuggling to serve other jihadist terrorist purposes in the future.

Our volume both opens and ends with a conceptual discussion and with theology. In Chapter 10, Serafettin Pektas examines the Muslim critiques and the counter-theological arguments against militant jihadism. The role of the wider Muslim, particularly Sunni, community will evidently matter for the future evolution of Islamist extremism and terrorism. Pektas provides a synoptic analysis of the counter theologies of four leading Sunni institutions that seek to defy terrorist jihadism, namely *al-Azhar al-Sharif* (Egypt), *Diyanet İşleri Başkanlığı* (Turkey), *Nahdatul Ulama* (Indonesia) and *al-Rabita al-Muhammadiyya lil-'Ulama'* (Morocco). He examines in what ways the institutional and national contexts shape their respective counter-religious strategy, and reflects on the dynamics that will affect their future success.

Our final chapter presents concluding remarks about what to consider and expect for the future of militant jihadism.

References

Barrett, R. (2017). 'Beyond the Caliphate: Foreign Fighters and the Threat of Returnees'. *The Soufan Center* [online]. Available at: http://thesoufancenter.org/wp-content/uploads/2017/11/Beyond-the-Caliphate-Foreign-Fighters-and-the-Threat-of-Returnees-TSC-Report-October-2017-v3.pdf [accessed 26 November 2018].

Dell'Oro. J. L. (2015). 'Combien y a-t-il de djihadistes en France et quels sont leurs profils?' *Challenges* [online], 20 November 2015. Available at: https://www.challenges.fr/france/combien-y-a-t-il-de-djihadistes-en-france-et-quels-sont-leurs-profils_45504 [accessed 26 November 2018].

Europol. (2018). *European Union Terrorism Situation and Trend Report* [online]. Available at: https://www.europol.europa.eu/activities-services/main-reports/european-union-terrorism-situation-and-trend-report-2018-tesat-2018 [accessed 26 November 2018].

Graham-Harrison E. and Surtees, J. (2018). 'Trinidad's Jihadis: How Tiny Nation Became Isis Recruiting Ground'. *The Guardian* [online],2 February 2018. Available at: https://www.theguardian.com/world/2018/feb/02/trinidad-jihadis-isis-tobago-tariq-abdul-haqq [accessed 26 November 2018].

Lipka, M. (2015). 'Muslims and Islam: Key Findings in the U.S. and Around the World'. *Pew Research Center* [online]. Available at: http://www.pewresearch.org/fact-tank/2017/08/09/muslims-and-islam-key-findings-in-the-u-s-and-around-the-world/ [accessed 25 November 2018].

O'Neill, S., Hamilton, F., Karim, F. and Swerling, G. (2017). 'Huge Scale of Terror Threat Revealed: UK Home to 23,000 Jihadists'. *The Times* [online], May 27 2018. Available at: https://www.thetimes.co.uk/article/huge-scale-of-terror-threat-revealed-uk-home-to-23-000-jihadists-3zvn58mhq [accessed 26 November 2018].

Orsini, A. (2018). *L'ISIS non è morto. Ha solo cambiato pelle.* Milano: Rizzoli.

Speckhard, A. and Yayla, A. (2017). 'The ISIS Emni: Origins and Inner Workings of ISIS's Intelligence Apparatus'. *Perspectives on Terrorism* [online], 11(1). Available at: http://www.terrorismanalysts.com/pt/index.php/pot/article/view/573/html [accessed 20 November 2018]. See also: https://www.youtube.com/watch?v=GJRRp7BKDUI [accessed 20 November 2018].

CHAPTER 1

Salafism, Jihadism and Radicalisation: Between A Common Doctrinal Heritage and The Logics of Empowerment

Mohamed-Ali Adraoui

Introduction

The imprint of Salafism and jihadism seems to be greater than ever on many Muslim societies and beyond. Some observe that the combination of these two currents can explain the matrix of the growing wave of radicalisations and commitments that we have been witnessing for several years. This chapter aims to shed light on the links between these three phenomena, namely Salafism, jihadism and radicalisation, within the specific framework of the territorial demise of the so-called "Islamic State" (IS). IS's recent defeat does not evidently mean a short-term end to the jihadist ideology. Numerous studies have attempted to understand and explain the religious, political and military movements organised on the basis of a martial, violent and transnational interpretation of "jihad." For many centuries, the Muslim tradition has understood jihad as an attempt to bring the letter of Islam (hotly debated though this may be) in line with its spirit. The twentieth century witnessed the emergence of groups entirely dedicated to fighting against those (inside or outside the majority Muslim societies) who were presented as the enemies of Islam in parallel with the growing visibility of an ethics based on a necessary return to the earliest days of Islam (*al-salaf al-salih*). This ethics forms the basis of a doctrinal heritage which is common to Salafism and jihadism. Moreover, the development of these two currents is mainly interpreted as a product of Salafist socialisation. Radicalisation is, then, presented as an essentially ideological, or more precisely a religious, phenomenon.[1] According to this explanation, the Islamic utopia is prevalent; a utopia that instigates some believers to construct a "state" which is supposed to extend the "Caliphate" of the early days and that legitimises violence as a means to establish it. This explanation views it as an idealistic vision in the philosophical sense of the term since it is a "religious" utopia. It then tends to describe Salafism as the framework that conditions and prepares jihadism. This idealist reading, however, stands in opposition to materialistic explanations. For instance, some focus on the "purely" political nature of the conflict where the power relations between the "dominant" and the "dominated" in the international system produce jihadist violence while some others emphasise the problems with regard to access to economic and socio-demographic resources.

This chapter seeks to shed light on the dialectic between Salafism and jihadism on the doctrinal, sociological and political levels. More specifically, it probes this dialectic within the framework of re-compositions that are present in several movements which seek to set up a sovereign entity governed by the most fundamentalist religious norm and designed to unite the Muslim *umma* under a common political power and which aim to realise this objective through revolutionary strategies immediately or in the long term. In fact, we need to consider several points that may help to analyse the porosities, affinities and rivalries between these different conceptions of present-day Islam. First of all, the successes achieved by certain jihadist movements compels us to investigate their doctrinal backbone in order better to understand the conceptual imagination promoted by their theoreticians and militants, although membership of a radical group involves a number of considerations that may sometimes not only relegate the founding ideology into second place but also replace it with other factors. Next, we need to analyse the jihadists' claim that they are Salafists. Do these different forms of Islamic revivalism mean the same? What is the difference, if any? Is it about inclination to violence and questioning the established order? Similarly, in terms of on-going changes, at sociological, political or ideological levels, how are different forms of Salafism interacting today? Do we witness an interpenetration or even fertilisation among these forms; or, on the contrary, do we see different dynamics of empowerment or even a definitive split? Finally, what about the role of certain players, particularly at state level? To what extent are their re-compositions that have opposed the various puritan movements within Sunnism responsible for the emergence of a globalised Salafist field? Although these movements have subscribed to a fundamentalist vision which insisted on breaking with many codes of the modern world, they have not generated politicisation and violence. How has this changed and who is to be held responsible for that?

This chapter is organised around three considerations. First, it addresses the purely doctrinal dimension of the connections between Salafist revivalism and violent jihadism. From a macro point of view, contemporary radicalisation espouses a form of religious morphology that stems from a Salafist approach. Both conceptually and discursively, these two manifestations of present-day Muslim puritanism seem to share a very similar epistemology whose grammar was historically developed as a response to a common matrix. Does this commonality reveal an absolute identity between the two or rather does the latter proceed from the former? Secondly, the chapter further questions a real homology between the two. The sociological trajectories of jihadist fighters are often different from those of many Salafists. Besides, Salafist acolytes have developed dissimilar political considerations. We observe an increasingly clear and explicit tendency where different sides of Islamic fundamentalism disqualify each other. A differentiation or even proliferation is observable in the Salafist field due to some factors that need clarifying. This leads jihadism to be perceived as a distinct school increasingly diverging from the Salafist fundamentalism. The third consideration is a sociological point of view. The geographical context and human resources of the jihadists who support religiously motivated violence differ from those of most Salafists who are likewise religiously fundamentalist but politically opposed to violence. Moreover, we see an ideologisation of Islam whose content substantially differs from that of the most common type Salafist preaching. A closer examination of jihadist phenomena shows that sociocultural isolation and alienation facilitates the adoption of jihadist views and that jihadists have different social profiles. The religious justification of violence as represented by IS also shows differences among other fundamentalists. This leads to the conclusion that the jihadist socialisation process is now largely detached from any prior fundamentalist processes and a new "jihadist ethics" is under construction.

Salafism and Jihadism: A Common Doctrinal Heritage

Salafism is a longstanding movement within the Islamic tradition; yet it is not fair to think of it as a totally coherent school of thought. It comprises diverse groups. The common assumption of the Salafist belief is that Muslims have deviated in time from the "original" Islam and thereby ended up with various groups that have differently and aberrantly interpreted the normative sources of Islam. Out of these groups, only one is considered to have indeed remained faithful to the original Islam while others have gone astray. This single faithful group is the one that carefully follows *al-salaf al-salihin*, or "the pious/virtuous predecessors/ancestors", that is, the early (three) Muslim generations. With this assumption, proponents of Salafism argue that being a true believer requires a threefold movement in time: First, to go back to early history of Islam so as to explore the footsteps of the *salaf*, secondly, to come back today with a puritanical ethic within which contemporary problems are cognitively filtered, and thirdly to move forward into the future with the aim of engendering forms of socialisation which are based on the perpetuation of an allegedly revitalised Salafist path (*al-minhaj al-salafi*). In this schema, the jihadists are then those who resort to violence to make the deviant interpretations and practices compatible again with the orthodoxy and orthopraxy set by this Salafist path.

Salafism is about the believer's quest for authenticity. Its followers hold that early Muslims represent the pure, most authentic models of Islamic faith and practice. They show the "straight path" as opposed to the deviation occurred in time; thus it must be resuscitated. In Salafism, the *salaf* is regarded as having put the ultimate paradigm for the subsequent generations and the Salafist is the one who "preaches" this paradigm in order to keep and reproduce the "state of authenticity" which is furnished by an exclusive moral, religious and social content. As such, Salafism (*al-Salafiyya*) is considered to be the Islamic form that contains the highest level of authenticity. Its religious ethic is consciously fundamentalist in the sense that it aims at restoring the primordial true model of belief, worship and action in a given society. The Salafists then share a common logic of restitution whereby the heritage of the *salaf* is kept and whatever contradicts it is traced down and set apart. This is why socialisation within Salafist circles is rich in both doctrinal and social debates over contemporary changes which must be either accepted or refused. This explains why the concept of "*al-wala wa-l-bara*" or allegiance and disavowal is key among Salafist circles (see e.g. Wagemakers 2012 on this concept). Salafist communities have proclaimed for centuries the imperative need to restore the true understanding of Islam, and more particularly that of the Divine Unity (*al-tawhid*), without which there can be no spiritual and material revivalism. They have, however, been deeply divided in identifying and following the appropriate ways to (re)create the original Islamic society.

Contemporary scholarship on Salafism tends to classify the Salfist matrix into three main groups (Wiktorowicz 2006). The first group are those Salafists who preach a particular position on political activism. They seek to serve their revivalist goals through classical political activism designed to bring a party to power wishing to reform the society in question in the direction of a greater "authenticity." The second group are those who give legitimacy to Muslim regimes and tend to suppress all other forms of political opposition contesting these regimes. They justify their position by arguing that any "*fitna*" or sedition which is not forestalled might endanger the socio-political order without which the religious orthodoxy could be threatened. The followers of the third group, on the contrary, justify the use of violence and incite the armed struggle aimed at overthrowing any enemy who, whether "nominally" Muslim or not, opposes the restoration of the "primordial" authentic model. These diverse, even antagonistic, Salafist positions within the same matrix can be explained by the different politico-religious constructions that stem from divergent understandings of the preaching of the leading Salafist ulama and their fundamental concepts.

Historically speaking, Salafism has evolved as a response to several crises that were responded by a number of influential scholars/clerics whose puritanical reform attempts in turn set the keystones of Salafist epistemology. In the views of these scholars, these crises paved way to certain deviant beliefs and practices, and in some cases they even put people out of Islam. Their puritanical reforms or counter-reforms were hence targeted to revive the "original Islam" and restore the norm again with reference to the "pious predecessors." Salafism thus became an epistemic framework whereby historical crises were responded to in a particular way (Amghar, 2011). In this epistemic framework, the concept of "*al-jihad*" has been put forward to restore the rights of an allegedly flouted doctrine. As a generic notion *al-jihad* refers to the attempt to bring the letter of Islam (hotly contested though this may be) in line with its spirit. For those who were eager to revive what they regarded as Islamic authenticity, *al-jihad* represented the preferred way of restoring the original norm. For some of them, it did (does) not simply mean a moral, spiritual or charitable struggle but a violent fight or even militancy.

Among the most renowned scholars whose preaching laid the foundations of the Salafist approach are Ahmad ibn Hanbal (d.855), Ahmad ibn Taymiyya (d.1328) and Muhammad Ibn Abd al-Wahhab (d.1792). They are revered by contemporary jihadists as well. Although they lived in different centuries and in different contexts, each initiated a puritanical (counter)reformation as a response to different politico-religious challenges that they commonly viewed as heretic or even *kufr*, unbelief. Ibn Hanbal, for instance, led the opposition to the rationalist Mu'tazilite school of his time. He refused to subscribe to a dogma of this rationalist school that he deemed "associationist" (*shirk*) in nature. As a result, he was himself subjected to the "great ordeal" (*al-mihna al-kubra*) ordered by the Caliph who was influenced by this school and sought to impose its rationalist doctrine as the official dogma. Ibn Hanbal, on the other hand, called for obedience to authority so as to avoid chaos which would be harmful to the security of society. He was, for instance, reported to state, "sixty years of tyranny are better than one night of anarchy." In another version of this report, he said: "sixty years with an unjust sultan are better than one night without a sultan" (Melchert, 2006).

Ibn Taymiyya was known for his famous fatwa that he issued in 1303 as part of his religious judgment on the Mongol authority that was fighting with the Mamluks (Rapaport and Ahmed, 2015). He was greatly suspicious about the conversion to Islam of Genghis Khan's descendants who dominated the Muslim Middle East at that time. Witnessing that the Mongol leaders were still keeping the *Yasa* (Mongolian "Great Law") as their legal code although their conversion to Islam should have led them to recognise only the Muslim legislation (*shari'a*), Ibn Taymiyya concluded that they were not in fact Muslims despite what they stated otherwise and excommunicated them. His fatwa accordingly stipulated that it was legitimate to overthrow them by violence. This fatwa forms the religious basis for many jihadist or revolutionary Salafists who targeted to topple the "ostensible" Muslim rulers who appeal, for instance, to Western type of governance and democratic elections and do not recognise Islamic law as the unique source of legislation.

In a similar manner, in the 18th century Muhammad ibn Abd al-Wahhab led a puritanical campaign. He was aggressively hostile to the practices of saint veneration and tomb visits that became commonplace in his day. For him, these practices were anathema because they were apparently undermining *tawhid*, the most fundamental element of Islamic teaching and had not been practised by the "pious predecessors." What is quite different in Ibn Abd al-Wahhab's case vis-à-vis the other two was his success in forming an alliance with Muhammad ibn Sa'ud, a tribal leader from the Najd region, who provided the military support in implementing his fundamentalist reform. The latter, in turn, was able to extend his power after his political authority was anointed with a religious blessing by this alliance. The first revolt of these two allies was defeated; however, their descendants were able to officially establish the Saudi Kingdom in 1932 after which it has become the official sponsor to export Salafism on a global scale. This alliance between Ibn Abd al-Wahhab and Ibn Sa'ud served as a model where religious and political authorities closely collaborate in order to implement a puritanical reform in a territory conquered for this purpose. It also defined again the distinctive roles of political and religious authorities in a Muslim society.

These three figures are the most prominent personalities of contemporary Salafism and they are equally referred to and revered by opposing Salafist factions. This makes their legacy contested. Doctrinally speaking these opposing groups share a common *épistémè*.[2] They, however, differ in terms of how to define its content. Achieving true *tawhid* or Divine Unity is the prime element of Salafist *épistémè*. It is the axial principle of Islam for them. The legitimist, revolutionary and jihadist Salafist groups all venerate One God. The implication of this veneration is that their "authentic" faith in One God cannot tolerate any form of idolatry, which can be symbolised by allegiance to systems or persons to the detriment of the Oneness. The jihadist Salafists – those who justify use of physical violence – are characterised, however, by an extensive understanding of the implications of *tawhid*. Although his legacy is disputed, they take Ibn Taymiyya's fatwa as an efficient way to achieve true *tawhid*. Based on this fatwa, as mentioned above, they have supported local and/or global insurrections that aim to replace an established political order accused of betraying or combatting Islam.[3] This has forged a moral and conceptual framework that legitimised jihadist violence as clearly exemplified since the end of the 20th century by such organisations as al-Qaeda and IS.

The jihadist Salafists also expand the scope of *tawhid*. In conventional Salafist literature, genuine *tawhid* requires asserting three types of *tawhid*: i.) *tawhid al-uluhiyya*, or the Oneness of God's Divinity; that is He alone is worthy to be worshipped as God; ii.) *tawhid al-rububiyya* or the Oneness of God's Lordship; that is it is only God Himself who is capable of performing certain acts such as creating, bestowing life and sustenance, bringing death, etc.; iii.) *tawhid fil-asma wa-l-sifat*, oneness of God's Names and Attributes, that is, God's description of Himself (in the Qur'an) implies an ontological specificity. He is the only One who perfectly claims greatness, perfection, power or knowledge. Although these categories exist in humans, they cannot be compared to what these terms cover when God speaks of Himself. There is a consensus among the Salafist groups on this tripartite understanding of *tawhid*. This consensus is also shared more generally within Sunnism. Jihadists, however, adds a fourth element, namely *tawhid al-hakimiyya*, or Oneness of God' Sovereignty. According to this latter jihadist extra, a society can be managed only by the strict respect of religious injunctions commanded by God Himself. More precisely, this conception is based on the idea that the structures of a society (political, legal, identifying, cultural, etc.) must never be in conflict with the divine commands. For example, according to this view, the Salafist reform cannot be limited merely to power in a given society. All that would be seen as a failure to unite Muslims and to defend themselves could legitimise the act of "turning against those in authority." Moreover, Islamic law (*shari'a*) represents one of the preferred means of serving *tawhid* on earth and is always superior to any regime, however nominally Muslim it may be. Besides, the sincerity of a Muslim believer, they argue, requires first and foremost allegiance to Islam, which is interpreted as an integralist, "uncompromising" and "radical" faith and practice.[4] As an extension of this argument, the jihadists claim that a "violation" of the *shari'a* authorises physical *jihad* and sanctions an uprising against a "failing" authority.

Saudi Arabia: A Modern Salafist State

Salafism is to be better viewed as a complex matrix rather than a clearly identified coherent current or school of thought. Different sides of this revivalist movement both share and dispute about a common doctrinal heritage. This allows us to see, on the one hand, that jihadism as a Salafist modality derives its legitimacy from a religious universe built up over several centuries. On the other hand, the re-formulation of *jihad* by certain modern Salafist clerics and thinkers, who were eager to restore the "original, pure, authentic Islam" today and to do it violently if necessary, brought conceptual and strategic novelties to jihadism, as appeared in the late 20th century. Jihadist Salafism thus demonstrates a new form of relationship to the state, to politics and to violence. Saudi Arabia as a modern Salafist state has played a significant role in the differentiation and acceleration of contemporary jihadist Salafism. This is because the re-conceptualisation of jihad and the jihadists' novel relationship with power and violence has, to a great extent, occurred as a form of reaction to the developments in Saudi politics for the last several decades. While the jihadists did not question the founding religious referent of this modern Salafist state, they opposed its exercise of an exclusive magisterium within the contemporary Salafist field. More concretely, theirs was a reaction to the increasing tension between the two opposing conceptions of the Saudi regime's missionary Salafist pan-Islamic agenda. Therefore, the Saudi kingdom has occupied both a positive and negative yet central position in the development and later fragmentation of the Salafist field in the 20th century. As shown by David Commins (2006) and Thomas Hegghammer (2010), without Saudi Arabia there would simply have been no Salafism and Jihadism in the 20th century. The difference between these two conservative and fundamentalist narratives has actually more to do with the Saudi conception of what Islam should be at some point. According to the changing historical and socio-political circumstances, the Saudi kingdom and the religious scholars who support its political leadership have reassessed to what degree the use of violence is considered more or less legitimate. The rise of the transnational jihadist movement over the last few decades has progressively meant the end of a possible convergence of visions and interests between the Saudi State and the jihadist groups that claim to defend Muslims worldwide. The latter have turned against Saudi Arabia itself, which they see as having betrayed Islam for allying, for instance, with Western countries and abandoning the oppressed Muslim people across the world, in particular the Palestinians and the Iraqis.

The Kingdom of Saudi Arabia (KSA) was officially founded in September 1932 as a result of the earlier alliance contracted between Ibn Saʿud's political authority and Ibn ʿAbd al-Wahhab's religious authority, as mentioned above. KSA is run by the Saudi royal family supported by a body of Salafist clerics divided between two main institutions, namely the Council of Senior Scholars and the Permanent Delegation for Islamic Research and Issuing Fatwas. Both are headed by the Grand Mufti ʿAbd al-ʿAziz ibn ʿAbdullah who is from the *al-Shaykh* family, the family of the descendants of Muhammad ibn ʿAbd al-Wahhab. The Council is the top religious authority in the kingdom and gives Islamic ratification to political decisions and provides religious advice first to the king and later other political players who embody the secular arm of power. In theory, the Council exerts the most substantive political impact in KSA. In practice, however, it functions to provide religious legitimacy to the king's decisions and policies. The Delegation, whose members are appointed from those of the Council, rather issues religious rulings on many fields ranging from purely theological to legal, social, cultural, economic or foreign policy-related issues. It also leads the KSA's research and education agenda.

Since its creation as a new socio-political order in the heartland of Islam, serving the cause of Salafism has been both the source of the kingdom's religious identity and the tool for its political legitimation. Moreover, as a missionary state,

KSA has become the central base for reinforcing and exporting Salafist norms throughout the world. As such, KSA has become the key player in implementing this dual form of Salafism. Inside the kingdom, its peculiar religious-political structure has produced the first form which gave rise to a legitimist political conservatism where the Salafist clerics entrust their fate to the incumbent regime even if it imperfectly served Islam. On the one hand, legitimist Salafism can be considered as a fundamentalism that indeed operates to secularise the two-tier political authority. The clerics achieve this through constantly impregnating the political power with their advice (*al-nasiha*) so that their advice is widely heard. They even sometimes remonstrate with the rival princes who, in exchange, ask to guarantee the obedience of the people to themselves. Legitimist Salafism, on the other hand, lets the clerics enjoy a genuine autonomy because they can assert legitimacy for another prescriptive regime to carry out the specific role of the Salafist state. Jihadist Salafism has emerged as a reaction to this distinction between these pragmatist and normative aspects of Saudi Salafism.

Outside the kingdom, KSA has supported Salafist preachers who have worked to apply their Salafist standards as the religious ideal in other states and governments. For several decades, KSA's foreign policy has also prioritised solidarity with and helped Muslim populations that have suffered war or difficulties as a religious obligation. The soaring oil prices have definitely been instrumental in pursing this goal. In supporting the "suffering" Muslims, on the one hand, KSA has promoted international organisations some of which it founded. Through them, it was able to exert a considerable degree of influence on an interstate diplomatic level. KSA-backed Salafist preachers, on the other hand, encouraged the idea of "pan-Islamic" help and support to Muslim *umma* worldwide, which has given rise to the de-nationalisation of both the "Muslim sufferings" in different parts of the world and of solidarity with fellow Muslims. The contemporary rise of jihadism can be regarded as an extension of KSA's Salafist efforts to de-nationalise and trans-nationalise this pan-Islamic solidarity, and as a response to its (perceived) failure to realise it. Those jihadists who were critical of Saudi Arabia — when the latter was (seemingly) unable to give necessary and effective support to other Muslims — emerged as private players in order to defend the "Islamic nation." As transnational actors without any national allegiance, they began to be involved in a global struggle against those they deemed the enemies of Islam. In other words, KSA'a promotion of the idea of de-nationalised pan-Islamic solidarity with the global *umma* has, in time, paved the way to a contemporary transnational jihadist venture where each jihadist can now help suffering fellow Muslims in any part of the world. In this respect, jihadism constitutes a novelty in the history of Muslim societies.

The similarities, porosities and divergences that we observe today between the legitimist and jihadist factions of Salafism are therefore more understandable, given the developments in the domestic and foreign policy of KSA and the tensions within the Saudi Salafist circles between serving authentic Islam and ensuring the kingdom's political stability. After 1945, in which KSA established an allegiance with the USA, the disagreement between these two distinct visions began to increase. The official clerics of monarchy backed this alliance. They argued that Saudi identity by nature necessitated service to religion, and such an alliance would consolidate the role of the kingdom as an effective international player, which would ultimately allow the global promotion of "authentic/orthodox" Islam. Other Salafist clerics, on the other hand, were harshly critical of such an alliance, arguing that particularly the Israeli expansion at the expense of Palestinians and the two Gulf wars demonstrated that the kingdom was indeed unsuccessful in fulfilling its religious duty of pan-Islamic solidarity. In their view, they made the "distant" enemy a "neighbouring" enemy. They also levelled sharp criticism against the Kingdom as the Saudi authorities had compromised certain Salafist morals in response to the modernisation brought about by the boosting of oil revenues since the 1970s while they continued to claim to defend Islam and the *umma*. The degree of divergence is perhaps best illustrated by the following quotations from the representatives of the legitimist and jihadist factions of contemporary Salafism. The first is an appeal issued by the Council of Senior Scholars as a response to public demonstrations held in Saudi Arabia in March 2011. The appeal denounces the demonstration and makes a religious call to restore public order. It also defends the regime as an organic support of Islam:

> The Council of Senior Scholars implores Allah to grant to all Muslims the help, the stability and the renewed union of the rulers and citizens around the Truth. The Council praises Allah for having granted the Kingdom of Saudi Arabia the favour of uniting His word and for closing ranks around the Book of Allah [Qur'an] and the Prophet's Tradition [Sunna] in the shade of wise governance, legitimised by a legal allegiance, may Allah grant it consolidation and permanence, and may Allah complete this blessing for us and make it lasting. ... Allah has granted that the people of this country come together, with their rulers, around the guidance of the Book and the Tradition, without causing them to diverge or to disperse their words on the

basis of currents of thought coming from elsewhere, or of parties holding antagonistic principles ... The Kingdom has succeeded in conserving this Islamic identity. Thus, in spite of the progress and development that the Kingdom has experienced, and the recourse to lawful earthly means, it has never allowed nor will it allow – by the strength of Allah and His Power – currents of ideas coming from the West or East to undermine this identity or to disperse this group (Salafs, 2011).

The second quotation comes from a jihadist Salafi website (Tawhid, 2011). It sets out the "sins" committed by the leaders of KSA and exposes, so to speak, how the Kingdom indeed betrayed its Salafist ideals:

The impiety of Saudi Arabia takes many forms such as having a seat at the UN General Assembly, organisation of municipal elections, authorisation of interest in international [financial] transactions, amendment of martial law concerning theft of a soldier..., being a member state of the UNESCO, King Fahd's wearing cross [referring to his carrying a cross shape medal during his visit to the UK in 1994], the alliance with the American infidels, their fight against the *Mujahidin* [the jihadists] ... The alliance with infidels, the abandonment of the jihad and the alliance with the crusading infidels against the Taliban and the Iraqis, the presence of American bases in Arabia, their fighter planes bomb Muslims and they send gifts and food to the crusading soldiers, not to mention the oil they sell to these infidels.

The two quotations clearly illustrate the "equivocal" nature of the contemporary Salafist norm in the 20th century as presented in the Saudi Kingdom. Therefore, the evolution of KSA as a modern Salafist state and the opposing views on its dual form of puritanical religious mission have conditioned another form of jihadist empowerment among Salafists, not only doctrinal but also geopolitical and strategic this time, which in turn caused notable disagreements and later divergence within the different faces of the present-day Salafist fundamentalism.

Jihadist Differentiation from Salafism

Various forms of conflict that take place within militant jihadism make it possible to seriously question, or at least qualify, the thesis that there is a structured continuity between the fundamentalist socialisation of Salafism and the violent commitment of jihadism. Al-Qaeda and IS are the two major representatives of the phenomenon of espousal of the jihadist conceptual imagination. Their respective interpretations of jihad, however, shed light on how today's jihadism has begun to differ from Salafism. The case of al-Qaeda exemplifies the reorganisation of Salafism as a jihadist ideology. The Afghan War in the 1980s, which took place against the backdrop of the final days of the Cold War, set the context for this reorganisation. Here we saw for the first time in the history of Islam a discussion on initiating a world revolution with the ultimate aim of bringing in a unique and exclusive sovereignty commanding the whole of the *umma*. Although the defence of fellow believers remained a central concern in the Afghan War, the later emergence of al-Qaeda triggered a new form of global jihadist insurgency that no longer claimed to unify the *umma* within a particular geographical area. In other words, jihad in this case ceased to be a form of violence limited to the duration of a particular war. This new form makes the claim of common identity between Salafism and jihadism more questionable. While its will to unite the Muslim *umma* may be understood as an illustration of reviving an original norm (e.g. a return to the times of the "well-guided Caliphs" of *al-Salaf*), an armed jihad has never been so disconnected from a specific time and place over the past centuries of Islamic history. This unbounded and perpetual nature is what constitutes the present-day novelty. On the other hand, even though the IS jihadists, unlike al-Qaeda, have sought to establish the Caliphate in a particular territory, their case exemplifies not a jihadist reorganisation of Salafism but another kind of differentiation from it. The case of IS indeed highlights two new phenomena: the growing sociological discontinuity between Salafism and jihadism, and the emergence of a new type of jihadist intent which is primarily motivated by total violence and which relegates concerns abut religious orthodoxy to second place to be replaced, instead, by an apocalyptic discourse that transforms the conventional Salafist focus on redressing this world.

Empowerment of Jihadism: Violence without Religious Socialisation
From a macro sociological point of view, the emergence of jihadism is often explained by the emergence of a Salafist paradigm during the course of the 20th century. On the micro sociological level, however, the causes of the current phenomenon of radicalisation increasingly represent a clear disconnection between Salafist socialisation and embracing the use of violence. As the Saudi experience shows, religious (Islamic) framing of contemporary violence has been

observed for a period of several years and in various countries. Yet, this was before violence was embraced as a consistent trajectory. Current jihadism distinguishes itself by a dynamic of empowerment of people whose itineraries leading to this ideology fail to follow those of puritanical careers, both in majority and minority Muslim contexts. The jihadist ideology, as we mostly observe in IS today, is now becoming a different school itself. Although it shares a common heritage with other forms of Salafism, it legitimises military struggle for Islam and aims to disrupt world politics in order to make itself a hybrid movement rather than an enduring force for reform. We still lack comparative, cross-sectional studies examining the number of people who were previously part of a Salafist community and subsequently espoused the jihadist conceptual imagination. Some research (Rabasa and Benard, 2014; Roy, 2017; Khosrokhavar, 2018) nevertheless suggests that in the majority of cases the profiles of combatants from Europe or predominantly Muslim societies who joined al-Qaeda, IS or claimed to act out of ideological affiliation with them are marked by an absence of an ordered fundamentalist socialisation that is observed within Salafist communities. This does not mean that the Salafist discourse does not generate or consolidate religious radicalism as we see a differentiation between Salafists and jihadists. It rather indicates that the social disruption that today fuels support for jihadism seems to be of another sort. Predisposition to embrace the legitimacy of the IS's strategy of total violence often stems from an appetite for physical violence and the apocalyptic utopia which in fact springs from a secular rather than a religious form of socialisation rather than any Salafist rooting that jihadists claimed at the outset.

Besides observing this Salafism-free jihadism in the life-path of most of the militants, present-day followers also demonstrate the emergence of a new ethics of violence that proceeds mainly from individual initiatives. This individuality is not only about individual ideological affiliation independently from a jihadist organisation, but also about the individual philosophy of violent action and its *modus operandi*. We see here a viral paradigm that illustrates the fact that Salafism and jihadism have now become mutually distinct realities, although the latter is empowered by the former. Nevertheless, IS theoreticians now trigger an independent jihadist form which is characterised by and is an essentially individual approach whereby identification, assimilation and implementation of the call to violence take place at the individual, instead of a collective, level. In short, a considerable number of this new jihadist generation define themselves in terms of viral jihadism. Armed combat here is a form of acculturation rather than the result of military commitment. The transition to violence works in a viral mode where hostility is first created or reinforced in certain individuals who then find reasons to nurture it as part of a relationship of violence which they will often themselves go on to decide just how to translate into acts. There is, indeed, a large share of personal creativity in this. While the ideological contours are already given (e.g. a state of permanent war, the designation of the enemy, etc.), the practical aspects of the terrorist act are usually left up to the perpetrator himself to work out. We see here not so much a sponsored action but rather the instigation of terrorist careers. Hostility to others is displayed in the form of Jihad whereas it might have been expressed in the (more classical) form of symbolic, verbal or physical violence. Terrorist radicalisation appears to espouse the jihadist agenda as it is put forward by IS; but it is actually driven by more complex mechanisms. Jihadism, essentially in its most recent form, leads to a dilution of the relationship with jihad. In this way, any phenomenon of hostility (even non-religious) comes to find expression through a conceptual imagination that has been fashioned in another part of the world. IS thus offers a way of converting existing social or interpersonal tensions into a sacred struggle. In this respect, the opportunities for armed jihad are much greater since they are atomised and personalised. The individual's trajectory spurs him to make use of the jihadist conceptual imagination to interpret the frustrations and malaise that are driving him to consider his environment through the lens of religious radicalism. The homology between personal psychological tensions and the desire to defend one's co-religionists in another part of the world largely explains terrorist radicalisation. Having the idea of a transnational ideological struggle in the background, local interactions, which may involve certain Muslims, can be "jihadised" without difficulty. The suicidal impulse, the desire to harm a hated group or the feeling of solidarity with fellow believers suggests that we consider the jihadist conceptual imagination as something that stems from a certain degree of opportunism. That is to say, it is not the ideological supply provided by Salafist or Islamist currents that creates the demand for appropriating the doctrinal system devised by IS. The new jihadist generation no longer operates solely through the jihadisation of a tangible conflict in a given part of the world. It instead (and even especially) operates through the jihadisation of social relations and tensions within societies, particularly within those that are not predominantly Muslim.

Apocalypticism of IS Jihadism

Al-Qaeda, the father of contemporary jihadism, primarily aimed to fight against "the enemies of Islam" and to proliferate the centres of conflict without any territorialisation strategy. Founded and headed by elders from al-Qaeda (as well as from the Iraqi Baathist regime) IS, rather, breaks with this agenda to replace it with a revival of the Apocalypse. While apocalypticism is not absent from the literature ascribed to the jihadist theoreticians of previous generations (Filiu, 2010[2]), IS distinguishes itself by a specificity which largely accounts for its current success and which above all prevents it from being identified as a classical Salafist movement.

Its perception of the future echoes the belief that it is now time to precipitate the end of this world as to hasten the final Day of Judgment. As such, IS explicitly sees itself as an essential agent of the "end of time" whose members (leaders, clerics, inhabitants, soldiers or whatever) form a community of those "saved" (*al-farqat al-najiyya*) and "victorious" (*al-tayfat al-mansura*); it is the only one that is able to correctly interpret the present time and the "signs of the hour" (*'alamat al-sa'a*) which herald the demise of the terrestrial world and the imminence of final judgment. Hence, the idea of establishing and expanding an "Islamic State" reflects the desire both to defeat the enemies of Islam and to prepare the *umma* to achieve its salvation. The newly restored "Caliphate" built on the ruins of "false" Islamic regimes is considered one of the most important signs heralding the "coming of the (final) hour." Establishing a political and religious structure claiming to be the ultimate one in history thus fulfils both an ideological purpose (ensuring Islam's triumph) and a soteriological one (ensuring the salvation of Muslims, for whom there is no longer any horizon other than that of the restored Caliphate). This is what makes IS such a specific movement as the first that follows an eschatological logic in realising its ultimate aim. As its teleological belief states that human history is inevitably leading to the Day of Judgement, IS holds that the future is already heralded by the warning signs. Accordingly, the future of humanity will witness the ultimate collision of the forces of "good" and "evil", a logic of self-fulfilling prophecy. In its eyes, any event involving IS should necessarily be interpreted in eschatological terms. At the root of IS's militant activities (military, political, religious, etc.) runs this fundamental apocalyptic logic. The advent of the End of Time, thus, must be greeted by membership of the organisation.

Therefore, the phenomena of jihadist radicalisation that have been unfolding before our eyes over recent years, whether they take the form of leaving for a war-zone like Syria to fight or committing terrorist violence in a peaceful society, Western or not, seem to bypass the traditional Salafist conceptual imagination. The offensive apocalyticism and the idea of the imminent end of the world had never been part of Salafist preaching. The ideological distinction from classical Salafism reaches a climax here. In classical Salafism, the relationship with time and history includes no notion of any possible appropriation by the believers themselves. The "End" will come, but without any deliberate attempt to restore the Caliphate through encouraging the "real" believers actively to join to the apocalyptic end. The ultimate purpose of Salafism has rather been purification and education (*al-tasfiyya wa-l-tarbiyya*) within a framework of worldly puritanism. In other words, Salafists do not call Muslims to bring the End because they prefer to share the same time frame with those who are not Salafists. The jihadism embodied by IS, on the other hand, is undeniably built upon a radically different concept of time and the believer's relationship with it.

Post-IS Jihadism

Although it is difficult for the moment confidently to forecast the future of IS's jihadist activities, we can still point to a certain number of potentially important changes to be expected over the coming years.

Considering its recent territorial demise, IS must today deal with three issues in particular. Firstly, how can it recover from the forced eviction from, and the disappearance of, the proto-state that the movement sought to build and extend? This represents the very foundation of its politico-military strategy and its conceptual imagination. Secondly if offensive Islamic apocalypticism meant a fundamental break with the al-Qaeda generation and made IS's hallmark, what will it do now with such a utopia one of whose founding and constitutive prophecies has already failed? That is to say, what future is there for the jihadists' apocalyptic illusion in the face of "unmet prophecies" (Bunzel, 2017)? Finally, rather than embodying the Salafist puritanical agenda, IS has emerged embodying total violence that was conditioned by Middle Eastern geopolitics. Should we expect the definite emergence of jihadism as an independent current different from Salafism which opts for an all-out belligerent ethic with a primary focus on violence, and as such no longer adheres to the latter's claim to embody lasting Islam in everyday life? In other words, should we expect a schismatic event to occur in the Salafist matrix we have been studying?

An answer to these three questions could be that IS represents a truly radical transformation of Salafism. On the one hand, it shares certain principles of contemporary Salafism (such as the need to disavow what Islam is supposed to oppose). On the other hand, its apocalyptic strategy and intransigent emphasis on armed jihad, which is only a small part of the Salafist doctrinal heritage, make it quite unique. In other words, through hyper-specialisation in a discourse of violence and total belligerence, the Islamic State distances itself from modern Salafist revivalism that pursued the setting up of a symbolic authority focused on extolling the early days of Islam to address the anomic crises that different Muslim groups have gone through over the past few centuries. IS certainly provides protection and meaning (under limited conditions) to social groups that demand violence; for instance, to some Sunni populations in the Levant, to the Western youth in rebellion or to the radicalised political players in the Arab world. However, it does not propose a lasting and genuinely structured narrative, unlike, for example, that of the non-violent Salafists. The latter's narrative can be more in tune with the codes and norms of the certainties of modernity, such as looking for material wealth while staying away from political activism (e.g. Adraoui, 2020), moral radicalism for a social and cultural change without resorting to violence, opposition to grand ideologies that advocate transforming the world through violence. The post-IS jihadism seems to be less Salafist.

Conclusion

The above analysis indicates that while Salafism has taken a form of ideologisation of Islam, jihadism has further taken an ideologisation of Salafism. Doctrinally and historically, both maintain a cognitive or political radicalisation which generates a clear dichotomy between "true" believers and "deviant" others. Notwithstanding, it would be misleading to conclude hastily that at the present time Salafism is the ideological infrastructure of jihadism. Such a generalisation holds a linear vision which assumes that wherever the former is adopted the latter necessarily emerges. It presumes a direct link between Salafism, radicalisation and jihadism, or between ideology and ideologisation. Salafism is believed to set the scene for the social and moral disruption which later prepares the ground for the acceptance of violent action, which finally ends up with jihadism. An intersectional approach seems to be more productive, however, in order better to understand and explain the absence of mutual identity that we empirically observe today between fundamentalist socialisation and the commitment to violence. In today's context, jihadism is the prerogative of actors who are radicalised as an opposition to the world and to the politics which harm them, and not necessarily by a pre-existing fundamentalist ethic. Non-violent Salafism, rather, constitutes a form of religious radicalism that is a response to broader dynamics of anomie, marginalisation and nihilism. Salafism, jihadism and radicalisation certainly interact, but they interact within the framework of socio-political contexts. The careful analysis of these contexts suggests distinguishing between religious intransigence and political radicalism, and to refute the systematic nature of any links between fundamentalism and violence. The majority of cases of present-day radicalisation do not occur among those who are seeking more and deeper religious practice.

Notes

1 Farhad Khosrokhavar (2014: 21) defines radicalisation as "the articulation between a radical ideological vision and the implacable will to implement it."
2 Michel Foucault (2002) defines *épistémè* as the framework that defines "the conditions for the possibility of knowledge." For Foucault, the *épistémè* has two dimensions: First, a "structural" dimension that contains the empirical contents to which the players have access and that represents "an imperceptible network of constraints." Secondly, it has an "archaeological" dimension, i.e. a specific way of seeing history, and particular forms of producing knowledge. In the case of Salafism, while the first dimension corresponds to the customs of *al-salaf-al-salihin*, the second dimension is manifested by their ways of reasoning.
3 Such an idea of "enemy" implies the one meant by Carl Schmitt (2017). The enemy could be either "close" (i.e. a "false" Muslim regime that claims membership of Islam but that "betrays" it by violating some of its obligations) or "distant" (i.e. any non-Muslim group or state accused either of attacking Muslim people or of reinforcing iniquity).
4 The "uncompromising" Salafist approach is similar to the intransigent attitude of French Catholics in the late 19th century as explained by Emile Poulat (1986). For Poulat, the "intransigent Catholics" were those who were totally loyal to the Church's teachings and commands, and so refused to make any concession to modern ideas that questioned the fundamentals of their faith. The Salafists examined here similarly are very loyal to what are regarded as authentic, unsurpassable Islamic origins and refuse any element they deem exogenous to this initial universe of Islam. In like manner, Jean-Marie Donegani (1993: 406) talks about "radical Catholics" of France who were highly critical of the clear

separation between church and state epitomised in 1905 French law and thus opposed to relegating faith to the mere private sphere. They rather desired to stay fully and radically Catholic and attempted to take advantage, for instance, of the growing autonomy of the economic sphere as private employers or trade unions in order to keep their influence on the state. The Salafist principle of Divine Unity (*al-tawhid*) regards Islam as not only a religious system but also a sovereign body. Salafists and jihadists today similarly react to the absence of compliance with Islamic law (*al-shari'a*) whose scope, in their view, extends to such other spheres as spiritual, social and political life. Their "radical" faith thus necessitates a unique form of allegiance to both an exclusive law and a political power. They are highly critical of any socio-political entity (even in majority Muslim cases) which fails to comply with Islamic norms in their totality.

References

Adraoui, M. A. (2020). *Salafism Goes Global: From the Gulf to the French Banlieues*. New York: Oxford University Press.

Bunzel, C. (2017). 'Caliphate in Disarray: Theological Turmoil in the Islamic State', *Jihadica* [online], 3 October 2017. Available at: http://www.jihadica.com/caliphate-in-disarray/ [accessed 4 October 2017].

Commins, D. (2006). *The Wahhabi Mission and Saudi Arabia*. New York: I.B. Tauris.

Donegani, J. M. (1993). *La liberté de choisir: Pluralisme religieux et pluralisme politique dans le catholicisme français contemporain*, Paris: Presses de la FNSP

Filiu, J. P. (2012). *Apocalypse in Islam*. Berkley, LA: University of California Press.

Foucault, M. (2002). *The Order of Things: An Archeology of the Human Sciences*. London: Routledge.

Hegghammer T. (2010). *Jihad in Saudi Arabia: Violence and Pan-Islamism since 1979*. Cambridge: Cambridge University Press.

Khosrokhavar, F. (2014). *Radicalisation*. Paris: EMSH

Khosrokhavar, F. (2018). *Le nouveau jihad en Occident*. Paris: Robert Laffont.

Melchert, C. (2006). *Makers of the Muslim World: Ahmad Ibn Hanbal*. London: Oneworld.

Poulat, E. (1986). *L'Eglise, c'est un monde: L'ecclésiosphère*, Paris: Editions du Cerf.

Rabasa A. and Benard, C. (2014). *Eurojihad: Patterns of Islamist Radicalization and Terrorism in Europe*. Cambridge: Cambridge University Press.

Rapaport, Y. and Ahmed, S. (2015). *Ibn Taymiyya and His Times*. New York: Oxford University Press.

Roy, O. (2017). *Jihad and Death: The Global Appeal of Islamic State*. London: Hurst & Company.

Salafs. (2011). 'Le Comité des Grands Savants exhorte au maintien de l'union et souligne la prohibition des manifestations'. *As-Salafs* [online]. Available at: http://www.as-salafs.com/2011/03/21/le-comite-des-grands-savants-exhorte-au-maintien-de-lunion-et-souligne-la-prohibition-des-manifestations/ [accessed 11 July 2011].

Schmitt, C. (2017). *The Concept of the Political*. Chicago: Univ. of Chicago Press.

Tawhid. (2011). *Tawhid wa al-Jihad Over Blog* [online]. Available at: http://tawhid-wa-al-jihad.over-blog.com/article-25372538.html [accessed 13 March 2011].

Wagemakers, J. (2012). "The Enduring Legacy of the Second Saudi State: Quietist and Radical Wahhabi Contestations of *al-Wala' wa-l-Bara*". *International Journal of Middle East Studies*, 44 (1), pp.93-110.

Wiktorowicz, Q. (2006). 'The Anatomy of the Salafi Movement'. *Studies in Conflict & Terrorism*, 29, pp. 207-239.

CHAPTER 2

The Libyan Jihadist Outlook: Origins, Evolutions and Future Scenarios

Arturo Varvelli

Introduction

Libya's contemporary history has been dominated by the interplay between the perpetual dynamics of religion, tribalism, oil, nationalism and ideology, further aggravated by 42 years of rule by an oppressive, pervasive and sometimes irrational regime. With Libya hidden behind its regime's curtain, it has been difficult from outside to understand the religious changes often happening under its surface.

Apparently, its social fabric shows little change: Libya – despite a fragile national identity – remains a very homogenous country from a religious point of view, with a huge majority of Sunni Muslims following the Maliki *madhhab*. Islamic identity arose as a preponderant element after the fall of the Qaddafi regime. With everyone recognising themselves as Muslim and with little conflict in the doctrinal sphere, Islam emerged as a legitimising element in society and in politics. At the same time, as representatives of this element of legitimacy, competition arose between new political parties, renewed religious figures (such as the Grand Mufti) and radical groups of various origins. Among these, jihadist groups, trying to impose the creation of a caliphate on Libya if necessary by using force, have found fertile ground due to the semi-anarchic situation.

Libya's current crisis has deep causes and distant origins, ranging from a weak national identity to legacies from the civil war of 2011, which did not end with the killing of Colonel Qaddafi (Baldinetti, 2010). The fall of Qaddafi opened up new spaces for Libya's Islamist groups, even those at the more extreme end of the spectrum. Libya is experiencing a very worrying phenomenon: it has rather quickly become a safe haven for local, foreign and international jihadist groups.

It is worth saying that all the attempts to rebuild the country after the fall of Qaddafi failed. There are multiple and complex reasons for this outcome: multiple identities (regionalism, localism, and tribalism), the progressive political polarisation after the failure of the "Arab Spring" – with Islamists fighting against military forces and nationalist movements. Above all, one should add the toxic role of international actors (Europeans included) that tried to favour the groups closer to them in an attempt to gain influence in the country.

Libya appears, now, as a fragmented composition of hundreds of militias, most of them divided into two coalitions: the first, the Fa'iz al-Sarraj's Government of National Accord (GNA), supported by the UN; the second led by Khalifa Haftar and linked with the Tobruk parliament. After the failure of the national reconciliation processes – exclusively based on weak figures with no leverage on the militias, which have the real power in Libya – it seems we have entered a new phase. Therefore, now there is an attempt to try to broaden the consensus towards the peace process through both the actions of the UN special envoy Ghassan Salamé and the meetings convened by countries like Italy and France.

The consequence of this stalemate is that Libya is still a sort of failing state – and failed states are the perfect place for the rise of jihadist movements and radicalisation processes. The most dangerous group to have emerged in Libya has been Islamic State (IS), above all because it was the strongest opponent of any agreement between political forces in Libya. IS is only the most recent terrorist group to have found a place in Libya and the Maghreb but, because of its peculiar structure and way of acting and the impact that there could have been on Libya, it is worth analysing its spread.

The Genesis of Radicalisation in Libya

Thanks to the religious moderation of most Libyans, up to now the Islamic mainstream has been relatively "temperate" from a doctrinal point of view. The definition of Libyans as religiously moderate may appear debatable, considering the high numbers of Libyan jihadists that fought outside Libya. Under Qaddafi's regime, jihadism represented one of the few practical responses available to personal religious or political dissatisfaction with the existence of a strongly illiberal system that prohibited activities by Islamist groups. In fact, global jihad outside Libya became a sort of substitute for Islamic activities within the country. This explains the high numbers of Libyan citizens (especially from Derna and eastern Libya) amongst Al Qaeda (AQ) groups or Salafi jihadist movements in Iraq and Afghanistan, where Libyan *mujahidin* form one of the most numerous national groups of foreign fighters.

It is interesting to note that this "jihadist attitude" is linked more to a traditional way of expressing discontent and dissatisfaction with the domestic situation (rooted in the Qaddafi period) than to real theological extremism. As has been shown (Torelli and Varvelli, 2014: 45-71), it seems to be a sort of "functional jihadism" more than a doctrinal one. However, there are indications that Libyan jihadists active in Afghanistan and Iraq — who have been exposed to the message and proselytism of Eastern movements such as the Deobandis and the Tablighi Jama'at — represent a channel of diffusion for radicalism, strictly based on their dogmatic approach to Islamic orthopraxis. At the same time, their rigid approach to ritual personal purity and absolute adherence to a very strict interpretation of Shari'a principles may further radicalise their activism and their militancy. According to documents seized by US forces in Iraq, Libyans formed the second-largest group among 700 foreign fighters who joined the al-Qaeda offshoot, Islamic State in Iraq (ISI), between August 2006 and August 2007. In relation to national population, the Libyans were first by a long way. Even more telling were the cities they came from. More than half originated from Derna.

Consequently, Libyan jihadists form the largest group per capita of foreign fighters supporting AQ and the other militias in Iraq and, since 2012-2013, in Syria. The important role of returnees in expanding the jihadist network across the Middle East (and in Western countries, too) is well known and has been widely studied. Jihadists returning from the front line to their towns and tribes are generally afforded greater status as *mujahidin*. They are, therefore, in a position to radicalise their original environment, with extremist proselytism being the favoured method; to create new jihadist groups and cells; to carry out the training of new members and upgrade local militants' combat capability; and to enlarge extremist networks, with the diffusion of Salafi jihadist ideology, thus delegitimising traditional local authorities.

According to Wolfram Lacher (Lacher, 2015), in the last 20 years three successive generations of Libyan jihadists have been shaped by very different experiences, and consequently responded differently to the possibilities opened up by Qaddafi's demise. The first generation began its formative experiences with the armed struggle in Afghanistan during the 1980s and 1990s. The second generation of Libyan jihadists was radicalised during imprisonment at Abu Salim prison or during the 2003 Iraqi war. Here they came into contact with what was then the most radical branch in jihadism. During the 2011 revolution and after the fall of the regime the third generation mobilised. Their radicalisation largely occurred during the struggle against Qaddafi when they came into contact with the other two generations and with other revolutionaries. After the fall of Qaddafi, jihadists benefitted from relationships created during the revolution. Many of them, for example, found places in parastatal units inside the new Libyan administration.

A good example of this merger is *Ansar al-Shari'a*, the group responsible for the murder of American ambassador Christopher Stevens in 2012. Since its "birth" in 2011, *Ansar al-Shari'a* has been not just a terrorist group. It also seems to be striving to gain the population's support through *da'wa*, or charitable works, and control of the territory as a replacement for the state, welfare state and Libyan institutions, with the aim of becoming something very similar to Hamas in the occupied Palestinian territories or *Hizbullah*. Since the 11 September 2012 attack, for instance, *Ansar al-Shari'a* has shown some openness and willingness to work within the boundaries of the state, trying to distance itself from accusations of being a member of al-Qaeda's network or even being merely a cover name for al-Qaeda. Although thousands of people took to the streets in Benghazi after the 11 September attack to demand the removal of the radical militias and show solidarity with the US, it is also true that Islamist militants in Libya are perceived as legitimate actors thanks to the role they played in the revolution. These militias also have an important role in territorial control and the provision of security in the power vacuum created by the collapse of the regime. During the post-Qaddafi period, the Libyan governments utilised many of them as part of the security forces, even if they were acting and operating quite independently (Torelli and Varvelli, 2014: 45-71).

Between 2012 and 2014, *Ansar al-Shari'a* groups expanded their activities in Derna, Benghazi, Ajdabiya and Sirte. Although the relationship between IS branches in Libya and *Ansar al-Shari'a* is very controversial, the dividing line between them was progressively seen as fluid. Both *Ansar al-Shari'a* and its various allied militias, especially those with younger members, appeared to admire the rise of IS in Iraq and Syria, creating ideal conditions for its diffusion in Libya. Between 2014 and 2015, parts of *Ansar al-Shari'a* joined forces with returnee jihadists to work under the flag of the Islamic State, especially in Sirte and Benghazi. Elsewhere it continued to exist as an autonomous group.

The Case of Derna

In Cyrenaica and Derna, a city of 80,000 on the Mediterranean coast, radicalisation has become well established over the past decade. However, the Syrian/Iraq campaign has significantly boosted it, creating a wave of veteran fighters that had a disastrous effect on the security situation in Libya. In October 2014, a local jihadist group, the Islamic Youth Shura Council (*Shabab al-Islam*), claimed Derna in the name of IS, thus showing IS's ability to break with traditional notions of territorial contiguity by creating an enclave outside its "borders" in Syria and Iraq. The Islamic Youth Shura Council was composed of elements of *Ansar al-Shari'a's* Derna branch and several other militias: the Rafallah al-Sahati Brigade; the February 17th Martyrs Brigade; The Shield of Libya; and *Jaysh al-Mujahidin*.

IS leadership accepted the proclamation a few weeks later and formally annexed the city. This seems to be the result of an expansion plan formulated in Syria and Iraq. Abu Bakr al-Baghdadi's first militants arrived in Libya in the spring of 2014, when the men of the al-Battar Brigade, composed entirely of Libyan volunteers, began returning from the war in Syria and Iraq. In Libya, the brigade was composed of 300 jihadists who had previously been deployed in Dayr al-Zur (Syria) and Mosul (Iraq). The Derna branch of IS was composed of about 800 fighters and operated in half a dozen camps on the outskirts of the town, having larger facilities in the nearby mountains as well (Benotman, 2014).[1]

In September 2014, aiming to help the al-Battar Brigade, al-Baghdadi sent to Derna one of his senior aides, Abu Nabil al-Anbari, an Iraqi veteran.[2] The city had an autonomous administrative organisation governed by a little-known Saudi (or Yemeni) preacher, Muhammad Abdullah, whose *nom de guerre* is Abu al-Bara' al-Azdi. Like many militiamen who founded the 'Province of Cyrenaica' (*wilayat al-barq*), al-Anbari and al-Azdi fought in Syria. Derna became the major new hub where fighters from North Africa, primarily Tunisia, are recruited. Out of the at least 3,000 Tunisians who have joined IS many have found protection in Libya (UN OHCHR, 2015).

However, under the name of the Mujahidin Shura Council (MSC), local Islamist militias, including the strong Abu Salim Martyrs' Brigade, created a coalition in order to confront and defeat IS (Heras, 2014). The Abu Salim Martyrs' Brigade mainly consists of Libyan fighters and was formed during the revolution. Its stance and ideology are very clear: it wants to establish an Islamic government in a Libya ruled by Islamic law. The Brigade provides and secures fuel supplies, protects banks from robberies and was led by 'Abd al-Hakim al-Hasidi and Salim Derby.[3] From a general point of view, the disputes between the groups are based, of course, upon an ideological difference: "local jihad" versus "global jihad". The Abu Salim Martyrs' Brigade is a local movement that seeks to establish an Islamic government in Libya, while the Shura Council of Islamic Youth in Derna is part of a global movement, "exogenous" to the Libyan tradition (The Maghrebi Note, 2015). In June 2015, Nasir 'Atiyya al-'Akar, a prominent al-Qaeda-linked jihadist in the Mujahidin Shura Council was murdered. The assassination, claimed by IS, set off a round of fighting. The MSC assaulted Islamic State positions around the city. A few of IS's key leaders in Derna were reportedly killed or captured. The two groups repeatedly clashed in the following months in disputes over power and resources. In July 2015, IS was driven out of a large part of Derna and, finally, in April 2016, definitively expelled from the area (Sehmer, 2016).

The Case of Sirte

The context of Islamic State's rise in Sirte is to a certain extent similar to the one that initially favoured IS's expansion in Iraq. The Iraqi government under Nouri al-Maliki marginalised large segments of the Sunni Iraqi population, which caused many Sunni tribes initially to consider IS as the lesser of two evils. In this context, mounting sectarian strife has created favourable conditions for the noticeable return of sectarian violence in Iraq's already fragmented society. Although Libya is not characterised by such a deep-rooted sectarianism, it is no coincidence that IS has expanded its activities in Sirte, the hometown of Muammar Qaddafi. On a beach in Sirte, IS beheaded 21 Egyptian Christians, as shown by the video circulated on the web in mid-February 2015. Sirte is a cradle of the Qaddafa tribe. Since Qaddafi's fall, the tribe has been expelled and ostracised by the Tripoli-based government. Other militias similarly accused it of conspiracy with the former regime. For this reason, it was eventually severely struck down. Part of the regime's rearguard as well as some tribal youth have thus joined Islamic State's cause mostly for political rather than ideological reasons (Varvelli, 2015). A consensus emerged about the evidence that IS attracted members from Ansar al-Shari'a and from the segments of the population that have been marginalised in the "new" Libya. However, as is evident in the case of Derna, some local armed factions and jihadists regard Islamic State as an infiltrator and competitor.

In August 2015, tribal fighting in Sirte began after IS assassinated Khalid ibn Rajab al-Firjani, a prominent imam from the local al-Farjan tribe, a substantial force in many of Libya's central coastal cities. Although the al-Farjan tribe has traditionally been strongly represented in the region's Sufi orders, the assassination came after local Salafists and al-Farjan tribesmen had refused to pledge allegiance to IS. Hasan al-Karami, one of the Libyan leaders of IS in Sirte, has family ties with and belongs to the clan of Isma'il al-Karami, head of the anti-drug agency during the Qaddafi regime and a Qaddafi militia leader during the revolution. This seems to confirm the fact that some supporters of the Colonel were recycled in IS (TMAITIC, 2016). He appears in some video propaganda of IS in Libya, preaching to the crowd in Derna in December 2014;[4] patrolling Sirte's market; speaking at a public meeting in which 40 officers of the Interior Ministry ask forgiveness for their lives (Raineri, 2015).

It is unlikely that IS will replicate the Sirte model in similar communities across Libya where there might be a perception of exclusion from the UN-led negotiations, but a potential risk persists. However the "tacit alliance" between IS and the tribal/local members appears to be very fragile. In April-May 2016, IS executed several members of the Qaddafa tribe in Sirte, demonstrating that tribes are not a monolith and support for the IS group is reversible.

On 5 May 2016 in Sirte, IS launched an offensive in eastern Tripolitania, named "Abu 'Ali al-Anbari" after a senior IS leader who was killed in an American raid at the end of March 2016 in eastern Syria. The attacks began with several suicide vehicles targeting checkpoints manned by militias from Misrata. Altogether, IS launched this offensive with up to 2,000 jihadists. According to Wolfgang Pusztai, a security expert and former Austrian Defence Attaché to Libya, "the relatively low number of IS fighters in Libya makes it necessary to concentrate forces for offensive operations while accepting a calculated risk on other frontlines" (cited in Varvelli, 2016: 102). The objective of the IS offensive in eastern Tripolitania seems to be to secure the western flank of its territory around Sirte and to foster important land lines of communication between IS in Libya and Boko Haram in Nigeria, and further to gain freedom of manoeuvre in the east, in the direction of the oil infrastructures (Pack and Sizer, 2016).

From Sirte and Sabratha to Where?

The ambivalence of relations between local communities and jihadist groups remains a central point in the analysis of radicalisation processes in Libya. For instance, the majority of the Libyan population did not support the rise of IS in the country. On its part, the Tripoli government initially refused to acknowledge the presence of IS in Sirte and in Tripolitania, and even went on to accuse former Qaddafi militias of fostering jihadist groups and aiding foreign infiltration. In reality, according to data from The Soufan Group and Italian diplomatic sources, the majority of the IS militants in Sirte (around 80%) are actually foreign fighters, of which half appear to be Tunisian nationals (Varvelli 2016). However, their presence in certain areas rather than others demonstrates that endogenous conditions make a difference. The intervention of Libyan troops, predominantly from Misurata under the formal direction of the Government of National Accord (aided by American bombings), made it possible to liberate Sirte in the autumn of 2016. Nonetheless, a proportion of the soldiers of the self-proclaimed Caliphate – whose total number reached somewhere between 5,000 and 6,000 jihadists at the height of combat (a figure sometimes exaggerated by the media) – managed to flee and disperse outside the city. Afterwards, an American raid targeted some of them in January 2017 on a rebuilt operational base in the south of the city (Schmitt, 2017). In the same month, there were accusations of looting and property seizure by Misuratan soldiers in Sirte, which suggests that there may again be systemic marginalisation of certain populations (Trew 2017). These events mirror dynamics in Iraq and Syria where NGOs and human rights agencies accuse the anti-IS militias of committing serious crimes in areas retaken from IS.

Furthermore, the heavy presence of Tunisian jihadists in Sabratha characterised what could be defined as a "third model" (differing from Derna and Sirte) of territorial takeover by IS in Libya. In Sabratha, Tunisian fighters affiliated with IS controlled an anti-Tunisia training camp. In February 2016, an American raid on another training camp in the city killed 40 IS militants accused of planning two large-scale attacks on Western tourists in Tunisia. The raid revealed the large number of Tunisian foreign fighters in Sabratha, and justified the West's increasing concern about the creation of a new base for IS troops in an illicit trafficking hub. In fact, Sabratha is a Mediterranean outlet of the trafficking corridor that runs from sub-Saharan Africa through Fezzan to the Libyan coasts. Illustrating a very different strategy compared to those used in Derna and Sirte, Sabratha can be taken as the third model of IS development in Libya. Indeed, the group proliferated in Sabratha avoiding IS's loud propaganda style with the aim of launching attacks into nearby Tunisia and not in Libya. The US air strikes had the immediate consequence of instigating military action by the local brigades against remaining IS troops, *de facto* ending a situation of *omertà* and tolerance towards the jihadist presence in the city. The local military council eventually forced IS to abandon Sabratha. According to a United Nations report, these IS troops are still operating in the area stretching from Tripoli to the Tunisian border, mainly in the rural zones. Some foreign fighters have crossed the Tunisian border, while others were retrenched in Sirte – at the time still in IS hands – in Tripoli and in the rural areas around Sabratha in the foothills of the Nefusa mountains. (UN SCR, 2016). This is a very worrying fact, more so because this area could become a recruiting base for terrorist attacks directed at Europe. Salman Abedi, the Libyan suicide bomber of the Manchester attack, travelled several times from Libya to Great Britain and had well-grounded connections in this area.

Militant Jihadists in Southern Libya

The southern region of Fezzan represents a different case, on the other hand. Radical groups tied to al-Qaeda in the Islamic Maghreb (AQIM), *al-Murabitun* and *Ansar al-Din* are still present and very active in this region, often engaging in illegal business. This evidence continues to make the area a possible "sanctuary" for criminal and terrorist organisations. In Fezzan, IS and AQIM conducted two rival campaigns while at the same time engaging in sporadic, circumstantial relations. Such relations were grounded on a substantial exchange of expertise, mostly regarding weapons, transport, and other fields of illegal trafficking (Shaw and Mangan, 2014). In January 2016, an AQIM video openly accused Italy of neo-colonialism for its attempt to mediate politically between the Libyan factions by hosting the Libyan summit meeting in Rome on 13 December 2015. The video featured Abu Yusuf al-'Anabi, AQIM's second in command. AQIM's interest in Libya seems to indicate that al-Qaeda has not relinquished its role in the country. AQIM is probably delegating its regional organisation in North Africa to spreading its influence with particular attention to the Fezzan theatre. However, with respect to this *communiqué*, the strategy seems aimed at mustering the Libyan factions against the new "invader" evoked by old ghosts; AQIM here proposed itself as the unifier combatting new colonialism (ANSA, 2016).

Since IS began its campaign in Sirte, it seemed to have different goals from al-Qaeda and the various local jihadist groups. At the same time, however, there were some tactical convergences on specific goals. IS sympathisers like *Ansar al-Shari'a* and former al-Qaeda members came together and united as the Benghazi Revolutionaries Shura Council to fight Haftar in the city of Benghazi. Elsewhere, as in Derna, the various jihadist groups fought one another. On the other hand, it is also true that the demarcation line between IS and *Ansar al-Shari'a* has become increasingly fluid over time. For instance, individuals or whole militias sided with IS, as the Sirte case demonstrated.

In the southern part of the country, the increasingly active pro-Haftar troops might once again facilitate a coalition among Islamic militias, the self-confessed jihadist militias and former IS soldiers withdrawn from Sirte. Most of the transnational jihadists active in southern Libya have a long history of local knowledge, a fact that stems from the Sahel insurrections of the 1990s and the Algerian civil war. During the 2011 revolution, these groups established relations with local armed forces and jihadists in the north, particularly in the north-eastern area of Benghazi, Derna and Ajdabiya. Fezzan's logistic corridor first shuffled groups of AQIM soldiers from the south towards the *Ansar al-Shari'a* networks, aiding the arrival of jihadists from Algeria, Mali and the Sahel in the northern training camps, and subsequently in Syria. In response, *Ansar al-Shari'a* stated that it had sent volunteers to Mali while training troops faithful to the Algerian jihadist Mukhtar Bilmukhtar, prior to the January 2013 attack on the Tiguentourine gas plant in Amenas, Algeria (Wehrey, 2012).

Local collaborators in Fezzan facilitated some of these movements. Among the most frequently cited in the UN report (UN SCR, 2016) on the jihadist presence in the area is the Border Guards Brigade 315, or Maghawir Brigade The Brigade is a militia based in the Tuareg-speaking city of Ubari and led by a former army officer and Islamist educator, Ahmed Umar al-Ansari, who resides in the southern part of the city along the route to Niger by way of the Salvador Pass. According to Frederick Wehrey (2017) from Carnegie Endowment for International Peace and several other analysts who were able to conduct on-site surveys, it should be acknowledged that enemies of the Tuareg have often exaggerated the gravity of extremist penetration in Ubari and Western areas of Fezzan. Despite the proven existence of jihadists and their camps around Ghat and in the mountain valleys of Aracus, this presence is mostly motivated by logistic reasons that can be traced to weak control by the government and the police rather than to widespread social support. For example, the group that conducted the attack on Amenas in 2013 passed through areas north of Ghat easily, precisely because the local brigades were unable to stop jihadist movement. For its part, although in the summer of 2016 AQIM appealed to its fighters to mobilise against Haftar's forces, it seems to concentrate specifically on the Sahel as a primary area of expansion through exploiting Libya to acquire logistic depth.

When relations exist between jihadists and local armed groups, they are based less on ideological affiliations and more on common interests in keeping borders free of control. The penetration of radical ideology in the southern areas controlled by the Tuareg – or more widely in the social weave of the south – is minimal, despite what is stated by the forces tied to Operation Dignity[5] and the Tebu population.[6] The various reports from the intelligence services of the different Libyan factions regarding the spread of IS after the fall of Sirte should be closely examined given their interest in depicting their adversaries as terrorists. In fact, IS never really extended its sphere of influence to southern Libya. Any attempt to influence or be present in the south will encounter not only a crowded market of armed groups tied to local communities and tribes, as already noted, but also networks affiliated with al-Qaeda. Even in north-eastern Libya, a good number of fighters who had defected from groups close to al-Qaeda or *Ansar al-Shari'a* to join IS are now returning to al-Qaeda. How this dynamic will evolve in the southern part of the country remains to be seen.

Indeed, the spread of IS through the south might have gone further. Last year independent sources reported that militants numbering between 60 and 80 were active near Girza, a town located 170 km west of Sirte. Another group of about 100 was located near Zalla and the Mabrouk oil wells (some 300 km south-east of Sirte). A third group was located in the al-Uwaynat area (near the border with Egypt and Sudan) (Lewis, 2017). IS demonstrated its ability to operate successfully in the area, as proven by the attacks on the power plants between Jufra and Sebha in 2017. In addition, as early as the summer of 2016, there were reports of the presence of pro-IS jihadists on the borders between Libya and Sudan, near the oases of Kufra and Tazirbu where the terrorist group – according to what was stated – reached an agreement with local smugglers to protect their northern supply lines (UN SCR, 2016).

Recent Political Developments and the Future of Jihadist Groups

It seems clear that political developments in Libya will influence the room for manoeuvre of jihadist groups in the country. The jihadist landscape seems characterised by a repositioning process. Despite the defeat and consequent disappearance of the most violent radical groups from cities like Benghazi and Sirte, IS and al-Qaeda remain present and active in the country. According to the UN special envoy Salamé, these jihadist groups have conducted various attacks since then. At the end of January 2017, 30 people died in two terrorist attacks in Benghazi. Significantly, the explosions were limited to the al-Salmani area which is controlled by Haftar's forces. Among the victims of the attack were, indeed, the officials of the local security services who responded directly to Haftar's commands. Together with the growth in attacks carried out in the area, counter-terrorism initiatives increased too, in particular those led by the US.[7]

The aim was to prevent the jihadist groups from gaining ground in the proximity of the city of Ubari. The airstrike was coordinated with Tripoli's GNA. While it was the first time that an attack had hit al-Qaeda members in the country, it followed the eight raids of the previous year that killed dozens of alleged terrorists mainly in the desert located to the south of Sirte. The attacks, conducted mainly with drones, helped to contain the terrorist menace which is still strong in this north African country. Both IS and al-Qaeda still retain the ability to conduct terrorist and other types of attacks. Consequently, they can undermine even more the already fragile and unstable security scenario. Nevertheless, the number of raids decreased compared to 2016 when 500 attacks were carried on in the city of Sirte in response to IS's expansion in Libya.

To cope with this unstable situation, French President Emmanuel Macron organised a conference on Libya in Paris on 29 May 2018. The conference concluded with a joint declaration from Fa'iz al-Sarraj, the president of the Government of National Accord, Aquila Selah Issa, the president of the Tobruk Chamber of Deputies, Khaled Mishri, the president of the Tripoli High Council of State and General Kahlifa Haftar, the head of the Libyan National Army. The four committed themselves to holding legislative and presidential elections on 10 December 2018, to facilitating a referendum before the elections for the approval of the constitution and to passing the necessary electoral legislation by 16 September. However, no referendum was called and there is still no agreement on new electoral legislation.

From this standpoint, they are committed to supporting the work of the UN envoy Ghassan Salamé and the national electoral commission, as well as working towards unifying the military and police forces under the leadership of the legitimate government. This is not the first document of this type. Aside from specifying dates, it is not very different from the one that was issued at the beginning of 2018 by the "Quartet for Libya" (the UN, EU, African Union and Arab League). What is new is the inclusion of the president of the High Council of State in a meeting organised through national diplomacy. In the previous meetings held in 2017 by national governments (in Cairo in February, in Abu Dhabi in May and in La Celle-St-Cloud in July) the High Council of State was not represented. The exclusion of this body led to the failure of the agreement proposed in the Salamé Action Plan in late 2017.

The coming months will show whether the four "guarantors" will be willing or able to follow up on their Paris commitments. The results of the summit are not encouraging. The French project is based on a vision that assumes the four Libyan leaders effectively have control of strong, compact coalitions. The project seems to aim to legitimise the four to the detriment of others. This approach risks being not only ineffective but also dangerous. On the other hand, the inclusive and broader approach of the United Nations and the National Dialogue Conference remains the best way to reduce the possibility of escalations.

On the one hand, the French project continues to wish to give *de facto* predominance to Haftar who, if elected as the President of the Republic, would also become the legitimate and civilian head of the country's armed forces and security services, an outcome that is totally unacceptable to the revolutionary and Islamist factions. At each attempt to legitimise Haftar, the galaxy of revolutionary and Islamist organisations bands together, which in turn destroys the centrist platform that the UN is still trying to strengthen as the only means towards a successful transition. The National Dialogue Conference is the latest attempt to create this platform, including and conciliating the myriad actors in the Libyan crisis. It has many weaknesses but also the merit of going in the right direction. The French project is not a contribution to the Conference but an alternative to it. On the other hand, Haftar's reported illness (Wintour, 2018) revealed the disunity of the forces that support him and the weakness of an eventual succession. It also highlighted Haftar's dependence on external actors such as France, Saudi Arabia or the United Arab Emirates. The siege of Derna is, at the same time, a show of force by Haftar and a factor that increases the revolutionaries' and Islamists' opposition to Haftar, uniting them on the political scene as well as on the military, as seen in the mid-May 2018 blitz on the oil crescent.

In addition, al-Sarraj also contributes to the current disaggregation of forces in Libya. His recent project to integrate the militias that supported him last year under the Ministry of the Interior – starting from the Salafists led by 'Abd al-Ra'uf Kara – is very similar to what the Libyan government did in 2012 which triggered the collapse of the state. The project increases neither his independence nor his leadership. On the contrary, it betrays his dependence as it may weaken the Government of National Accord over which he presides and which is desired precisely by the UN. This policy could, in addition, be very troublesome for Misurata and fragment the Tripolitania front.

Conclusions

Libya remains a very fragile country, sensible to radicalisation processes and to the presence of terrorist organisations. The reasons behind this are many: chronic instability, collapse of the state with a huge black market, fragmented security apparatus, jihadist tradition in some historically marginalised areas of the country, border porosity. Despite the IS defeat in Derna, Sirte and Sabratha, the group's members are now professionalized, and it appears difficult for them to find a different occupation. Furthermore, many of those fighters who came from outside will be unlikely to be able to return to their countries of origin. It is possible that some of those fighters will join other terrorist groups in the Sahel like AQIM. Alternatively, the IS-linked groups may choose to operate clandestinely. They may possibly adopt guerrilla tactics and attack, especially in the light of the next general elections which are planned to take place in 2019.

Notes

1 Noman Benotman is a former Libyan jihadist who is now involved in terrorism analysis at the Quilliam Foundation, UK.
2 Al-Anbari and al-Baghdadi met in a prison camp in Iraq prior to fighting together in the ranks of IS (Benotman, 2014).
3 Derby was killed in fighting with IS militants in June 2015.
4 See for instance the video at: https://archive.org/details/Moltaqa_1 [accessed 31 August 2015].

5 Confirming his growing strength and influence, General Khalifa Haftar on 16 May 2014 launched "Operation Dignity" with the aim of eradicating terrorist groups from Benghazi.
6 Tebu is a clan-based ethnic group inhabiting northern Chad, southern Libya, north-eastern Niger and north-western Sudan. They live as herders, nomads or as farmers near oases.
7 For instance, in March 2018 US forces announced that they had killed two al-Qaeda members. Among them was Musa Abu Dawud, an AQIM leader in Libya. Moreover, the US regularly patrols the Libyan skies.

References

ANSA. (2016). 'Al-Qaeda Threatens Italy'. *ANSA* [online], 14 January 2016. Available at: http://www.ansa.it/english/news/world/2016/01/14/al-qaeda-threatens-italy_bf3677bf-a525-45c2-ab8a-9d39f8fc448a.html [accessed 15 September 2018].

Benotman, N. (2014). 'IS Comes to Libya'. Interviewed by P. Cruickshank, N. Robertson, T. Lister and J. Karadsheh for *CNN* [online], 18 November 2014. Available at: https://edition.cnn.com/2014/11/18/world/isis-libya/index.html [accessed 14 May 2015].

Baldinetti, A. (2010). *The Origins of the Libyan Nation: Colonial Legacy, Exile and the Emergence of a New Nation-State*. Oxford: Routledge.

Heras, N. (2014). 'Libyan Islamist Militia Leader Salim Barrani Darbi Forms New Coalition in Derna'. *The Jamestown Foundation Militant Leadership Monitor* [online], 5(12). Available at: http://www.jamestown.org/single/?tx_ttnews%5Btt_news%5D=43227&tx_ttnews%5BbackPid%5D=381&cHash=bd474a8d1e337146eb3e49c0286218df#.VL_H9SuG-Lg [accessed 15 September 2018].

Lacher, W. (2015). "Libya: A Jihadist Growth Market", in Steinberg G., Weber A. (eds.), *Jihadism in Africa: Local Causes, Regional Expansion, International Alliances, Research Paper*. Berlin: SWP. Available at: https://www.swp-berlin.org/en/publication/libya-a-jihadist-growth-market/ [accessed 15 September 2018].

Lewis, A. (2017). *Islamic State Shifts to Libya's Desert Valleys after Sirte Defeat*. *Reuters*. Available at: https://www.reuters.com/article/us-libya-security-islamicstate/islamic-state-shifts-to-libyas-desert-valleys-after-sirte-defeat-idUSKBN15P1GX [accessed 15 September 2018].

Pack, J. and Sizer, L. (2016). *ISIS Fuels Discord in Libya. Using Oil to Weaken the Unity Government. Foreign Affairs*. Available at: https://www.foreignaffairs.com/articles/libya/2016-05-17/isis-fuels-discord-libya?cid=nlc-twofa-20160519&sp_mid=51416474&sp_rid=YXJodXJvLnZhcnZlbGxpQGhvdG1ha WwuaXQS1&spMailingID=51416474&spUserID=NTA0ODY1MzkyODES1&spJobID=922408674&spReportId=OTIyNDA4NjcoSo [accessed 15 September 2018].

Raineri, D. (2015). "La catena di comando dello Stato islamico in Libia". *Il Foglio* [online], 19 March 2015. Available at: https://www.ilfoglio.it/esteri/2015/03/19/news/la-catena-di-comando-dello-stato-islamico-in-libia-82035/ [accessed 31 August 2015].

Schmitt, E. (2017). *Warnings of a 'Powder Keg' in Libya as ISIS Regroups. New York Times*. Available at: https://www.nytimes.com/2017/03/21/world/africa/libya-isis.html [accessed 15 September 2018].

Sehmer, A. (2016). 'Libya: Islamic State Forced out of Derna'. *The Jamestown Foundation Terrorism Monitor* [online], 14(9). Available at: http://www.jamestown.org/single/?tx_ttnews%5Btt_news%5D=45373&tx_ttnews%5BbackPid%5D=7&cHash=b21308f283125 1226bf6e563b15459d2#.VytE_oSLTct [accessed 15 September 2018].

Shaw, M. and Mangan, F. (2014). *Illicit Trafficking and Libya's Transition: Profits and Losses*. Washington D.C.: United States Institute for Peace. [Online]. Available at https://www.usip.org/sites/default/files/PW96-Illicit-Trafficking-and-Libyas-Transition.pdf. [accessed 15 September 2018].

The Maghrebi Note. (2015). 'ISIS in Libya: The Origins of ISIS in Libya and Its Methodology'. *The Maghrebi Note* [online], February 2015. Available at: https://themaghrebinote.files.wordpress.com/2015/03/isis-and-its-origins-in-libya-themaghrebinote.pdf [accessed 15 May 2015].

TMAITIC (The Meir Amit Intelligence and Terrorism Information Center). (2016). "ISIS in Libya: A Major Regional and International Threat". *TMAITIC* [online], 20 January 2016. Available at: http://www.terrorism-info.org.il/en/article/20943 [accessed 20 May 2017].

Torelli, S. M. and Varvelli, A. (2014). 'New trends in North African Jihadism: Ansar al-Sharia in Tunisia and Libya', in Plebani A. (eds.), *New (and Old) Patterns of Jjihadism: al-Qa'ida, the Islamic State and Beyond*. Milan: ISPI, pp. 45-70. Available at: https://www.ispionline.it/it/pubblicazione/new-and-old-patterns-jihadism-al-qaida-islamic-state-and-beyond-11099 [accessed 15 September 2018].

Trew, B. (2017). 'Libyan-backed Fighters Accused of Looting City Seized from Isis'. The Times [online], 27 January 2017. Available at: https://www.thetimes.co.uk/article/libyan-backed-fighters-accused-of-looting-city-seized-from-isis-qgz5m5bkc [accessed 20 May 2017].

UN OHCR (UN Office of the High Commissioner for Human Rights). (2015). 'Preliminary Findings by the United Nations Working Group on the Use of Mercenaries on Its Official Visit to Tunisia – 1 to 8 July, 2015'. *OHCHR*. [Online]. Available at: http://www.ohchr.org/EN/NewsEvents/Pages/DisplayNews.aspx?NewsID=16219&LangID=E [accessed 15 September 2018].

UN SCR (United Nations Security Council Report). (2016). *Report of the Secretary-General on the Threat Posed to Libya and Neighbouring Countries*. UN Security Council. [Online].

Available at: http://www.securitycouncilreport.org/atf/cf/%7B65BFCF9B-6D27-4E9C-8CD3-CF6E4FF96FF9%7D/s_2016_627.pdf [accessed 20 May 2017].

Varvelli, A. (2015), *Libya's fight for Survival – Defeating Jihadist networks*. Brussels: European Foundation for Democracy. Available at: http://europeandemocracy.eu/2015/09/libyas-fight-for-survival-defeating-jihadist-networks/ [accessed 15 September 2018].

Varvelli, A. (2016). 'The Libyan Radicalization Hotbeds: Derna and Sirte as Case Studies', in A.Vravelli (ed.), *Jihadist Hotbeds: Understanding Local Radicalization Processes*. Milan: ISPI, 93-106. Available at: http://www.ispionline.it/it/EBook/Rapporto_Hotbeds_2016/JIHADIST.HOTBEDS_EBOOK.pdf [accessed 20 May 2017].

Wehrey, F. (2012). *The Struggle for Security in Eastern Libya*. Washington D.C.: Carnegie Endowment for International Peace. [Online]. Available at: http://carnegieendowment.org/2012/09/19/struggle-for-security-in-eastern-libya-pub-49425 [accessed 15 September 2018].

Wehrey, F. (2017). *The Challenge of Violent Extremism in North Africa: The Case of Libya*. Washington D.C.: Carnegie Endowment for International Peace. [Online]. Available at: https://carnegieendowment.org/2017/03/29/challenge-of-violent-extremism-in-north-africa-case-of-libya-pub-68446 [accessed 15 September 2018].

Wintour, P. (2018). 'Libyan Military Chief Khalifa Haftar Severely Ill After Stroke – Reports'. *The Guardian* [online], 11 April 2018. Available at: https://www.theguardian.com/world/2018/apr/11/libyan-military-boss-khalifa-haftar-severely-ill-after-stroke-report [accessed 15 September 2018].

CHAPTER 3

The "Unreturned": Dealing with the Foreign Fighters and Their Families who Remain in Syria and Iraq

Nadim Houry

Introduction

Tens of thousands of individuals from over 80 countries travelled to join Islamic State (IS) in Iraq and Syria. While foreign fighters espousing jihadist ideology have participated in military conflicts in recent decades, such as in Afghanistan, Bosnia, or Chechnya, the scale of travel to IS-held territory as well as the substantial percentage of women and children who undertook the journey was unprecedented.[1]

With IS's loss of its self-proclaimed "caliphate," international attention has mostly focused on the risk posed by the potential return of these foreigners to their home countries. But the flood of "returnees" that was feared did not materialise and returnees so far represent a relatively small percentage of those who travelled to live under IS. Cook and Vale (2018) noted that out of the 41,490 foreigners who became affiliated with IS only 7,366 (i.e. 17%) are known to have actually returned to their home countries.

What happened to those who did not "return"? While many died in anti-IS military operations, those who are still alive fall into three broad categories: (1) those detained by authorities and local groups in Iraq and Syria, (2) those still living in small pockets that remain under the control of IS in eastern Syria, and (3) those who are hiding in local communities in Syria, Iraq or neighbouring countries, notably Turkey, after paying smugglers to cross battle lines or borders.

This chapter focuses on those who are in detention in Iraq and Syria.[2] These IS-affiliated foreigners are very diverse in profile, with a significant percentage of women and children. The chapter begins with a quick overview of those who constitute these "unreturned" foreigners before delving into the challenges and difficulties they currently face. The main issue in northern Syria is the legal void they are in as the US-backed Syria Democratic Forces (SDF) which are holding them have stated that they do not intend to prosecute them and would like to transfer them to their home countries. However, with very few exceptions, most home countries have refused to take them back. For those held in Iraq, the issue is not a lack of trials but rather the absence of fair trials with Iraqi courts sentencing most of them to death or life in prison following rushed proceedings that fail to take into account a suspect's individual actions or role in IS. Not only does this situation affect the rights of the accused, it also denies justice to victims of IS who are not included in any proceedings. The current approach has also left IS-affiliated foreign children, who ended up in Syria and Iraq through no fault of their own, stranded in extremely vulnerable situations.

The "Un-returned:" A Quick Mapping

Most estimates put the number of foreigners who travelled to join IS or lived in its self-proclaimed "caliphate" at around 40,000 (RAN, 2017; Barrett, 2017). Cook and Vale (2018) review all publicly available information on those who travelled and counted 41,490 IS affiliates in Iraq and Syria whom they broke down as follows: 75% men, 13% women, 12% children. Of those, their study counted 7,366 IS returnees.[3] These numbers should be taken as best estimates because many countries did not properly track their nationals and no one really knows how many children were born to foreigners in Syria and Iraq.

The estimates of returnees are lower than initially expected or feared in security circles.[4] Studies suggest that there is a difference in the "rate of returns" depending on nationalities. As of July 2017, the Radicalization Awareness Network (RAN) estimated that about 30% of the approximately 5,000 residents of the European Union thought to have gone to Syria and Iraq had returned home (RAN 2017). Percentages were lower for nationals from Russia and the former Soviet Republics with the Soufan Group, a security consultancy, estimating that just over 10% of these foreigners had returned (Barrett, 2017). The lower number of returnees may be related to the fact that a large proportion of foreign fighters and their families were killed in the fighting or in airstrikes on IS-held territory. General Raymond Thomas, head of US Special Operations, stated that the US and its allies "have killed in conservative estimates 60,000 to 70,000" IS followers (Aspen Institute, 2017). This number does not distinguish between foreigners and locals and does not specify whether these IS followers were all combatants. Lt. Gen. Kenneth F. McKenzie Jr., the director of the Pentagon's Joint Staff, was quoted as saying, "We're not seeing a lot of flow out of the core caliphate because most of those people are dead now. Some of them are going to go to ground" (cited in Schmitt, 2017). Local authorities in Raqqa and Mosul continue to find bodies and mass graves in the rubble of their cities (HRW, 2018c; al-Jumma, 2018). In addition to those killed in the fighting, IS has also executed many within its own ranks, especially as it became increasingly worried about spies (Abdul-Zahra and Mroue, 2016).

But the lower numbers of returnees are also due to the fact that starting in 2015, it became harder for foreigners to leave Syria and Iraq. Many of their countries by then had issued arrest warrants for them or revoked their citizenship to deter or prevent them from returning.[3] Turkey, which was the only international gateway to access IS-controlled territories, also tightened its border control in late 2015, making it much harder for people who had joined IS to cross back and try to make it to their home countries (Soguel and Batrawy, 2016). By September 2016, Turkish forces and their local Syrian allies finally expelled IS from the last strip of territory it controlled along the Syrian-Turkish border effectively sealing it from the outside world (Mroue and Bilginsoy, 2016). For the foreigners who remained in Syria and Iraq, the options for leaving narrowed drastically.

The IS-affiliated foreigners who remain in Syria and Iraq are very diverse in profile with more than 80 nationalities represented. Based on available information about those detained in these countries, the group includes a significant percentage of women and children, many of them very young or born locally. Most of their home countries have indicated that they do not want them back and have left it to Iraqi and US-backed local authorities in northern Syria to deal with them despite the immense challenges already facing these authorities.

Legal Void in Syria

As SDF forces took areas from IS, they rounded up thousands of suspected IS members and their families, including many foreign men, women and children.

While the SDF has not released statistics about the number of foreigners it is holding, US officials told CNN in April 2019 that after the fall of the last IS enclave in Baghouz, the SDF is holding more than 2,000 men from over 50 countries (Browne & Hansler, 2019). The US is helping the SDF to run and secure its detention facilities.[6]

The Kurdish-led authorities in northern Syria have adopted distinct strategies for dealing with nationals and foreigners who are accused of joining IS. Syrian nationals are eventually transferred by the SDF to local ad hoc counter-terrorism courts, known as the People's Protection Courts, and some have their situations regularised as part of locally negotiated amnesties. However, with the exception of a few Iraqi nationals, the Kurdish-led authorities have not prosecuted any foreigner accused of IS affiliation. The official position of the local authorities in northern Syria is that the foreigners are a burden and their preference is that their countries take them back. A spokesperson for the SDF told the author that the foreigners were a "legal and logistical challenge. As much as possible, we try to contact their countries usually through the civilian administration. We are ready to hand them over. But many countries do not want to take them back" (Omar, 2018).

The overwhelming majority of countries have been reluctant to take their nationals back, citing fears that they represent a security threat. Some have also indicated concern about evidentiary and legal challenges that would prevent them from prosecuting these IS suspects (Savage 2018). Some countries, such as France, have explicitly said that they would prefer their nationals to be tried locally (BFM TV, 2018). However, the court system set up in northern Syria suffers from serious shortcomings and is not recognised internationally. Key issues include the absence of any role for a defence lawyer and the lack of any formal appeals process. Local critics also noted that the courts are not fully independent of the local authorities and lack adequately trained prosecutors and judges.[7]

Even if there was a local and international will to build up the local judicial system to ensure fair trials, the SDF is an unlikely long-term jailor. Its future control over northern Syria is uncertain and it has recently entered into negotiations with the Syrian government which may eventually lead to a return of government forces to the area (Francis, 2018). Given the record of Syrian government forces in abusing detainees and the abysmal record of Syria's counter-terrorism courts, an eventual transfer of SDF-held detainees to Syrian government custody would violate international norms and so far has not been discussed by international policy-makers as a desirable or viable option.[8]

The future of foreign IS members held in northern Syria was discussed at a meeting of key defence ministers of the "International Coalition to Defeat ISIS" in Rome in February 2018 but no agreement was reached (Castelfranco, 2018). Shortly thereafter, a number of local and international news outlets reported that the SDF exchanged some IS detainees for SDF fighters held by IS in secret exchange deals (Alani, 2018; Ensor and Boscolo, 2018). The SDF denied such exchanges and details of how many detainees, if any, may have been exchanged remain unknown.

In the absence of a collective agreement for transferring detainees to their home countries, the US began transferring some of the detained men to their country of origin through bilateral arrangements. A senior US Defense Department official was quoted in July 2018 as saying that about two dozen men had been returned while "another 100 or so are in the process of being sent back to their countries" (Lubold, 2018). The official did not provide specifics about the countries involved, but media outlets later reported that Lebanon and Macedonia had taken back some of their nationals (al-Amin and Murtada, 2018; Munoz, 2018). The US also repatriated two American citizens held by the SDF in northern Syria (Jarrett and Browne, 2018).

The current US-led approach to transferring detainees to their countries of origin may reduce the numbers of foreign detainees but it does not address the issue of what will happen to those – currently a majority – whose countries continue to refuse to allow them to return. France, for instance, has repeated its refusal to take them, and this position was emphasised again in July 2018 by Frederic Parisot, the French director of civil-military operations for the anti-IS coalition.[9] Britain's defence secretary also reiterated that the two British men accused of being members of an IS group implicated in the torture and beheading of a number of foreigners "should never be allowed to return to the UK," and media reports indicated that the UK may have already stripped them of their citizenship (Kirka, 2018).

In addition, the US would be in breach of its international obligations if it transferred these detainees to countries of origin or other third countries where they might be tortured. The United Nations Convention against Torture, to which the US is a party, as well as international humanitarian law prohibits the transfer of detainees to a country where "there are substantial grounds for believing" they would be in danger of being tortured or would otherwise face mistreatment. The concern is amplified by the fact that these transfers are being done through military channels and in secrecy, and therefore it is unclear whether detainees are being provided with the opportunity to contest their transfer.

If progress is not made with respect to the situation of the foreign men detained in northern Syria, hundreds of them are likely to remain there in a legal vacuum for the foreseeable future. What is needed is increased international cooperation to ensure accountability for IS's horrific crimes in trials where victims can participate if they wish to. In the absence of local trials, a clear framework is needed to arrange for transfers to other destinations where trials could take place. For those who cannot be sent back to their countries of origin because of fear of torture, there needs to be a serious effort to relocate them to a third country.

Detained in Camps: Foreign Women and Children

In addition to the almost 2,000 foreign men in its custody, the SDF is also holding IS-affiliated foreign women and children. Unlike the men, the SDF is not holding them in prisons but in three camps for the displaced in northern Syria, namely in Roj, 'Ayn 'Issa and al-Hawl. While the SDF have not released any statistics, visits to the camps by the author in January 2018, September 2018 and Februray 2019 as well as discussions with local camp administrators indicate that there were about 1,200 women and children from over 50 countries.

Like the men, the women and children are in legal limbo. The SDF says it is holding them temporarily until their countries take them back (Omar, 2018; Khalil, 2018); but in the absence of a return programme, their situation is beginning to resemble indefinite detention without legal basis. While the SDF has conducted investigations with the women, it has not prosecuted or referred any of them to trial. Some women complained that their SDF interrogators, usually women, beat them during interrogation, including some who reported beatings that would amount to torture (Ahmad, 2018). Many of the foreign children in the camps are under the age of six, including a significant number of those who were born while their mothers lived in areas under IS. Health conditions are poor. While there are doctors who visit the camps, specialised care is not readily available and diseases spread easily, especially among the children. During a visit by the author to the camps in January 2018, there was a Hepatitis A outbreak, and two months later cases of Tuberculosis were reported in Roj camp and led to the death of a Russian-speaking woman (whose nationality was not communicated to the author). There are no rehabilitation programmes or counselling for the women and children in the camps to treat the trauma they were exposed to. Many women expressed worries about their future, especially after reports that some women were part of the detainee exchanges with IS.

By May 2019, only Russia, Indonesia, Kazakhstan, Kosovo and the US were publicly known to have taken some of their nationals back from these camps.[10] France and Sweden have taken back a handful of children who were orphans. Russia initially made the most active effort to return women and children from Iraq and Syria. In August 2017, Ramzan Kadyrov, the head of Chechnya, organised efforts, with the support of the Kremlin, to repatriate women and children. Between August 2017 and February 2018, over 90 children and women arrived in Russia on special flights to Grozny, Chechnya's capital (Lokshina, 2018; Arutunyan, 2018). According to a Kurdish local official, an estimated 35 of those came from the camps in Syria (Hubbard, 2018). But these returns appear to have stopped in February 2018 without any explanation.

Other countries take the view that while they would not stop women and children from returning if they manage to reach a consulate or embassy, they will not exert any particular effort to return them from northern Syria. Given that these women and children are not free to leave the camps, let alone cross a border, these policies amount to perpetuating the indefinite detention currently in place in northern Syria.

Many officials justify their lack of initiative by arguing that their countries no longer have consular representation in Syria. But the real reason appears to be a political reluctance rooted in concern that the women and even the children could present a threat which governments feel ill-prepared to deal with because they may not have grounds to prosecute them.

The governments' attitudes started to harden towards women who travelled to join IS in 2016. Before then, policy towards women was more lenient as it was based on a generally accepted assumption that the women who left were victims of male relatives or recruiters. But since the participation of women in IS-inspired attacks in Europe, many security officials have reversed their assessment and a number of experts have noted that women's roles in IS's "caliphate" were not limited to care giving, with some participating in recruitment.[11] Attitudes hardened not only in Western countries but also in countries like Morocco and Tunisia (Tafnout, 2018).

Official hostility has also recently extended to the return of children who lived under IS as security officials began warning of the danger they could represent without necessarily substantiating these claims. Germany's head of domestic intelligence, for instance, warned of the "massive danger" posed by children returning to Europe, saying, "We have to consider that these children could be living time bombs. There is a danger that these children come back brainwashed with a mission to carry out attacks" (cited in Shalal and Siebold, 2018). Similar views – often sensationalised by media outlets – were expressed by British and French officials.[12]

But a potential threat cannot be the basis for condemning these women and children to indefinite detention without trial in camps in northern Syria. Women should either be referred to a judicial process if there is any evidence that they committed a crime or be released. If the local authorities in northern Syria cannot or do not wish to conduct such trials, then they need to transfer them to their countries of origin or release them. The current situation is particularly troubling for the children who remain in the camps. Most are very young, under the age of six, and their exposure to recruitment attempts by IS is probably minimal and in any case not subject to criminal responsibility. Even if the children attended IS's schools or fought for IS, international law is clear: anyone under the age of 18 who has been recruited into armed or terrorist groups is, without exception, the victim of crimes committed by adults. In the event that these children committed crimes, international juvenile justice standards call on relevant authorities to make efforts to seek alternatives to prosecution, and to prioritise rehabilitative measures with the aim of reintegrating children into society. By leaving them in the camps in northern Syria, their countries of origin deny them the support they need to reintegrate into society and, ironically, could be laying the ground for these children to end up as "time bombs."

Unfair Trials and Harsh Sentences in Iraq

Iraqi authorities have also detained large numbers of foreigners affiliated with IS as they have regained control of their territory (HRW, 2017). Iraq has not provided details of the number of foreign IS-affiliated nationals in detention, but media outlets managed to report on some information relating to foreign women and children. A security source (cited in AFP, 2017) stated that most of the foreign women and children held in Iraq belonged to a group of more than 1,300 foreigners detained by Iraqi forces in August 2017 during the battle for Tal Afar in Iraq's north-west. The group was composed of 509 women and 813 children. A large proportion of these women and children are Turkish nationals according to Iraqi Prime Minister al-Abadi (cited in AP, 2017b). The overall number of foreign women and children in detention is believed to be slightly higher based on information from sources close to the penitentiary system in Baghdad (HRW, 2018b).

Unlike the local authorities in northern Syria, Iraq has proceeded with trials against foreigners on charges of membership of or assistance to IS as well as illegal entry into the territory.[13] Such prosecutions of foreign nationals have encompassed men, women and children over the age of nine. The Iraqi authorities have not published any information about the number of foreigners tried in Iraq on IS-related charges. Abdul Zahra and George (2018) reported in March 2018 that the Iraqi government has detained more than 19,000 people, most of them Iraqis, on terrorism-related charges and convicted at least 8,861 since 2013. Of these, at least 3,130 were sentenced to death on terrorism-related charges, with at least 250 having been executed. However, these statistics do not mention how many are foreigners.

There are serious shortcomings in Iraq's current legal proceedings against individuals accused of IS affiliation. Trials are rushed and end in harsh sentences without taking into account the individual actions of suspects. Human Rights Watch (HRW, 2017) reported one judge stating that he had recommended the death penalty for an IS cook because "how could an ISIS fighter have executed someone if he had not been fed a good meal the night before?"

Opportunities for a meaningful and substantive defence are lacking in the cases reviewed by human rights groups and foreign journalists. Trials often last around ten minutes and sentences are often issued on the same day as the trial (Coker and Hassan, 2018). The overwhelming majority of cases that have been reported publicly ended with a life sentence, which in Iraq amounts to 20 years in jail, or the death penalty. Victims play no part in the proceedings and the current approach, with its lack of emphasis on individual actions, is unlikely to provide victims with closure or establish an essential record of the terrible crimes committed by IS.

A particular worry is that Iraq is carrying out its death sentences, which the UN has warned risks "resulting in gross, irreversible miscarriages of justice" (UN OHCHR, 2016). Two mass hangings of 42 and 38 convicted IS members took place in September and December 2017 (The New Arab, 2017; BBC, 2017). The true number of executions may be even higher but remains unknown due to lack of transparency by the government. Not only combatants but also civilian employees of IS are being sentenced to death.

Iraq applies the same strict approach to foreign women even though it initially seemed that it might adopt a different approach. In September 2017, shortly after the detention of a large group of foreign women and children near Tal Afar, Prime Minister Haider al-Abadi stated in an interview that many of the women and children were not guilty of any crime, and that his government was "in full communication" with their home countries to "find a way to hand them over" (cited in AP, 2017b). He noted that "it is not in our interest to keep families and children inside our country when their countries are prepared to take them." But Iraq appears to have changed its approach and began referring these foreign women for prosecution in large numbers starting in January 2018.

In trials of foreign women monitored by human rights groups, Iraqi authorities did not sufficiently examine the actual role and participation – if any – of these women in IS activities. Judges often asked the women the same set of questions about when and how they entered Iraq, where their husbands were, if they believed in IS ideology, and if they received any money from the extremist group. Many women ended up with sentences of 20 years in prison or the death penalty merely because they married an IS fighter or received a monthly stipend from IS after the deaths of their husbands.

There has been little discussion about what will happen to foreign men and women after they finish serving their sentences in Iraq. Will their countries of origin accept their "return" and, if not, where will they be deported to? In addition, what measures will the Iraqi authorities take to ensure that the time spent in prison helps in the future reintegration of IS-affiliated inmates. The current situation raises some concerns. The largest concentration of those with IS-related convictions is in Nasiriyah Central Prison, a maximum-security complex holding most of those sentenced for terrorism-related offences. According to a prison official, cells originally designed to hold two prisoners were in fact holding six (cited in Abdul Zahra and George, 2018). The official said that overcrowding made it difficult to segregate prisoners charged with terrorism from others and that an inadequate number of guards meant IS members are openly promoting their ideology inside the prison.

Countries with nationals facing trials in Iraq should work with Iraqi authorities to ensure fair trials, provide their nationals with access to consular services, and seek ways to improve detention conditions. They should also consider initiating discussions with Iraqi authorities about the possibility of having their nationals serve their sentences in their home countries to relieve Iraq's overcrowded prisons.

Trials of Foreign Children

Iraqi judicial authorities also prosecute foreign children over the age of nine on terrorism-related charges and sentence them in some cases to up to five years in prison for IS membership and up to 15 years for participating in violent acts (HRW, 2018b). Iraq's approach to these children seems to follow an age breakdown. A lawyer who has represented many foreign children accused of terrorism summarised the situation:

> For children between the ages of nine and thirteen, the courts are more lenient, though you can still be prosecuted for illegal entry and in some cases, for membership in IS. If you are just prosecuted for illegal entry, your sentence is usually between six months and one year. For membership, you get three to five years. If you are accused of participating in a violent act, like planting a bomb, then you can get between five and fifteen years (Qader, 2018).

He said that Iraq has conducted about 400-500 trials of children accused of affiliation with IS, including dozens of cases of foreign children, who are also charged with illegal entry into the country. Children as young as ten are sentenced for entering the country illegally even though their parents brought them there and they probably had no choice in the matter (HRW 2018b). Older children are subject to harsher sentences. An Iraqi court sentenced a 16-year-old German national whose case garnered much media attention to six years in jail – five years for IS membership and one year for entering Iraq illegally (Charter, 2018).

Iraq's current approach emphasises punishment in opposition to international juvenile justice standards which call on national authorities to make efforts to seek alternatives to prosecution, and to prioritise rehabilitative measures with the aim of reintegrating children into society. Even those children who may have been responsible for terrible acts of violence are often also victims of forced recruitment by IS. Therefore, international norms emphasise that authorities should incarcerate children only as a measure of last resort and for the shortest appropriate period. In 2007, the UN Committee on the Rights of the Child found holding children below the age of twelve criminally responsible "not to be internationally acceptable" (UN CRC, 2007). A report of the United Nations Office of the Special Representative of the Secretary-General for Children and Armed Conflict (UN SGCAC, 2011) similarly suggested that when dealing with children who took part in armed groups "more effective and appropriate methods, other than detention and prosecution are encouraged, enabling children to come to terms with their past and the acts they committed." Iraq's approach to children who are only accused of membership of a group like IS and not of any specific violent act is particularly troubling. In 2016, the UN Secretary-General (2016) criticised countries that respond to violent extremism by administratively detaining and prosecuting children for their alleged association with such groups.

Little information is available about the services available to children detained in Iraq. Foreign children under the age of three are usually kept in jail with their mothers in often overcrowded cells. Those between three and nine are usually separated from their detained mothers and put in foster institutions run by the Iraqi state. Those between nine and eighteen are held in juvenile detention facilities. Foreign orphans are kept in local orphanages.

While some foreign children have been transferred to their home countries, many others are still waiting to be transferred. Iraqi NGOs complain that many countries seem to delay or procrastinate in seeking the return of children who are their nationals.

Stateless Children

One particularly vulnerable group of children still in Iraq and Syria are those born to foreign parents living under IS and who do not have recognised birth certificates, which puts them at risk of statelessness. At least 730 infants from 19 countries were born under IS, including 566 recorded to have been born to a Western European parent (Cook and Vale, 2018: 30). However, due to considerable data gaps, particularly for the Middle East and North African region, the number of children born to at least one foreign IS parent is expected to be significantly higher. Some unverified estimates have suggested that up to 5,000 children were born to foreign parents (Chulov, 2017).[14]

The documentation problem for these children lies at two levels. First, if there are records, such as marriage or birth certificates, these tend to be issued by IS and such unofficial documentation is not recognised by the Iraqi or international authorities. Secondly, in many cases, most of these documents are no longer available as they were destroyed during the fighting.

In northern Syria, the SDF and the local administration started to issue birth certificates to children born to foreign mothers while living in SDF-run camps, but no measure has yet been taken for children previously born under IS. The situation is complicated by the fact that no country has diplomatic representation in northern Syria, which makes the process of proving lineage and issuing identity documents challenging.

The Iraqi government is working with some countries of origin to grant identity papers to children born to foreign parents. It conducts some DNA tests on foreign children as well as on their parents (Mostafa, 2018; Arraf, 2017). But many children are separated from their parents and there is no clear mechanism in place to compare DNA test results with those of extended families in home countries. The current system largely depends on the level of engagement with the countries of origin, which differs greatly. This creates a situation where many children are likely to fall through the cracks.

The current approach in Iraq and Syria for identifying children born to foreign parents is not adequate to handle the scale of the challenge. Some sources estimate that as many as 1,000 Russian minors have been orphaned or abandoned inside the conflict zones of Syria and Iraq (Ayres, 2017). ICSR estimates that 70% of children with a Belgian parent and currently present in Syria or Iraq were born under IS (Cook and Vale, 2018). Similarly, ICSR estimates that half of the children in Syria and Iraq with a Dutch or French parent are believed to be under four and five years old respectively, suggesting that many were born under IS.

There is an urgent need for states to take active steps to ensure that no child remains stateless. The home countries of foreign fighters should prepare to take back greater numbers of minors. Without clear political will and better coordination there is a risk that many of these children will fall through the cracks and end up living a life of stigma on the margins of Syrian and Iraqi society. Those bearing the "IS" label may find such societal stigma to be the fuel for future radicalisation.

Conclusion

The "un-returned," or those who travelled to join IS and remain today in Syria and Iraq, are unwanted. Their countries of origin overwhelmingly hope they can just remain there, and to this end have turned a blind eye to the legal and rights issues that affect their nationals, including very young children. But this approach – while it may be politically convenient for home countries – is short-sighted and fails to address pressing needs around providing fair trials for IS suspects, ensuring accountability for their crimes, guaranteeing safe and decent detention conditions, and promoting the safety and well-being of foreign children who ended up in IS territories through no fault of their own. After all, the failure to push for fair trials does not just affect the rights of suspects; it also denies victims their day in court. The absence of serious attempts to distinguish between those IS members who committed very grave crimes and those who simply married members of the group is not just unfair to some individuals but ultimately dilutes responsibility for the group's actions. and leads to overcrowded prisons in Iraq and Syria.

Those born in IS-controlled territories face the additional risk of remaining stateless as they usually lack recognised identification documents. Yet, instead of taking back foreign children – most of whom have extended families in their home countries who are waiting for their return – officials in many home countries have painted them as "time bombs" to be kept as far away as possible and have transferred the responsibility of handling them to the under-resourced authorities in Syria and Iraq.

The current situation not only raises major human rights concerns but also carries serious security risks. The US has voiced concerns that foreign detainees in northern Syria could escape from local prisons or help radicalise other inmates setting the stage for a renewed IS-inspired insurgency (Manson et al. 2018). This appears to be the main reason why it has tried to convince its allies to take their nationals back – with limited success so far. The handful of US-orchestrated transfers of foreign men that have recently taken place from northern Syria are shrouded in secrecy, raising concerns about possible transfers to torture or other ill-treatment.

A new approach is needed with the clear goal of ensuring fair trials that determine the individual culpability of those foreigners who travelled to join IS. The international community should work with Iraq to promote fair trials and ensure victim participation. If fair trials cannot be held locally in northern Syria, then they should be held in countries with a nexus to the perpetrators or the victims if conditions in those countries allow for such trials. There should be discussions about the possibility for foreigners convicted in trials in Iraq – or possible future trials held in northern Syria – to serve their sentences in their home countries to reduce overcrowding or deal with the uncertain future of northern Syria. The wellbeing of children should be a priority for all parties involved and accelerated measures should be adopted to issue them with identification documents, reunite them with their extended families, and provide them with psychological and educational support to reintegrate them.

Finally, there needs to be a discussion about the future of those in detention who have a legitimate fear of torture if sent back to their home countries and accordingly cannot be transferred back there. In interviews with the author, many women held in northern Syria expressed concern about their treatment if they were transferred to their countries of origin. Alternatives should be discussed for those who cannot return to their countries, including possible relocation to a third country. These discussions will not be easy. But waiting for the situation of foreigners who joined IS to somehow resolve itself will only make it more complicated.

Notes

1. For example, Thomas Hegghammer (2010: 60) found that of almost 20 conflicts that attracted foreign fighters with jihadist ideology, 13 involved fewer than 300 foreigners, while only 6 involved more than 1,000. For a broader discussion of the participation of foreign fighters in conflicts see Malet, 2017.
2. In the case of Syria, the focus is on those held by Syrian Democratic Forces (SDF) in north Syria. No information is publicly available about those held by the Syrian government.
3. Other studies suggest similar ranges. For example, Barrett (2017) estimates that "there are now at least 5,600 citizens or residents from 33 countries who have returned home." The European Parliamentary Research Service (EPRS, 2018) provides a good breakdown of returnees to European countries.
4. See for example comments by N.J. Rasmussen, Director of the United States National Counter Terrorism Centre, at the Aspen Forum in July 2017, saying that "fewer had returned than anticipated and assessing that most would likely stay to defend the caliphate" (cited in Barrett, 2017). See also comments by Peter Neumann from ICSR who notes that "I've been saying for a long time that there will not be a 'flood' of returnees, rather a steady trickle, and that's what we are seeing" (cited in Schmitt, 2017).
5. For a good discussion of deprivation of citizenship by European countries in the context of foreign fighters see EPRS 2018. Australia has also stripped citizenship from five IS supporters captured in Syria (McGuirk, 2018).
6. The New York Times reported that US Special Operations forces visit the prisons multiple times in a week to offer expertise in running them, train guards, and help process new detainees using biometrics and interrogation. On a visit to one detention facility a US military official was reportedly denied his request to speak with a detainee (Savage, 2018).
7. The author visited these local counter-terrorism courts in July 2017 and January 2018. Some of the findings from these visits can be found in HRW, 2018a.

8   Human rights groups and the UN Commission of Inquiry set up to investigate abuses in Syria have documented systemic human rights abuses of detainees by Syrian government forces including torture and large-scale deaths in detention. See for example HRW (Human Rights Watch), 2012. For an assessment of Syria's counterterrorism courts see Violations Documentation Centre, 2015 and Ekman, 2017.
9   When asked if France was working on repatriating its nationals, his answer was, "Well, on this question, it's quite clear. First of all, the government of France said that they do not want these people back. So I mean, that's a policy statement" (cited in US Department of Defense, 2018).
10 The US has only repatriated one female national with her four US children. For more details see Childress & Baker, 2018. Indonesia took back an extended family with at least 15 members in summer 2017 (Associated Press, 2017a). While some Western countries have repatriated children from Iraq, none have been repatriated from northern Syria so far, at least not publicly.
11 The study of Renard & Coolsaet (2018) from the Belgian Egmont Institute found that in Belgium, Germany, and the Netherlands "[u]ntil recently, women were treated with more clemency, but this has now come to an end." See also Mekhennet & Warrick, 2017 for the news reporting about the potential threat of women.
12 See, for example, the statements by Commander Dean Haydon, the head of Counter-Terrorism Command of London's Metropolitan Police Service (cited in Davenport and Hall, 2018) and comments by French Public Prosecutor François Molins (cited in RTL, 2018).
13 Since Iraq is a federal country, there are two judicial systems in charge of prosecuting IS affiliates: federal courts and courts operating in the Kurdistan Region of Iraq. Each has its own counter-terrorism laws. This chapter focuses on prosecutions before the federal courts where most foreigners have been tried. For more on Iraq's judicial prosecution of IS see HRW, 2017.
14 Iraq's Ministry of Interior surveyed the areas of Salaheddin, Kirkuk, Diyala and Anbar, and suggested that up to a third of marriageable-age women in these cities married members of IS, including foreigners, highlighting the potential number of foreign children. See reporting in al-Jibouri, 2016.

References

Abdul-Zahra, Q. and Mroue, B. (2016) 'Islamic State Kills Dozens of Its Own in Hunt for Spies', *Associated Press*, [online] 5 June 2016. Available at: https://apnews.com/98512c11

bc72441c95f5a6657837d9ca/islamic-state-kills-dozens-its-ownhunt-spies [accessed 15 October 2018].

Abdul-Zahra, Q. and George, S. (2018) 'Iraq Holding More than 19,000 Because of IS, Militant Ties', *Associated Press*, [online] 21 March 2018. Available at: https://www.apnews.com/aeece6571de54f5dba3543d91deed381 [accessed 15 October 2018].

AFP (Agence France Press). (2017) 'Iraq Set to Expel 500 Wives of IS Jihadists', [online] 18 September 2017. Available at: https://www.yahoo.com/news/iraq-set-expel-500-wives-jihadists-140520690.html [accessed 15 October 2018].

Ahmad, M. (anonymous). (2018). Interview by Nadim Houry for *Human Rights Watch* (HRW). Unpublished interview. 23 January 2018.

Al-Amin, I. and Murtada, R. (2018). 'A Very Secret US Operation in Beirut' [in Arabic]. *Al-Akhbar* [online] 2 August 2018. Available at: https://al-akhbar.com/Politics/255408/ [accessed 15 October 2018].

Alani, S. (2018). 'An Exchange between ISIS and SDF with 104 Women as Its Victims' [in Arabic]. *ANA Press* [online] 27 April 2018. Available at: http://anapress.net/a/519743184764168 [accessed 15 October 2018].

Al-Jibouri, G. (2016). 'Sins of the Father: Extremist Fighters' Children Live in Stateless Limbo in Iraq'. *Niqash* [online] 12 May 2016. Available at: http://www.niqash.org/en/articles/society/5267/ [accessed 15 October 2018].

Al-Jumma, K. (2018). 'Corpses Recovered from Zoo, Other Mass Grave Found' *Hawar News Agency* [online] 30 July 2018. Available at: http://hawarnews.com/en/haber/corpses-recovered-from-zoo-other-mass-grave-found-h2858.html [accessed 15 October 2018].

Arraf, J. (2017). 'Kidnapped, Abandoned Children Turn Up At Mosul Orphanage As ISIS Battle Ends'. *NPR* [online] 23 December 2017. Available at: https://www.npr.org/sections/parallels/2017/12/27/569396126/kidnapped-abandoned-children-turn-up-at-mosul-orphanage-as-isis-battle-ends?t=1534513177371&t=1539617047036 [accessed 15 October 2018].

Arutunyan, A. (2018). 'ISIS Returnees Bring Both Hope and Fear to Chechnya'. *International Crisis Group* [online] 26 March 2018. Available at: https://www.crisisgroup.org/europe-central-asia/caucasus/chechnya-russia/isis-returnees-bring-both-hope-and-fear-chechnya [accessed 15 October 2018].

Aspen Institute (2017). 'Aspen Security Forum 2017 Socom: Policing The World'. *Aspen Institute* [online] 21 July 2017. Available at: http://aspensecurityforum.org/wp-content/uploads/2017/07/SOCOM_Policing-the-World.pdf#page=7 [accessed 15 October 2018].

AP (Associated Press). (2017a) 'Indonesia Releases Family Detained for Joining IS in Syria'. *Associated Press* [online] 14 September 2017. Available at: http://www.dailymail.co.uk/

wires/ap/article-4883486/Indonesia-releases-family-detained-joining-IS-Syria.html [accessed 15 October 2018].

AP (Associated Press). (2017b) 'Iraq's Abadi: Half of IS Families Detained Near Mosul Are Turkish'. *Associated Press* [online] 16 September 2017. Available at: https://www.voanews.com/a/iraq-abadi-half-of-islamic-state-families-near-mosul-are-turkish/4032230.html [accessed 15 October 2018].

Ayres, S. (2017). 'Thousands of Russians Joined Islamic State and Brought Their Children Now Relatives Are Trying to Bring Them Home'. *Los Angeles Times* [online] 26 October 2017. Available at: http://www.latimes.com/world/europe/la-fg-russiaisis-baby-20171026-story.html [accessed 15 October 2018].

Barrett, R. (2017). *Beyond The Caliphate: Foreign Fighters and the Threat of Returnees*. The Soufan Center [online]. Available at: http://thesoufancenter.org/wp-content/uploads/2017/11/Beyond-the-Caliphate-Foreign-Fighters-and-the-Threat-of-Returnees-TSC-Report-October-2017-v3.pdf [accessed 15 October 2018].

BBC. (2017). 'Iraq Hangs 38 on Terrorism Charges'. *BBC* [online] 14 December 2017. Available at: http://www.bbc.com/news/world-middleeast-42356155 [accessed 15 October 2018].

BFM TV. (2018). 'Jihadistes françaises en Syrie: "Si leur défense est assurée, elles seront jugées là-bas", dit Griveaux'. *BFM TV* [online] 4 January 2018. Available at: https://www.bfmtv.com/politique/djihadistes-francaises-si-leur-defense-est-assuree-au-kurdistan-irakien-elles-seront-jugees-la-bas-1341391.html [accessed 15 October 2018].

Browne, R. & Hansler, J. (2019), 'US Officials Say More Than 2,000 Suspected Foreign ISIS Fighters Being Held in Syria.' *CNN* [online] 17 April 2019. Available at: https://edition.cnn.com/2019/04/17/politics/foreign-isis-fighters-syria/index.html [accessed 29 May 2019].

Castelfranco, S. (2018). 'Mattis: Syria Foreign Fighters Should Face Justice at Home'. *Voice of America* [online] 12 February 2018. Available at: https://www.voanews.com/a/mattis-syria-foreign-fighters-should-face-jsutice-home/4250186.html [accessed 15 October 2018].

Charter, D. (2018) 'Linda Wenzel, German Teen Who Joined Isis, Is Jailed for Six Years in Iraq'. *The Times* [online] 18 February 2018. Available at: https://www.thetimes.co.uk/article/linda-wenzel-german-teen-who-joined-isis-is-jailed-for-six-years-in-iraq-r07k8lg76 [accessed 15 October 2018].

Childress, S. & Baker, J. (2018). 'American Mom Who Lived Under ISIS Charged with Lying to FBI'. *PBS* [online] 24 July 2018. Available at: https://www.pbs.org/wgbh/frontline/article/american-woman-who-lived-under-isis-charged-with-lying-to-fbi/ [accessed 15 October 2018].

Chulov, M. (2017). 'Scorned and Stateless: Children of Isis Fighters Face an Uncertain Future'. *The Guardian* [online] 7 October 2017. Available at: https://www.theguardian.

com/world/2017/oct/07/children-isis-fighters-syria-raqqa-orphans-uncertain-future [accessed 15 October 2018].

Coker, M. & Hassan, F. (2018) 'A 10-Minute Trial, A Death Sentence: Iraqi Justice for ISIS Suspects' *The New York Times* [online] 17 April 2018. Available at: https://www.nytimes.com/2018/04/17/world/middleeast/iraq-isis-trials.html. [accessed 15 October 2018].

Cook, J. & Vale, G. (2018) *From Daesh to 'Diaspora': Tracing the Women and Minors of Islamic State*. The International Centre for the Study of Radicalisation and Political Violence [online]. Available at: https://icsr.info/wp-content/uploads/2018/07/Women-in-ISIS-report_20180719_web.pdf [accessed 15 October 2018].

Davenport, H. & Hall, A. (2018) 'Top Counter Terror Officer Warns of Threat Posed by Jihadi Children Returning to UK'. *Evening Standard* [online] 1 February 2018. Available at: https://www.standard.co.uk/news/uk/terror-threat-of-isis-children-returning-to-britain-to-commit-atrocities-top-counter-terror-police-a3755281.html [accessed 15 October 2018].

Donnelly, M. Sanderson, T. and Fellman, Z. (2017). *Foreign Fighters in History*. Center for Strategic and International Studies [online]. Available at: http://foreignfighters.csis.org/history_foreign_fighter_project.pdf [accessed 15 October 2018].

Ekman, M. (2017) *ILAC Rule of Law Assessment Report: Syria 2017. International Legal Assistance Consortium (ILAC)* [online]. Available at: http://www.ilacnet.org/wp-content/uploads/2017/04/Syria2017.pdf [accessed 15 October 2018].

Ensor, J. and Boscolo, B. (2018) 'European Isil Jihadists Released under Secret Deals Agreed by UK's Allies in Syria'. *The Daily Telegraph* [online] 15 June 2018. Available at: https://www.telegraph.co.uk/news/2018/06/15/european-isil-jihadists-released-secret-deals-agreed-uks-allies/ [accessed 15 October 2018].

EPRS. (2018). *The Return of Foreign Fighters to EU Soil, Ex-Post Evaluation*. European Parliamentary Research Service [online]. Available at: http://www.europarl.europa.eu/RegData/etudes/STUD/2018/621811/EPRS_STU(2018)621811_EN.pdf [accessed 15 October 2018].

Francis, E. (2018). 'Syrian Kurdish-led Council Visits Damascus for New Talks: Co-Chair'. *Reuters* [online] 14 August 2018. Available at: https://www.reuters.com/article/us-mideast-crisis-syria-talks/syrian-kurdish-led-council-visits-damascus-for-new-talks-co-chair-idUSKBN1KZ0GA [accessed 15 October 2018].

Hegghammer, T. (2010). 'The Rise of Muslim Foreign Fighters: Islam and the Globalization of Jihad,' *International Security* [online] 35(3). Available at: https://www.mitpressjournals.org/doi/pdf/10.1162/ISEC_a_00023 [accessed 15 October 2018]

HRW (Human Rights Watch). (2012). *Torture Archipelago: Arbitrary Arrests, Torture, and Enforced Disappearances in Syria's Underground Prisons since March 2011*. HRW [online].

Available at: https://www.hrw.org/report/2012/07/03/torture-archipelago/arbitrary-arrests-torture-and-enforced-disappearances-syrias [accessed 15 October 2018].

HRW (Human Rights Watch). (2017). *Flawed Justice: Accountability for ISIS Crimes in Iraq*. HRW [online]. Available at: https://www.hrw.org/report/2017/12/05/flawed-justice/accountability-isis-crimes-iraq [accessed 15 October 2018].

HRW (Human Rights Watch). (2018a) *Ensure Fair Trials of Syria ISIS Suspects*, HRW [online]. HRW [online] 13 February 2018. Available at: https://www.hrw.org/news/2018/02/13/ensure-fair-trials-syria-isis-suspects [accessed 15 October 2018].

HRW (Human Rights Watch). (2018b) *Iraq: Change Approach to Foreign Women, Children in ISIS-Linked Trials*. HRW [online] 21 June 2018. Available at: https://www.hrw.org/news/2018/06/21/iraq-change-approach-foreign-women-children-isis-linked-trials [accessed 15 October 2018].

HRW (Human Rights Watch). (2018c) *Syria: Mass Graves in Former ISIS Areas*. HRW [online] 3 July 2018. Available at: https://www.hrw.org/news/2018/07/03/syria-mass-graves-former-isis-areas [accessed 15 October 2018].

Hubbard, B. (2018) 'Wives and Children of ISIS: Warehoused in Syria, Unwanted Back Home'. *The New York Times* [online] 4 July 2018. Available at: https://www.nytimes.com/2018/07/04/world/middleeast/islamic-state-families-syria.html [accessed 15 October 2018].

Jarrett, L. & Browne, R. (2018) 'American Accused of Supporting ISIS in Syria Transferred to US for Prosecution'. *CNN* [online] 25 July 2018. Available at: https://edition.cnn.com/2018/07/24/politics/us-citizens-accused-isis-transferred/index.html. [accessed when?]

Khalil, R. (2018). Interview with Redur Khalil (Head of external relations at the SDF) by Nadim Houry for *Human Rights Watch* (HRW). Unpublished interview. 20 January 2018.

Kirka, D. (2018). 'UK Defense Chief: Don't Let 2 British ISIS Suspects Return'. *Associated Press* [online] 11 February 2018. Available at: https://kval.com/news/nation-world/uk-defense-chief-dont-let-2-british-is-suspects-return [accessed 15 October 2018].

Lokshina, T. (2018). 'Will Russia Bring Home Children Who Lived Under ISIS/the Islamic State?'. Foreign Policy in Focus [online] 14 August 2018. Available at: https://fpif.org/will-russia-bring-home-children-who-lived-in-islamic-state/ [accessed 15 October 2018].

Lubold, G. (2018). 'U.S. Weighs Destinations for Islamic State Detainees in Syria'. *Wall Street Journal* [online] 18 July 2018. Available at: https://www.wsj.com/articles/u-s-weighs-destinations-for-islamic-state-detainees-in-syria-1531951090 [accessed 15 October 2018].

Malet, D. (2017). *Foreign Fighters: Transnational Identity in Civil Conflicts*. 2nd edn. New York: Oxford University Press.

Malet, D. (2018). 'The European Experience With Foreign Fighters and Returnees,' in T. Renard and R. Coolsaet (eds), *Returnees: Who Are They, Why Are They (Not) Coming Back and How Should We Deal with Them?* Brussels: Egmont Institute [online]. Available at: http://www.egmontinstitute.be/content/uploads/2018/02/egmont.papers.101_online_v1-3.pdf?type=pdf [accessed 15 October 2018].

Manson, K., Solomon, E. and Bond, D. (2018). 'US Urges Allies to Help with Captured Foreign Isis Fighters' *Financial Times*, [online] 12 February 2018. Available at: https://www.ft.com/content/9d76776e-0f71-11e8-940e-08320fc2a277 [accessed 15 October 2018].

McGuirk, R. (2018). 'Australia Strips Citizenship From Five ISIS Supporters Captured in Syria' *Associated Press* [online] 9 August 2018. Available at: https://www.yahoo.com/news/australia-strips-citizenship-islamic-state-supporters-232905564.html?guccounter=1 [accessed 15 October 2018].

Mekhennet, S. and Warrick, J. (2017). 'The Jihadist Plan to Use Women to Launch the Next Incarnation of ISIS'. *Washington Post* [online] 28 November 2017. Available at: https://www.washingtonpost.com/world/national-security/the-jihadist-plan-to-use-women-to-launch-the-next-incarnation-of-isis/2017/11/26/e81435b4-ca29-11e7-8321-481fd63f174d_story.html [accessed 15 October 2018].

Meleagrou-Hitchens, A., Hughes, S. and Clifford, B. (2018). *The Travelers: American Jihadists in Syria and Iraq*. Washington D.C.: Program Extremism George Washington University [online]. Available at: https://extremism.gwu.edu/sites/g/files/zaxdzs2191/f/TravelersAmericanJihadistsinSyriaandIraq.pdf [accessed 15 October 2018].

Mostafa, N. (2018). 'Foreign IS Members' Children in Iraq to Undergo DNA Tests Before Returning Back to Homelands'. *Iraqi News* [online] 4 February 2018. Available at: https://www.iraqinews.com/iraq-war/foreign-members-children-iraq-undergo-dna-tests-returning-back-homelands/ [accessed 15 October 2018].

Mroue, B. and Bilginsoy, Z. (2016). 'Turkey: ISIS Has Lost All Territory along Syria-Turkey Border'. *Military Times* [online] 4 September 2016. Available at: https://www.militarytimes.com/2016/09/04/turkey-isis-has-lost-all-territory-along-syria-turkey-border [accessed 15 October 2018].

Muñoz, C. (2018). 'Pentagon Praises Macedonia for Repatriation of ISIS Foreign Fighters' *Washington Times* [online] 7 August 2018. Available at: https://www.washingtontimes.com/news/2018/aug/7/pentagon-praises-macedonia-repatriation-isis-forei [accessed 15 October 2018].

Omar, A. K. (2018). Interview with Dr. Abdel Karim Omar for Human Rights Watch (HRW) by Nadim Houry. Unpublished interview. 22 January 2018.

Radicalization Awareness Network. (2017). *RAN Manual, Responses to Returnees: Foreign Terrorist Fighters and Their Families* [online]. Available at: https://ec.europa.eu/home-affairs/sites/homeaffairs/files/ran_br_a4_m10_en.pdf [accessed 15 October 2018].

Renard, T. and Coolsaet R. (2018). *Returnees: Who Are They, Why Are They (Not) Coming Back and How Should We Deal with Them?* Brussels: Egmont Institute [online]. Available at: http://www.egmontinstitute.be/content/uploads/2018/02/egmont.papers.101_online_v1-3.pdf?type=pdf [accessed 15 October 2018].

RTL. (2018). 'Les enfants de jihadistes sont des bombes à retardement'. *RTL*, [online] 31 January 2018. Available at: https://www.rtl.fr/actu/debats-societe/francois-molins-sur-rtl-les-enfants-de-jihadistes-sont-des-bombes-a-retardement-7791948055 [accessed 15 October 2018].

Qader, K. (anonymous). 2018. Interview with Iraqi lawyer for Human Rights Watch (HRW) by Nadim Houry. Unpublished interview. 18 June 2018.

Savage, C. (2018). 'As ISIS Fighters Fill Prisons in Syria, Their Home Nations Look Away' *The New York Times*, [online] 18 July 2018. Available at: https://www.nytimes.com/2018/07/18/world/middleeast/islamic-state-detainees-syria-prisons.html [accessed 15 October 2018].

Schmitt, E. (2017). 'ISIS Fighters Are Not Flooding Back Home to Wreak Havoc as Feared'. *New York Times*, [online] 22 October 2017. Available at: https://www.nytimes.com/2017/10/22/us/politics/fewer-isis-fighters-returning-home.html [accessed 15 October 2018].

Shalal, A. and Siebold, S. (2018). 'Brainwashed Children of Islamist Fighters Worry Germany: Spy Chief'. *Reuters*, [online] 31 January 2018. Available at: https://www.reuters.com/article/us-germany-security-children/brainwashed-children-of-islamist-fighters-worry-germany-spy-chief-idUSKBN1FK1FJ [accessed 15 October 2018].

Soguel, D. and Batrawy, A. (2016). 'Turkey Tightens Jihadist Highway Near Syria Border, Pressuring ISIS'. *Associated Press*, [online] 6 July 2016. Available at: https://www.haaretz.com/middle-east-news/turkey/turkey-tightens-jihadi-highway-1.5406263 [accessed 15 October 2018].

Tafnout, A. (2018). *Le Maroc refuse de rapatrier 200 veuves et orphelins des jihadistes en Syrie*. *H24info*, [online] 11 July 2018. Available at: https://www.h24info.ma/maroc/le-maroc-refuse-de-rapatrier-200-veuves-et-orphelins-des-jihadistes-en-syrie/ [accessed 15 October 2018].

The New Arab. (2017). 'Iraq Carries Out Biggest Mass Execution of Prisoners This Year'. *The New Arab*, [online] 25 September 2017. Available at: https://www.alaraby.co.uk/english/news/2017/9/25/iraq-executes-42-prisoners-in-one-day [accessed 15 October 2018].

UN CRC (UN Committee on the Rights of the Child). (2007). General Comment No. 10 (2007), Children's Rights in Juvenile Justice, CRC/C/GC/10, 25 April 2007. Available at: https://www2.ohchr.org/english/bodies/crc/docs/CRC.C.GC.10.pdf [accessed 15 October 2018].

UN OHCR (UN Office of the High Commissioner for Human Rights). (2016). 'Iraq: Fast-Tracking executions will only accelerate injustice – Zeid'. *OHCHR*, [online] 1 August 2016. Available at: https://www.ohchr.org/en/NewsEvents/Pages/DisplayNews.aspx?NewsID=20324&LangID=E [accessed 15 October 2018].

UN Secretary-General. (2016). *Children and Armed Conflict: Report of the Secretary-General*. [Online]. Available at: http://www.un.org/ga/search/view_doc.asp?symbol=S/2016/360 [accessed 15 October 2018].

UN SGCAC (United Nations Office of the Special Representative of the Secretary-General for Children and Armed Conflict). (2011). *Children and Justice During and in the Aftermath of Armed Conflict*. [Online]. Available at: https://childrenandarmedconflict.un.org/publications/WorkingPaper-3_Children-and-Justice.pdf [accessed 15 October 2018].

US Department of Defense. (2018) *Press Briefing by French General Parisot via Teleconference from Baghdad, Iraq. US Department of Defense*, [online] 24 July 2018. Available at: https://www.defense.gov/News/Transcripts/Transcript-View/Article/1583421/department-of-defense-press-briefing-by-french-general-parisot-via-teleconferen/ [accessed 15 October 2018].

Violations Documentation Centre. (2015). *Special Report on Counter-Terrorism Law No. 19 and the Counter-Terrorism Court in Syria*. [Online]. Available at:, http://www.vdc-sy.info/pdf/reports/1430186775-English.pdf [accessed 15 October 2018].

CHAPTER 4
Cyber Jihadism: Today and Tomorrow

Laith Alkhouri

Introduction

Technological advancements have effectively become the backbone of the human race. Cyber technology is unarguably one of the world's greatest achievements. It has supremely accelerated the interconnectedness of people around the globe, helping shape our economies, policies, and behaviour. Cyberspace sits at the heart of our growth, seamlessly fashioning how we act towards others and how we present ourselves to them. Criminals of all sorts are no exception; they also utilise cyber technology to advance. The international community is especially concerned with Violent Non-State Actors (VNSA), among these criminals, as they continue to proliferate and grow. Their need for networking requires constant integration of cyberspace and digital technology into their ecosystem. Indeed, their reliance on the Internet is inseparable from their reliance on new recruits, new funds, and new PR platforms — all of which are critical to these groups' very existence.

The history of cyber jihadism is quite recent. When al-Qaeda launched the 9/11 attacks, its media apparatus consisted of embarrassingly low quality VHS tapes that partially aired on al-Jazeera, and one simple website that included written statements and lectures by al-Qaeda leaders. By the time the US invaded Iraq two years later, a jihadist social networking web messaging board was distributing full-length al-Qaeda in Iraq (AQI) videos. Then, unbeknownst to the international community, the administrator of the website, known as Muntada al-Ansar, was

19-year-old Younis Tsouli, a technically savvy young man of Moroccan descent living with his parents in England.

Tsouli represented a unique gateway into the evolution of today's online jihad; an online channel that bridged hardened battleground jihadists with aspiring individuals. Users of the online forum regularly spoke about their intention to leave their homelands and join al-Qaeda, and in some instances pointed to the administrator as a key link. Others indeed attempted to join or attempted to launch terror attacks at home. The head of the Metropolitan Police Counter Terrorism Command explained that Tsouli "provided a link to core al-Qaeda, to the heart of al-Qaeda, and the wider network that he was linking into through the Internet" (Akhgar and Yates, 2013). Although by 2005 the web forum went offline and Tsouli was arrested and sentenced to nearly 10 years in prison in the United Kingdom, his emergence represented the metaphorical keystone in the online jihadist community's quick and persistent integration of cyberspace into its activities.

This chapter discusses the possible scenarios about how cyber jihadist terrorists would be using technology and cyberspace in the near future, including their online platforms and technology tradecraft. Illuminating this area is critical in order better to understand the adaptive and innovative cyber behaviour of VNSA and might help to shed light on the bigger picture of cyber terrorism. It raises awareness of the evolving scope of terror threats, their potential scale, challenges and impact.

Possibilities versus Probabilities

Our collective fear of terrorists' use of advanced technology is notably reactive. We fear the possibilities of their success, an enormously wider range of variables than, say, the probabilities of their success. For legitimate reasons, we want to cover the gaps in security measures against them regardless of their criticality. Dave Mosher and Skye Gould conducted a study (2017) on how much threat terrorists pose to US citizens, using national health statistics. While an assault by gun has lifetime odds of 1/358 and suicide at 1/98, death by foreign-born terrorists is at 1/45,808. This means, they conclude, "terrorists pose a very small threat to Americans." Although currently statistical analyses on measuring terror groups' use of cyber technology and the direct impact on human lives are not available, we can assume that the lifetime odds of death by "IS cyber actors" are significantly lower. But here we speak about the potential cyber skillset of IS and those in its ilk, and ask whether we should be concerned when pondering upon the potential consequences.

The realisation that online social networking connects people of mutual interest must elicit attention as to how criminals of all sorts use it to enhance their capabilities and advance their operations. We can only consider what terror groups have been able to do without an imperative need for the Internet; hijack planes, conduct assassinations and raise money, to name a few. With cyber technology, terror groups are able to enhance their networking and drive their agenda even further than at any time before.

Indeed, the Internet has pushed us to limitless possibilities. It did so also for IS; it represents a virtual haven for the crumbling Caliphate. The group remains relevant precisely because its online footprint is steadfast, allowing it to continue radicalising and attracting people from around the world. Its main success criterion, however, is the decentralisation of terrorism: creating an avenue for individuals to take on what equals individual responsibility or find a sense of belonging, and conduct attacks out of inspiration by the group's cause. Jacob Olidort (2016) observes that "brand control is more important to [IS] than territory," arguing that "insofar as the group's sights are set on 'inspiring' others to its cause, it can use or do away with governance as the group considers helpful toward this end."[3] In other words, IS's lore is more of a cause than a group membership, and the decentralisation of its terrorism in the age of technology allows it to garner sentimental support and further cement its ideology without directly communicating with its supporters.

Decentralising Terrorism Online

When IS emerged as the strongest, most well-funded terrorist organisation in 2013 as the successor of what was al-Qaeda in Iraq, it seized large swaths of land and drove its operations in a centralised fashion. As the leaders directed and foot soldiers were executed, it quickly transformed into a *de facto* governing body in areas it dominated. It succeeded in attracting thousands of fighters from nearly 100 countries, swiftly and brutally controlling areas altogether larger than the land of several sovereign countries. Just four years later, the group is crumbling faster every day. However, IS has made gains from all these losses. They are illustrated in its massive online footprint and successful outreach to the "touch-screen generation."

What has pushed IS to continue decentralising is the efficacious scrutiny it has gradually and consistently faced from government agencies and tech companies, to hackers and online activists. The constant vigilance has driven many IS supporters to adapt, pivot, and innovate. They have released dozens of Information Security (infosec) instructional manuals authored by the jihadists, thousands of online IS followers have reverted to using encryption technology, and many of them have continued to confine themselves on "deep web" messaging boards, which are password protected and vetted online communities that shut down registration to new members and operate within an elite but hardline decentralised collective. The Internet is their most imperative avenue to drive their cause, and they are at a constant cyber war, so to say, with their enemies. The persistent challenge to remain relevant and to cement a sense of belonging has given birth to some innovativeness among them, the consequences of which may pose significant harm to individuals and industries. Without IS's territorial control, for now, there is a growing need to understand and counter the decentralisation of its terrorism. Among the priorities is to counter its online footprint; but, more importantly, to study the methods and procedures used by its followers and come up with robust solutions in a proactive fashion.

Viral Consumption

Countless discussions on IS's use of technology have come to the fore since its early metamorphosis. The group has focused on growing its audience through disseminating its propaganda online and recruiting tech savvy individuals. This has placed the group at the top of many governments' security agendas. IS's significant footprint online is partially due to its outreach to the smartphone generation — seamlessly fusing its messages into easily accessible formats in rapid dissemination and consumption.

IS declared its Caliphate in summer 2014 and since then has run a well-oiled media machine with nearly 30 media units in multiple languages. Until the end of 2015 when it started suffering major setbacks on the Open Web — the online environments that are indexed, discoverable, and searchable by search engines like Google — Twitter was arguably IS's most mainstream channel. According to Berger and Morgan (2015), IS's supporters pushed out over 200,000 tweets on daily average, and probably out-tweeted their opponents during their era of highest success. Based on data mining and content analysis, Badawy and Ferrara (2017) explored the theory that "theological and violence related issues compose a little over 30 percent of all the tweets."

The viral nature of the Internet facilitated such logistics and ensured the group's online longevity. Before IS, cyber jihadism had largely been confined within the Deep Web — a large part of the Internet that is not indexed by search engines. It comprises membership-based communities that stand behind password protected walls and its administrators very thoroughly scrutinise and vet newcomers. These underground environments, or web forums, have maintained a repository of jihadist propaganda and militant material. While IS exploited the "mainstream" Internet in unprecedented ways, it still maintains a robust and comprehensive database of its own multimedia on its top Deep Web forums. Uploading much of this content back on to the Open Web has not been an issue because every time social media companies suspend it, the cyber environment can still remain accessible to the public at large.

IS followers are adapting to a wide array of emergent cyber technology, such as encryption, hacking, and cloud technology. In other words, we are witnessing an evolution in the group's digital DNA. Even with its imminent defeat on the ground in Iraq and Syria, the group is taunting the international community with its quick adaptation and, indeed, reliance on obfuscating its cyber footprint.

Birth of a New Beast: Encrypted Platforms

We today witness the increasing use of encryption technology by IS supporters. Jihadists' dabbling in the use of encryption and security programs is not unknown. In 2007, the administrators of an online jihadist messaging board created a basic encrypted communication software known as "*asrar al-mujahidin*" or *mujahidin* secrets (Ullah, 2018). The software was not too disconcerting as far as intelligence agencies were concerned. The issue today is that IS has tailored its messages to the touch-screen audience, utilising a global technology available to the average citizen. This has widened its outreach network to such a global level that ensures a solid follower base, which equals to or transcends in value having territorial control. Killing a message with military power has no effect here, and for IS cyber terrorism becomes the practical utilisation of cyberspace as a main arena of operations.

The amplified suspension of the radical jihadist accounts and the removal of violent propaganda by video sharing platforms like Youtube, Twitter and Facebook are significant victories against the terror group. Yet, such scrutiny has helped to unleash noticeable innovative techniques among the IS online community. This is a crucial evolution for the sake of the group's survival. In May 2017, Facebook watchmen identified more than 1,300 posts on the site as credible terrorist threats in a single month and faced a "mission impossible" to control the amount of content proliferated by extremists (Hopkins, 2017).

Less than a year later, Facebook, Youtube, Twitter and Microsoft released the first technology union – The Global Internet Forum to Counter-Terrorism (GIFCT) – to stand against IS's abuse of tech platforms. This is an important and unprecedented initiative that speaks to the big problem at hand. Despite its infancy, GIFCT has partnered with the United Nations Counter Terrorism Executive Directorate (UN-CTED) as well as with Tech Against Terrorism, a UN-backed NGO that works closely with member states, tech companies, academia and other entities to combat online propaganda and cyber exploitation by violent extremists. However, this union faces the problem of cyber jihadists' persistent and evolving adaptation to the scrutiny. For instance, online jihadists have begun implementing countermeasures by employing link-shorteners, a cyber technology that shortens the original download link and makes it harder to detect.

Although faced with this imposed scrutiny, IS as an organisation embraced the use of encrypted messaging platforms to disseminate its messages. Telegram, for example, has become its main frontier in terror propaganda release. It has helped in evading the imposed Western social media probe and has ensured a consistent distribution channel for its radical messages. Telegram is an application that offers end-to-end encryption that provides a tremendous layer of obfuscation. It eases the consumption of multimedia, it operates on most smart devices, and it facilitates encrypted, group and individual chat sessions, creating hurdles for anti-terrorism law enforcement to eavesdrop on conversations between terror actors. Furthermore, Telegram's distribution mechanics via a proprietary cloud service allows jihadists to securely download the content directly to their hard drives. This is a huge advancement *vis-à-vis* the use of temporary upload links that takes remarkably longer to unlock videos and is infested with pop-ups. Similarly, downloading explosive-building videos and militant manuals has become easily available via extremist Telegram channels.

In essence, IS is in desperate need to stay online in order to keep its followers engaged. Thus, evading scrutiny is indispensable for its survival. Jihadists' wide use of Telegram is important to underscore because the platform provides an unprecedented one-stop-shop for the IS online community. This is critical given the fact that the group is losing key media staffers and suffering a noticeable decrease in the percentage of media releases. Today we have thousands of Telegram channels used by IS jihadists. They maintain the terror group's ability to stay connected with a large audience. The group officially has run hundreds of channels throughout its time on Telegram since 2014.

Thousands of non-official channels supporting the group continue to operate. Even without the broad following IS once enjoyed on Twitter, Telegram's easy use and operability have carved a pathway for jihadist black markets and networking, raising the bar that in the future it is possible jihadists may abuse the platform. For instance, channels for selling weapons, known as *suq* (meaning, "market" in Arabic), are making guns and ammunition available for certain groups, mainly in the Middle East. These market "channels" allow sellers to advertise the sale of their weapons to buyers. The sellers post their WhatsApp numbers or resort to using Telegram private messages to communicate directly with the buyers' other channels. The latter include those for "terror tactics" or "lone wolves" that are dedicated to inciting terrorist operations and providing the know-how with explosive building manuals, countermeasures advice, and other operational instructional content, including the architecture of operations. Some channels, on the other hand, offer human smuggling between Turkey and Syria and between Lebanon and Syria.

Online search engines do not index Telegram's channels, which are similar in concept to Facebook pages. Hence, it is not possible publicly to scrutinise its content. In the past three years, we have witnessed major public engagements such as flagging Youtube videos containing terror content and creating Twitter accounts to counter-troll IS fan boys. With the advent of more secure Telegram channels, such public engagements have become less and less effective. Though many Telegram channels are regularly suspended, it does not appear to have a major impact on the online jihadist community at large and it seems still to have insignificant impact on the future.

Jihadist Use of File-Sharing Technology

Since the emergence of cyber jihadism, what has been notionally consistent is that any new initiative by online jihadists could turn into a norm if the conditions for its success are met. The evolution of the jihadist propaganda logistics has been amongst the clearest examples of jihadists' cyber adaptation to the increasing scrutiny of tech companies. With restrictive measures on using streaming platforms like Youtube, IS followers have expanded their use of file-sharing technology and have engineered ways to create accounts on and share propaganda through such services as Google Drive, Microsoft OneDrive and DropBox. Even with the restrictions imposed by these companies, users are able to abuse the free trial and cloud storage features and share several videos before accounts are potentially suspended. In a similar fashion to IS, the Global Islamic Media Front (GIMF), a pro-al-Qaeda logistics media unit, recently deployed proprietary file-sharing for its propaganda, calling it "Epic Drive." Other al-Qaeda media arms, while still using Telegram, deploy their own website called *al-Risala* and use it to post links to new video releases.

Jihadists' inventive use of cyber technology could pave the way for new methods to influence and terrorise individuals around the world. To keep their momentum, they must always stay engaged with their support base. Therefore a top priority for cyber jihadists will be to ensure that sound and robust file-release-and-share methods are in place. In future, we will be witnessing IS followers and other jihadist groups building more proprietary websites to keep their followers abreast of propaganda and developments.

Online Security of IS

In the past two years, pro-IS infosec groups have also emerged on the scene with the aim of providing advice and assistance to the group's followers on obfuscating their digital fingerprints. The group, called "Horizons", the most notable one, has released a few dozen infosec manuals on topics ranging from security features and upgrades for smart phones to the use of Virtual Private Networks (VPNs), software that masks potentially traceable digital fingerprints when browsing the Internet. Instructions on using encrypted browsers, secure operating systems, encrypted e-mail and messaging services as well as cloud and file-sharing services are available for jihadist Telegram users. This collective of manuals, even though not officially produced or sanctioned by any specific individual or group, has so far laid a path made of a solid level of personal security for many jihadists, creating a niche follower base that seeks to stay safely online while supporting IS.

For instance, IS supporters have regularly mentioned the importance of using The Onion Router, or TOR, which is an encrypted network containing thousands of nodes that routes Internet connections in a secure way (Alkhouri and Kassirer, 2016). TOR has a browser that enables users to access websites securely. This means that it protects the end user's identity by obfuscating their access points. Furthermore, the TOR browser enables users to access the Dark Web, which contains thousands of undiscoverable ".onion" domains. These domains are not yet displayed via the Google or Bing search engines. Because of the latter's added security layer, many malicious actors prefer to build websites using this domain for their illegal activities such as maintaining black markets, providing hacking tutorials and cryptocurrency exploitation kits. While TOR is needed to access the Dark Web, it is also used as a secure way of accessing Open Web domains – something that many IS followers use when they access IS-supportive blogs and websites, or log into social media platforms. Future IS actors will probably continue to optimise their utilisation of TOR and Telegram.

Bankrolling Terrorism

In the overall picture, intelligence agencies have achieved major victories in tracking and preventing the use of funds intended for terrorist activities, especially against individuals and self-proclaimed charities. Financial institutions' potential monetary and reputational liabilities pushed them to design outstanding anti-money-laundering (AML) and anti-terrorism-financing measures against terror groups. This is not to say that this has stopped jihadist groups' bankrolling streams. IS was arguably the richest terror group in 2014 and 2015 according to the Global Terrorism Index (GTI, 2017: 83-84), which measures the impact and the status of terrorist groups and operations annually. In 2015, IS bankrolled a whopping two billion dollars from oil, taxation, ransoms and the sale of antiquities (GTI, 2016: 53). It could thus function without much need for wire transfers. The group, however, lost control of oil resources and now operates more as a collective of guerrilla groups. The IS leaders and commanders who once enjoyed a certain level of freedom and mobility are now dead or no longer in the forefront. The critical need for funds has currently placed the group in a difficult position. We can speculate with a high degree of confidence that in order to meet their needs IS and its networks will employ various types of other fundraising activities, including online.

The financial activities of the terror groups are vigorously scrutinised like those of cybercriminals, fraudsters and hackers, although the motivation of the terrorist organisations is political and they are usually ideologically driven. Unlike financially motivated actors, pro-IS actors are not sophisticated in garnering money through illegal cyber means, like forgery, black markets and individual and organisational fraud. They rely very much on individual donations and locally unsanctioned transactions. Thus a trust-or-fear dynamic is at play. However, as the terror-funding landscape is now changing, it is simply impractical for IS to disregard bankrolling through online means.

The increasing criminal abuse of cryptocurrency may provide a glimpse into the potential future fundraising campaigns of terror groups and their supporters. It is therefore highly probable that pro-IS actors may revert to using under-regulated cryptocurrency to finance their attacks across the world. That is not without precedent. For instance, in January 2018, analysts at New York based business risk intelligence company Flashpoint identified instances where jihadists on Telegram had sought Bitcoin donations, for "*mujahidin* in Syria" (e.g. al-Sadaqah Telegram Channel, 2018).[1] In another case, multiple sources reported that the Bitcoin wallet of IS's faction in Gaza was posted on its Telegram channel (McCoy, 2017). The channel had released digital posters with price tags attached to its weaponry. The administrator of the channel underscored what the money had been funding: military weapons and gear, and explosive-building experiments (Ibn Taymiyya Media Center Telegram Channel, 2015). Notwithstanding, the IS followers are largely far less experienced in their cyber skills in comparison to the money-hungry cybercriminal and hacking collectives. Since the latter are mostly driven by financial gains, their *modus operandi* has no specific concern in relation to political affiliation or ideology. Therefore their knowledge could be transferable and be employed to finance terrorist activities as well. IS supporters can conveniently benefit from them if they act accordingly. Given that it simply needs funds to finance its attacks, it is more likely to see in the future that the followers of IS would engage in more sophisticated frauds and exploit their know-how in furthering the group's cause.

Use of Unsophisticated Yet Impactful Cyber Technics

The offensive skillset of pro-IS cyber actors remains insignificant. Their most remarkable cyber attack was on 12 January 2015 when they hacked the Twitter account of the US Central Command (CENTCOM), the US military body that spearheads decision-making and directs US military entities in times of war (Gompert and Libicki, 2015). This attack gave rise to a degree of panic among the public. The fact is that the so-called "Cyber Caliphate" of the IS was never able to penetrate any sensitive data systems or to steal critical information beyond the short-lived hijacking of the Twitter account (Gompert and Libicki, 2015). Yet, the mere success against the highly secure US CENTCOM elevated the perceived notoriety of IS's cyber actors. It rightfully raised questions about their immediate and near future capabilities. The attack, however, created a blurry perception because the entire initiative was carried out by one IS fighter who had a hacking background, namely the British national Junaid Hussain who was killed in a 2015 airstrike in Syria. Moreover, it was never acknowledged publicly by the IS's central media. If the ultimate goal of the terror groups is to create confusion and fear, IS as a terrorist organisation was successful in this instance without claiming responsibility. However the question whether this is the success of a group or simply of an individual remains to be answered.

On the other hand, the cyber-savvy followers of IS are more successful in some other less sophisticated but much more consuming and detrimental cyber activities. They have been cost-effectively able to push the public and private sectors to expend their resources on otherwise negligible, if opportunistic, threats. For instance, IS-supportive hacking collectives, like the United Cyber Caliphate (UCC), have harvested personally identifiable information (PII) of innocent individuals and repackaged the data into their "hit lists." They have distributed via private Telegram channels the names, addresses, phone numbers of people, thousands of PII sets affecting Americans, Canadians, Saudis, Egyptians and others. In their messages, the hackers underscored that these individuals must be targeted as enemies despite the fact that most of them had no political affiliation or never publicly expressed an anti-IS sentiment. This was a prominent tactic between 2015 and 2017, when the UCC and other hacking teams released the PII sets on their respective Telegram channels (Katz, 2016). Just in New York, 3,000 names were released on one list in 2016, which prompted the FBI to notify all of those named and clarify the circumstances behind why their names ended up on a so-called IS hit list. Though brought about by simple means, this ordeal caused not only a huge call on government funds and resources, but also imaginably had an impact on the mental wellbeing of the citizens. The release of the PII sets was meant to strike fear and exhaust security resources more than to be used as a directive to kill. In this regard, this is one of the simplest and most effective cyber tactics employed by jihadists online.

Weaponised Drones and Possibilities

If we distill the collective threat down to mere possibilities, it is quite disconcerting. Several examples speak to such heightened concerns today, which all security authorities should be cognizant of. IS, for instance, has been able to weaponise commercial drones in order to conduct reconnaissance and to drop small explosive devices from the air. On the one hand, this has enabled it to preserve its human resources on the ground to a considerable extent. On the other hand, using RC radio controllers, mounted HD cameras and small improvised explosive devices attached to these drones, IS has been able to scatter and wound soldiers as well as wreak havoc at military posts and in urban areas with scenes prominently featured in its propaganda videos during 2017 (Warrick, 2017). In one instant, IS released a video in February 2017 showing its drone dropping small explosive devices over targets in Mosul. The advancement came after IS had been utilising drones for surveillance purposes, using small quadcopters to monitor targets from a safe distance.

While featuring the tactic with the drones in a number of videos, IS followers on the Deep Web began brainstorming about the weaponisation of the drones in even more dangerous ways. Several discussions with experimental ideas on top IS messaging boards have kept certain technical followers engaged. One 2016 manual, released by a self proclaimed IS supporter on one of the group's top web forums, known as "*Minbar*," provides realistic instructions on building explosive-laden drones to target aircraft (Minbar, 2016). The idea floated as a suggestion to particularly counter the coalition war jets in Iraq and Syria. However, several Youtube videos feature drone enthusiasts and their engineering modifications to make drones faster, more controllable and destructive.[2] Jihadists suggested some other targets as well: fuel and power stations, airports, taxiing aircraft, frigates, boats, even Industrial Control Systems (ICS) that automate the distribution of electricity, water and gas.

In an interview, a US Department of Homeland Security official indicated that drones — also known as "unmanned aerial vehicles" or UAVs — "continue to provide a significant challenge to special event security ... In the civilian special event environment, there are no safe mitigation technologies available at this time" (cited in Winter, 2018). Concerts, stadiums and cities do not often have a ceiling to physically protect their audiences against the attacks of such explosive drones. Furthermore, the current measures to limit the illegal use of drones are at an initial stage.

In 2017, DJI company, the maker of the commercial UAVs whose quadcopter drones have reportedly been used by IS, made some moves to counter the reputational and physical risks posed by the fans of IS. It designated certain "no fly zones" for its products across Iraq and Syria and attempted to make adjustments in its application in order to prevent the use of its products by the IS terrorists (Dalton, 2017). This was an important step, but it does not prevent terror actors in most parts of the world from using them in individual operations. UAVs may be potentially dangerous to human lives and property in the hands of terrorist groups or their sympathisers. There are no precedents for an effective anti-drone measure in place. This failure highlights a major gap that terror actors could exploit. While the disciples of Usama bin Laden hijacked planes, today's aspiring terrorists may have their hands on small "kamikaze" drones in the foreseeable future. The innovative tactics and techniques with the drones prove the proverb "Necessity is the mother of invention." It is thus critical to consider that terrorist groups such as IS are smart enough to adapt, especially during times of crisis.

Hacking for IS 3.0

The aforementioned hacking of US CENTCOM's Twitter account in 2015 was opportunistic but provides a glimpse into the type of targets that future IS cyber actors may set their sights on. Hacking a Twitter account is met with a simple incident response measure. It is also a reminder to switch on "two-factor authentication" – a measure that requires a second step to verify the legitimate account owner, such as sending a verification code to an associated phone number – to prevent many types of cyber attacks. The actual target, however, is what gives rise to more concern. The IS cyber actors zoomed in on US CENTCOM, the body that is spearheading the military coalition against IS. Sensitive military data can be of tremendous leverage for terror groups which they could exploit in a range of ways from spying on military personnel to terrorising their families, to directing political blows at governments and highlighting their weaknesses in protecting civilian and military data. Data are, henceforward, a major influential tool for swaying political decisions. Terror groups would use civilian and military data to try to level the playing field and expend fewer resource in order to gain significant victories.

On 15 October 2015, the federal prosecutors made public a criminal complaint against the Kosovo citizen Ardit Ferizi, who is believed to have been the leader of the hacking collective "Kosova Hacker's Security." The criminal complaint charged Ferizi with providing material support to IS and committing "computer hacking and identity theft violations in conjunction with the theft and release of personally identifiable information of the US service members and federal employees" (Office of Public Affairs, 2016). Ferizi targeted servers in the US and stole thousands of individuals' personal information. He then allegedly provided the information of more than 1,000 American government personnel to Junaid Hussain, the founder of "Cyber Caliphate," for public release. Hussain subsequently watermarked it with an IS flag and released the data as a hit list (Office of Public Affairs, 2016). The Hussain-Ferizi connection itself is an evolution from the hacking of Twitter accounts and releasing PII sets. We can call their relationship "hacking for IS 2.0." In essence, it means seeking connections to skilled hackers outside IS's orbit. What we witnessed was a plot similar to "hacker-for-hire." This example sheds light on the jihadist potential to benefit from an already dangerous underground cabal of hired hackers, or what are labelled "black hats."

The market for offensive tools against sensitive electronic and information systems is enormous. Black hats on the Dark Web would be a logical choice for terrorists to hire. Many of them are able to develop malware or help in orchestrating attacks, depending on the service. This potential relationship should be taken seriously because it requires the investigation of the money trail between the buyer and the seller. Black hats are highly sophisticated in their transactions. If IS invests in engaging with them, this engagement, even in trial and error, will undoubtedly enhance IS's learning curve.

IS is still very far from the path towards a sophisticated cyber offensive. Most of its achievements so far have been against targets of opportunity; easy targets that have few or no added layers of cyber security and are behind on updating outdated software. The trajectory of pro-IS cyber attacks has fluctuated in number and type since their inception in 2014. Moreover, most of them have been low-hanging fruits that were repurposed to intensify the perceived threat. Offensive cyber jihadist initiatives are emerging on the scene in scattered and under-sophisticated ways. They are nevertheless making some headway through experimentation. For instance, an IS supporter on a password-protected and vetted jihadist messaging board, who proclaimed to be a software developer, released multiple proprietary software including an encrypted communication tool and distributed denial of service (DDoS) attack tool, which he named "Caliphate Canon" (Wolf, 2017). Known as Turgeman al-Khawarzmi, he claimed to have targeted seven Middle Eastern government domains, allegedly penetrated two of them successfully, including the domain of the Iraqi Ministry of Oil. Al-Khawarzmi's activities are early indicators of the potential of further integration of technology that IS can employ to support activities and get their feasible impact. This example is key to understanding the following: the cyber success of IS supporters is gradual and based on a grassroots approach. The need they feel first stimulates them to understand and learn more about the possibilities, which in turn leads to the employment of more technology. This developmental approach seems to be continuing into the foreseeable future.

Conclusion

It may be up to the security authorities to take a more proactive approach to understanding the tactics, techniques and procedures of online terror actors to mitigate their further risk. IS as an organisation on the ground in Iraq and Syria is shrinking. However, it is highly powered by its followers, some of whom could remarkably contribute to the group's objectives with their cyber knowledge and technical crafts. These cyber actors are advancing and the online methods that they use may cause significant physical harm. They must be critically considered in the global fight against the ruthless terrorist group they assist. The manuals prepared by the cyber jihadists are a good place to start. It is no less important to keep an eye on non-jihadist cyber criminals as well. The efforts against cyber jihadism will be ineffective unless how those criminals are operating and how their *modus operandi* is transferrable are tracked and revealed.

Notes

1 The present author works for this intelligence company as Co-founder and Senior Director. The sources cited in this article from this company's publications are freely available online.
2 For a video sample mentioned in the manual see https://www.youtube.com/watch?v=PTScNHvVbyc by Aerofred Van H. Youtube Channel, 2013.

References

Aerofred Van H. Youtube Channel. (2013). *A RC-plane Fires Successfully at a Second RC-Plane with an Airsoft Machine Gun.* [Online]. Available at: https://www.youtube.com/watch?v=PTScNHvVbyc [accessed 20 November 2018].

Akhgar, B. and Yates, S. (2013). *Strategic Intelligence Management: National Security Imperatives and Information and Communications Technologies.* Oxford: Butterworth-Heinemann.

Alkhouri, L. and Kassirer, A. (2016). *Tech For Jihad: Dissecting Jihadists' Digital Toolbox.* New York City: Flashpoint. Available at: https://www.flashpoint-intel.com/wp-content/uploads/2016/08/TechForJihad.pdf [accessed 20 November 2018].

Al-Sadaqa Telegram Channel. (2018). *Telegram.* [Online]. Accessed by Laith Alkhouri on 19 January 2018.

Badawy, A. and Ferrara, E. (2017). *The Rise of Jihadist Propaganda on Social Media.* Los Angeles: University of Southern California, Information Sciences Institute.

Berger, J. and Morgan, J. (2015). *The ISIS Twitter Census: Defining and Describing the Population of ISIS Supporters on Twitters.* Washington D.C.: Center for Middle East Policy at Brookings Institute. Available at: https://www.brookings.edu/wp-content/uploads/2016/06/isis_twitter_census_berger_morgan.pdf [accessed 20 November 2018].

Dalton, A. (2017). 'DJI Grounded its Drones in Iraq and Syria to Lock Out Extremists'. *Engadget*, [online], 26 April 2017. Available at: https://www.engadget.com/2017/04/26/dji-no-fly-zones-grounded-drones-iraq-syria/?guccounter=1 [accessed 22 November 2018].

Gompert, D. and Libicki, M. (2015). *Decoding the Breach: The Truth About the CENTCOM Hack.* Santa Monica: The RAND Corporation. Available at: https://www.rand.org/blog/2015/02/decoding-the-breach-the-truth-about-the-centcom-hack.html [accessed 20 November 2018].

GTI. (2016). *Global Terrorism Index 2016.* Sydney: Institute for Economics and Peace. [Online]. Available at: http://economicsandpeace.org/wp-content/uploads/2016/11/Global-Terrorism-Index-2016.2.pdf [accessed 20 November 2018].

GTI. (2017). *Global Terrorism Index 2017*. Sydney: The Institute for Economics and Peace. [Online]. Available at: http://visionofhumanity.org/app/uploads/2017/11/Global-Terrorism-Index-2017.pdf [accessed 20 November 2018].

Hopkins, H. (2017). 'Facebook Struggles with Mission Impossible to Stop Online Extremism'. *The Guardian* [online], 24 May 2017. Avilable at: https://www.theguardian.com/news/2017/may/24/facebook-struggles-with-mission-impossible-to-stop-online-extremism [accessed 20 November 2018].

Ibn Taimiyyah Media Center Telegram Channel. (2015). *Telegram*. [Online]. Accessed by Laith Alkhouri on 17 January 2015.

Katz, M. (2016). 'Are You On The ISIS Hit List of Random New Yorkers?'. *The Gothamist* [online], 29 April 2016. Available at: http://gothamist.com/2016/04/29/isis_nyc_art_all_whatever.php [accessed 20 November 2018].

McCoy, O. (2017). *Bitcoin for Bombs*. N.Y. City: Council on Foreign Relations Center for Preventive Actions. Available at: https://www.cfr.org/blog/bitcoin-bombs [accessed 20 November 2018].

Minbar. (2016). *Al-sayf al-battar la-isqat ta'irat al-kuffar* (The Sharp Sword in Confronting the Aircraft of the Infidels). *Al-Minbar Al-I'lami Forum* (www.mnbr.info/vb). Accessed on 2 December 2016 through https://justpaste.it/saifbattar, (now offline).

Mosher, D. and Gould, S. (2017). 'How Likely Are Foreign Terrorists to Kill Americans? The Odds May Surprise You'. *Business Insider UK*, [online], 1 February 2017. Available at: https://www.businessinsider.com/death-risk-statistics-terrorism-disease-accidents-2017-1 [accessed 20 November 2018].

Office of Public Affairs. (2016). 'ISIL Linked Kosovo Hacker Sentenced to 20 Years in Prison'. *US Department of Justice* [online], 23 September 2016. Available at: https://www.justice.gov/opa/pr/isil-linked-kosovo-hacker-sentenced-20-years-prison [accessed 21 November 2018].

Olidort, J. (2016). 'Brand Control Is More Important to ISIS Than Territory'. *New York Times* [online], 21 October 2016. Available at: https://www.nytimes.com/roomfordebate/2016/10/21/does-isis-need-territory-to-survive [accessed 21 November 2018].

Ullah, H. (2018). *Digital Rebels: Islamists, Social Media and the New Democracy*. New Haven: Yale University Press.

Warrick, J. (2017). 'Use of Weaponized Drones by ISIS Spurs Terrorism Fears'. *The Washington Post* [online], 21 February 2017. Available at: https://www.washingtonpost.com/gdpr-consent/?destination=%2fworld%2fnational-security%2fuse-of-weaponized-drones-by-isis-spurs-terrorism-fears%2f2017%2f02%2f21%2f9d83d51e-f382-11e6-8d72-263470bf0401_story.html%3f&utm_term=.b93bf4a55402 [accessed 24 November 2018].

Winter, J. (2018). 'What Would Happen if Terrorists Attacked the Super Bowl With Drones?'. *Foreign Policy Magazine*, [online], 3 February 2018. Available at: https://foreignpolicy.com/2018/02/03/what-would-happen-if-terrorists-attacked-the-super-bowl-with-drones/ [accessed 22 November 2018].

Wolf, K. (2017). *Cyber Jihadists Dabble in DDoS: Assessing the Threat*. New York City: Flashpoint. Available at: https://www.flashpoint-intel.com/blog/cyber-jihadists-ddos/ [accessed 23 November 2018].

CHAPTER 5

The Role of Women in Post-IS Jihadist Transformation and in Countering Extremism

Anita Perešin

Introduction

Many jihadist organisations have recognised the importance of women in jihad and have systematically used them for their activities for decades. Female jihadists can be found in different jihadist organisations – from Afghanistan, Chechnya and Palestine to Syria, Iraq and the African continent – where their role is viewed as being as important as that of their male counterparts. The presence of female jihadists in Western countries is also on the rise.

With the proclamation of the Caliphate of the Islamic State (IS) in Syria and Iraq, the role of women in jihadist organisations received global publicity. By presenting and encouraging women as essential for the establishment of the new Muslim *umma* and preserving its longevity, IS introduced a new phase in its employment of women for the jihadist cause. The group succeeded in attracting more women from the West, both convert and born Muslims, than any other jihadist group had been able to do in the past. It also introduced a broad spectrum of roles that could be filled by women, not only in the territory where IS had gained control but also in their home countries. By giving the same importance to *muhajirat*[1] and domestic female jihadists, and by promoting both passive and active roles for them in jihad, IS created a new generation of female jihadists and a "network of sisters", motivated by a sense of empowerment and willing to support the group's long-term objectives.

Strategically planned female jihadist activities, supported by a continuous promotion of their roles via the Internet, have made it possible for IS to continue to employ women for its global operations, even after the collapse of the Caliphate. The transformation of the group and its loss of "credibility" in governing the so-called Islamic State did not, in fact, diminish or extinguish its attractiveness for women. The group has given women the ability to keep their roles in the post-IS transformation era and has afforded itself the capacity to continue to be a prominent actor on the global jihadist scene. Such global promotion of women in jihad can motivate other jihadist groups to increase the employment of female cadres for their cause or to motivate radicalised women to act as lone wolves.

There are already many examples of women's engagement in jihadist activities in Western countries. According to the European Union Terrorism Situation and Trend Report (EUROPOL, 2017: 22), one in four people arrested in 2016 for terrorism-related offences were women. The 2017 report of the Dutch Intelligence Service (AIVD) on jihadist women warns that the threat women pose should not be underestimated (AIVD, 2017). A report from The Heritage Foundation in the same year also notes "a marked jump in the involvement of women in terrorist plots in Europe over the previous two years"[2] (Barret, 2017: 24). Such dramatic growth of female involvement in jihadist terrorism leads to the "feminisation of jihad" (Brill Olcott and Haqqani, 2004),[3] a trend that is expected to rise in the future. But it also offers the opportunity to take advantage of the presence of women in the counter-terrorism field, to more effectively counter jihadist narratives and plans, thanks to the former's better insight into the mentality and approaches of the female terrorists.

The Prospect of Female Fighters

The role of women in jihad is a topic that has long been debated among the jihadist community. Classical and contemporary Muslim religious literature leaves much room for different interpretations and open questions due to its lack of clarity on the subject. There is no consensus on the role of women in combat within the Islamic community as well as within the most prominent jihadist organisations. There are some sources showing examples of women companions of the Prophet Muhammad who participated in battles alongside men. However, the information concerning the nature of their participation is limited and shows them in predominantly supporting roles, "usually by accompanying the fighters, encouraging the men, or by providing medical care and assistance after the fact." (Cook, 2005: 376).

Classical religious authorities, while being fairly negative on women participating in violent jihad except in extraordinary circumstances, did not explicitly forbid it. This ambiguity regarding jihadist female fighters provides theological space for women to fill militant roles in the modern jihad (De Leede et al., 2017). Using Muhammad Khayr Haykal's[4] explanation, Cook (2005: 378) distinguishes between two types of jihad: *offensive jihad* (defined as a community obligation, or *fard al-kifaya*) and *defensive jihad* (defined as an individual obligation, or *fard al-'ayn*). In the first case, there is no necessity for women to fight, but women should have that option if they wish to volunteer. Under the condition of the latter, girls and women have to fight, even without parents' or husbands' permission.

There are a handful of jihadist terrorist groups which have long supported the idea of women playing an active role in jihad. These groups, such as Hamas in Palestine and the Islamic Jihad Union (IJU) in Afghanistan and Pakistan, have been trying to associate women more closely with actual fighting in many conflict zones. In Article 12 of its Covenant (1988), Hamas clearly states that women are expected to play such role in jihad:

> Resisting and quelling the enemy becomes the individual duty of every Muslim, male or female. A woman can go out to fight the enemy without her husband's permission. (Hamas, 1998)

As such, the women of Hamas have actively carried out this role in the field for decades.

Others argue that even in extreme circumstances, when the necessity for jihad is incumbent upon the entire Muslim community, women fighting remains an option, not an obligation (Cook, 2005: 381), placing the supportive role of women in front of an active one. Even within a group, there can be disagreements regarding the place of women in jihad, as was the case with al-Qaeda's leadership. The only jihadist leader who formally addressed the jihadist community on women's role in jihad and explicitly called on women to take part in fighting is Abu Mus'ab al-Zarqawi, the leader of al-Qaeda in Iraq until he was killed in 2006. From his statements it is clear that al-Zarqawi believed that women should take a more active role in jihad and even requested them "to perpetrate martyrdom-seeking operations" (cited in Winter and Margolin, 2017: 24). His call on "systematic militarization of women" resonated with a Belgian woman, Muriel Degauque, who attacked a US military convoy near Baghdad in 2005, acting as the first European female suicide bomber.

However, al-Zarqawi did not exclude the importance of female supporting roles, such as raising children and encouraging their husbands and sons to fight jihad. Thus, Lahoud (2014: 788) argues that al-Zarqawi's statement "If you [Muslim men] are not going to be chivalrous knights in this war (*fursan al-harb*), make way for women to wage it", could rather be interpreted as his attempt to shame Muslim men who had not taken up jihad than as genuinely calling on women to enter the battlefield. The then number two and current al-Qaeda leader Ayman al-Zawahiri has never shared al-Zarqawi's standpoint. In response to a female questioner during an open interview with jihadist forum members in April 2008, he clearly advocates that there is no role for women in al-Qaeda and that the women of the *mujahidin* should only have a domestic role:

> Al-Qaeda has no women, but the women of the *mujahidin* do their heroic part in taking care of their homes and sons in the roughness of the immigration, movement, unity, and expecting the Crusader to strike (cited in INSITE, 2008).

There is no indication that al-Qaeda will officially change its stand in the near future. However, al-Zarqawi is still perceived as one of the most influential jihadist ideologists whose speeches still inspire many from various jihadist organisations and lone actors who are attracted by the jihadist ideology.

IS, on the other hand, with no clear statement of its leadership on this issue, successfully combines both passive and active female roles by deploying female jihadists in varying capacities as deemed desirable. In the document entitled "Women of the Islamic State: A Manifesto on Women by the *al-Khansa'* Brigade," IS demonstrates the group's position on the role of women and endorses their participation in both supportive and active roles (Winter, 2015).[5] However, in this document it is clarified that the designated role of women under IS is primarily domestic: to raise the new generation of jihadists. A combat role for women is not excluded, but only in extreme situations of an enemy attack against the country, an insufficient number of available men to engage the enemy, or a fatwa issued by an imam. The image of IS female fighters promoted online should primarily be seen as an IS propaganda tool to lure Western women. However, the efforts IS invests in women by providing them with training on how to use and fabricate weapons and carry out suicide bombings prove the group's intention to have women ready to take active roles when the need arises.

The fact that the women's right to play an active role in jihad is not fully accepted among conservative Muslims does not prevent IS from attempting to legitimise such a possibility, as they did in 2015 with the IS's Manifesto and the introduction of an example of IS' marriage certificate. This certificate, approved by both parties, gives the woman the right to impose conditions on accepting the marriage. It is written that the husband would not deny the wife's wish to carry out a suicide attack if the IS leader approves it: "If the leader of the faithful [al-Baghdadi] consents to her to carrying out a suicide mission, then her husband should not prohibit her" (cited in Saul, 2015). This shows how the decision over her life or death relies upon the IS leader.

In August 2015, the IS-linked al-Zawra'a Foundation released a treatise entitled "Valuable Advice and Important Analysis on the Rules for Women's Participation in Jihad" (Winter and Margolin, 2017: 26). It clarifies the conditions in which women may engage in combative jihad, but advises them rather to be focused on female domestic roles. IS has continued intensively to discuss the role of women in combat in various publications like *Dabiq*, *Rumiya* and *al-Naba',* making clear that women should prioritise their support for the jihad carried out by the Islamic State. The arguments against the use of women in combat – such as disapproval of the mixing of sexes on the battlefield, the sufficiency of male fighters and the inability to protect the honour of women – were put aside in extraordinary circumstances, as in recent times when IS has continued to lose territory in Syria and in Iraq. The July 2017 issue of the IS magazine *Rumiya* endorses the prospect of female combatants whose time had come to take up arms in combative jihad and "to rise with courage and sacrifice in this war," (Winter and Margolin, 2017: 24) not due the lack of male fighters, but rather due to their religious obligation and the desire for heaven. In addition, in February 2018, the first IS video praised women for their contributions in combat by promoting female fighters who were fighting alongside men on the front lines (Gartenstein-Ross *et al.,* 2018).

These calls provoked many negative reactions and comments among IS male sympathisers on social networks and did not get much attention in IS publications. A prompt reaction came from al-Qaeda with the headlines in the new women's magazine entitled "Baytuki" ("Your Home") showing al-Qaeda's position on the role of women in jihad: "Prepare the food that your husband loves, prepare his bed after that and do what he wants" (cited in Svirski, 2018).

From the Islamic jurisprudential point of view, any obstacle to women actively participating in *defensive jihad* could be a double-edged sword for jihadist organisations. Lahoud (2014: 781) warns all the groups who have either purposely refrained from calling on women to fight alongside men or have explicitly excluded such possibility that such exclusion represents "the Achilles' heel of jihadist ideology." With the exclusion of women from combat, Lahoud elaborates, jihadists would lose the credibility of the *defensive jihad* they have declared they are waging and have justified through classical religious doctrine. On the other hand, she argues, the call on women to join men in combat could cause the loss of sympathy from conservative Muslims and distract possible male recruits.

The IS experience shows that jihadist organisations will not refrain from using female fighters in the future in exceptional circumstances and that the tactical successes and benefits of using female fighters will prevail over negative attitudes towards them among more conservative cadres. Their limited usage, as was the case in the final battle for Mosul in 2016-2017, did not "compromise the group's power system" (Peresin and Cervone, 2015: 506), nor provoke "a sexual revolution that would supplant jihad" (Lahoud, 2014: 798), as was previously feared. Thus, the future involvement of female fighters in conflict zones could be expected to rise, even within jihadist organisations that attribute more conservative gender roles to women. While some jihadist organisations show no indication of possible change in accepting female fighters, IS, by accepting them even in a limited way, will keep the image of the most attractive jihadist group for women.

The Rise of Female Suicide Bombers

Martyrdom operations are perceived differently from fighting, and also require religious legitimacy. Jihadist ideologues and leaders, while not being so open as to call on women to join them on the battlefield, more openly support women who volunteer to carry out martyrdom suicide operations. Lahoud (2014: 783) explains that the role of female suicide bombers can be easily justified because a martyrdom operation can be carried out by a woman without having to be in the company of a male who is not her *mahram*,[6] to avoid accusations that jihadists permit sacrificing or violating women's honour. Although it has been mainly associated with the conflicts in Chechnya and Palestine, or amongst the so-called more progressive jihadists, currently the participation of women in suicide missions has become greatly exploited by more active jihadist terrorist organisations in different areas. In the past few years, we have witnessed a rise in the number of martyrdom operations carried out by women in the name of various jihadist organisations.

According to Bloom (2014) there are four primary changes within the jihadist terrorist organisations which support such a rise: (1) an ideological shift with the issue of fatwas on women's obligation for jihad; (2) the change in the structure of terrorist organisations, which now host numerous regional affiliates that are more open to employing women for such operations; (3) a change from hard to soft targets that are more accessible to women; and (4) a new mobilisation strategy where the use of women helps to mobilise men into terrorist organisations.

The pursuit of martyrdom is as desirable for female jihadists as it is for males, even though the reward aspect of female martyrs is different from that of males and therefore significantly less attractive. The employment of women in suicide attacks could not be seen as an act of desperation, due to the lack of male suicide attackers, but most probably as the desire of a jihadist organisation to skew the profile of the typical suicide attacker and to spread more fear and uncertainty among the population. No less important is the fact that female suicide bombers receive much more media publicity than male ones, which brings significant benefits to the jihadist cause without compromising their conservative credentials.

Among the jihadist terrorist groups which deploy women in suicide missions, Boko Haram, also known as the Islamic State in the West Africa (ISWA), has proven to be more notorious than any other organisation. Research conducted by Warner and Matfess (2017) finds that Boko Haram is the first terrorist group in history to employ more women suicide bombers than men. According to this research, since 2011 at least 244 of the 338 attacks were carried out by women. In 2017 alone, Boko Haram sent 80 women on suicide missions. If the current trend continues, Boko Haram is expected to quadruple its female suicide bombing attacks from previous years. A rationale behind using more women than men, according to a former militant for this research, is that "women are cheap, angry for the most part, and using women saves male fighters" (Warner and Matfess 2017: 29).

IS has regularly attracted and deployed female suicide bombers not only in Syria and Iraq, but also in other regions either through its own branches or through its affiliates, including in Western countries. The 26-year-old Hasna Aït Boulahcen, the cousin of Abdelhamid Abaaoud, the suspected IS mastermind of the Paris attack in November 2015, became the first female jihadist suicide bomber in Europe.

Even so, women's martyrdom operations remain controversial among jihadist terrorist organisations, including both IS and al-Qaeda, and are not always officially supported and approved. Such was the case of Amina, the wife of the prominent jihadist cleric Anwar al-'Awlaqi.[7] After the latter was killed, her intention to carry out a martyrdom operation was thwarted by Sheikh Abu Basir, the leader of al-Qaeda in the Arabian Peninsula (AQAP). Abu Basir was concerned that such an operation carried out by a sister "would bring a lot of problems for them [AQAP]" (Lahoud, 2014: 784). Similar to this was the official reaction of IS after the Mombasa attack in 2016. Carried out by three female suicide bombers, the attack was at first approved and welcomed by IS, even though it belittled the role of the women, describing them not as "female soldiers" of the Islamic State but only as "supporters," in contrast with how they had embraced male suicide bombers. However, a stricter reaction followed in a subsequent issue of the IS newspaper *al-Naba'* (2016 Issue 50), with a message addressed to all women, using the Qur'anic verse (33:33): "O [Wives of the Prophet], sit still in your homes" (Lahoud, 2017: 68). The author of the essay clearly wished to remind readers of IS's position on women's main role in society.

Despite such inconsistency in public support and approval of the use of female suicide bombers, jihadist organisations, including IS, will not be likely to abandon the benefits female martyrs can bring to jihad. They consider it irrational not to exploit the undisguised desire of some women to die a martyr's death, repeatedly expressed in public. All these facts, which foster the revival of a female suicide bomber phenomenon, will fuel its tendency to rise in the future.

The Feminisation of Jihad

Pictures posted online of female jihadists carrying Kalashnikovs and suicide belts have flooded social networks and internet platforms – calling out to women to become female martyrs and providing explicit directions to women returnees to be prepared for jihadist missions in their home countries. They have promoted women as important actors in modern jihadism. By giving women the same roles as men and importance in the Caliphate and in their home countries, IS has identified women as essential jihadist players and has assured long-term support of women for the jihadist cause. Combined with the rising need to have more women in jihadist ranks, the ever-growing number of both convert and born Muslim women who willingly join terrorist jihadist organisations shows a trend towards the "feminisation of jihad" and the creation of a new generation of female jihadists. These women are empowered to fill at once both passive and active roles that jihadist organisations now offer, and to act globally in such roles.

More women on the jihadist scene could translate to more power and increasingly more important roles for women. The rise in their number would lessen the diversity between passive and active roles and give women the opportunity for more active participation. This will especially be the case with women who are interested in participating as lone actors for the jihadist cause, without strict ties to any one organisation.

Female jihadists present a new security challenge for western countries. As is the case with male terrorists, the possibility that IS will send female operatives to carry out terrorist attacks once they return home cannot be ruled out. Gartenstein-Ross *et al.* (2018) see three main future threats from IS female returnees: (1) plotting external operations, since women are still considered in many countries as less threatening or capable of violence than men. This notion could be easily exploited in the case of female returnees who may play the role of naïve victims and as such avoid the scrutiny of security checks or prosecutions; (2) radicalising and recruiting others in their home countries and serving as a connection or conduit between the newly radicalised and established jihadists; (3) assisting lone actors or small group attackers as "virtual planners" by supporting attacks through conceptualisation, target selection, timing and direct technical assistance.

There is ample evidence to suggest that women are prepared for such tasks, from weapons training for women in the IS-controlled territory in Syria and Iraq to calls for home-grown attacks in the West. Yet in 2016 in France, the first all-female terrorist cell emerged, composed of women who had plotted to set off a car bomb near the Cathedral of Notre Dame of Paris (Allen, 2016). Recently, a Belgian foreign fighter testified how IS had trained three women, one Dutch and two Belgians, to commit terrorist attacks in Europe (Pieters, 2018). At the same time, Western female IS sympathisers continuously express a degree of frustration on the lack of active roles for women in the West. A French letter posted on the Telegram channel on 2 February 2018 and attributed to the women of IS expressed a desire for physical participation in jihad and the pursuit of martyrdom. In their message addressed to IS leader al-Baghdadi, Umm Abdullah and Umm Abd al-Rahman affirm women's aspirations to receive the same status jihadist men have and to become martyrs, and to earn paradise:

> [O]ur problem is that we are girls! But we are not like other girls! ... Death for us is life ... and life for us is jihad! ... We want a path to jihad! And our biggest hope is for death in martyrdom. And do not say 'you are girls' because we know this! But we are girls with the souls of men! (cited in Maza, 2018)

Additionally, women are aiming to take over from men the task of coordinating jihadist networks across Europe. Female jihadists are trying to fill the gap left by their detained husbands and to take over their roles in establishing and coordinating jihadist networks during their detention. This trend can be seen within the most radical Salafist communities, such as the one in Germany. German authorities identified an Islamist network made up of approximately 40 women in North Rhine-Westphalia which follows "a strict Salafist doctrine – from how to raise children and cook ingredients to how to interpret Islamic rules and stir up hatred against the so-called 'non-believers'" (Deutsche Welle, 2017). For the same source, the German Head of the Office for the Protection of the Constitution (BfV) confirmed that the Islamist women's network is also active in advertising and proselytising an extremely conservative Salafist ideology on the Internet. Moreover, they indoctrinate children from an early age to follow their ideology and way of life. These women won the approval of their male counterparts for this role, who have noticed that "women can network much better and are therefore more capable of expanding the scene and keeping it active."

The idea of the Caliphate and the extreme IS ideology will live as long as the group has the support of sympathisers who will spread its ideology. The role of jihadist sisters, mothers and wives is crucial in this process due to the influence women have on their family members, especially on children. The collapse of the IS Caliphate will not diminish jihadist ideology and goals, as long as there are women like Zarah, a former member of *al-Khansa'* Brigade from Morocco. After she returned home from Syria, she promised that jihadist women "will bring up strong sons and daughters and tell them about the life in the Caliphate." Even if the enemies of the Caliphate try to destroy it, Zarah is convinced that "it will live on as long as we spread the idea of the Islamic State. Even if we had not been able to keep it, our children will one day get it back" (cited in Mekhennet and Warrick, 2017).

The Role of Women in Raising Jihadist Children

The women of IS are constantly reminded of the importance of their direct contribution to IS goals through motherhood and spousal support. Moreover, this domestic duty has been repeatedly glorified in all propaganda materials and promoted as a spiritually righteous obligation of women. As declared in the Manifesto on Muslim Women "the greatness of her position, the purpose of her existence is the divine duty of motherhood" (Winter, 2015: 18).

IS ideologists have demonstrated a clear vision of the importance of women in its ranks. From the time of the declaration of the Caliphate in 2014, they have been systematically trying to lure women from the West, both those who were willing to move to the IS-controlled territory in Syria and Iraq and those unable to travel but willing to support IS goals in their home countries. First, it needed wives for thousands of Western foreign fighters, to keep them in the IS-controlled territory and to raise their children – a new generation of jihadists. At the same time, they also needed wider support from mothers abroad – to raise children in the spirit of the jihadist ideology or to support those who are willing to wage jihad. There are many examples of how mothers supported violent actions of their children in the IS-held territory and abroad (both minors and adult children), and even co-opted them in terrorist actions.

Since the proclamation of the Caliphate, IS has constantly promoted the importance of children[8] for the existence and the future of the Caliphate. Exposure to and growing up in cultures of violence promotes the desensitisation to and acceptance by children of violence and even the need for violence as a value-based justice system. Of the 41,490 international citizens from 80 countries who became affiliated with IS in Iraq and Syria, up to 12% are recorded to be minors (Cook and Vale, 2018: 3). Current findings show complex and multi-layered processes through which children were recruited, enlisted, trained, and deployed by IS, quite often with the support of their parents. Barret (2017) declares that from 2014 to 2016, IS recruited and trained more than 2,000 boys between the ages of 9 and 15 as "Cubs of the Caliphate". IS has invested heavily in the indoctrination and weaponisation of jihadist children in order to create a generation of radicalised youngsters and provide the organisation with the transgenerational capability to support a protracted jihad. IS hoped that children who were either indoctrinated through familial ties or otherwise recruited to be the next generation of jihadists would outlive the impending collapse of the Caliphate and would carry on its vision.

Their success in doing so was displayed in video materials featuring children, who look no older than five, executing prisoners or child soldiers fighting on the frontline alongside adult fighters. On social networks, mothers or both parents sometimes publicly supported such actions of their children or expressed the pride they would feel if their children were martyred one day. Such was the case of a 10-year-old son with his mother Sally Jones, a British Muslim convert who was on the list of the world's most wanted female terrorists before she was killed by a US drone strike in June 2017. After she denied that one of the child executioners was her son, she publicly declared how she "would be very proud" if it was him (Dearden, 2016). There are more such examples of how mothers dreamed of martyrdom for their children, their sacrifice for the Islamist cause and, in their eyes, the reward of paradise.

The deployment of children as suicide bombers is an alarming new phenomenon. The death of Hudhayfa al-Badri, the son of IS leader Abu Bakr al-Baghdadi reported to be 14 years old in a suicide mission in July 2018, was used in the editorial page of the pro-IS magazine *al-Anfal* to encourage other parents to support children's martyrdom. His suicide mission was promoted as a jihadist role model on how important it is to eschew worldly pleasures for jihad, even for children:

> Have a good example in your brother Hudhayfa. So roll up your sleeves and declare the mobilisation. Shake from yourselves laziness and weakness. Join your brothers the *mujahidin*, and if you cannot, then do not hesitate in supporting them (al-Anfal, 2018).

As IS continued to lose territory across Syria, there are also many examples of shifting of women's roles to a more militant stance. A trend is that mothers take children to die with them in suicide bombings. Parents co-opting their own children to carry out attacks is an even more worrying trend present not only in IS-held territory, but also in other areas under IS influence. On 13-14 May 2018, in Surabaya (Indonesia's second largest city), three families linked to the Indonesian IS affiliate *Jamaah Ansharut Daulah* carried out attacks in which the attackers used their own children as suicide bombers. The children were aged between 9 and 18. Some authors see what could be considered a parent's rational choice at the root of the decision to take children into a terrorist attack. The decision is based on the religious belief that the reward for their '*amaliya* (the term jihadists use to refer to field action) is waiting for them in the afterlife and in the promise of heaven for the entire family. Others explain that as women are taking a more active role in terrorism, mothers will find it hard to leave their children without being able to ensure that they will follow jihadist ideology. Therefore, they choose to do the '*amaliya* together with their children (Rohmah, 2018).

Several cases illustrate the willingness of mothers to act together with their children or to encourage them to carry out terrorist attacks in Western countries. For instance, in the UK, a mother and her two daughters pleaded guilty to the preparation of terrorist acts as part of the country's first all-female terrorist cell (BBC, 2018). Similarly, the mother of one of the most wanted jihadists in Bosnia and Herzegovina posted a video in July 2016 in which she called upon Muslims worldwide to kill Christians. She said she was proud of her jihadist son, and could not wait for him to become a martyr. "If I had ten more sons, they would go to jihad and fight for Allah," she added for the local newspapers (cited in Slobodna Dalmacija, 2016).

These examples show not only a shift in women's roles in violent extremism but also in supporting terrorist activities by family members, including children. Women and minors affiliated with or inspired by IS have already established their prominence as a security threat, with numerous foiled and successful attacks plotted and carried out globally. Therefore, the mothers' influence on the future activities of their jihadist children should not be underestimated. Their influence could, however, be felt in both directions, either in further radicalisation or in de-radicalisation. As such, the latter requires further analysis and commensurate reactions.

Women in Counterterrorism

While they are valuable for the jihadist cause, women can also be precious partners in counter-terrorism efforts. Their potential aid in the prevention of radicalisation and countering violent extremism is yet often ignored or underestimated. In many countries, traditional counter-terrorism efforts still do not recognise the advantages of the involvement of women just as some still do not recognise the real threat female jihadists pose to the society.

Women, mothers and sisters are recognised in many cases as the main force behind men's decisions to join jihad. They support the actions of male jihadists, encourage other women to join the ranks, raise jihadist children and are willing to die as martyrs themselves. As a result, female jihadists show a face incompatible with stereotypes depicting women as tender and delicate in contrast to men.

On the other hand, there are women who were first lured by the jihadist propaganda and joined militant jihadist groups but were later disillusioned. They decided to leave and to cut former connections with jihadist networks. These women – with personal experience of having lived among jihadist communities – could be the most valuable contributors to successful counter-terrorism efforts. Those who understand the mind-set of female jihadists can be invaluable in the creation of measures used to cut a "fatal attraction among women and jihadism" (Perešin, 2015) – and thwart female jihadists in carrying out their particular roles. The strong position women have within the family unit may also be used to challenge extremist narratives at home, at schools and in society. They may prove to be instrumental in the character formation of their children and key to influence the decisions and actions of other family members. The Vienna-based NGO Women Without Borders conducted a study entitled "Can Mothers Challenge Extremism?" Based on 1,023 interviews with mothers in Pakistan, Israel and Palestine, Northern Ireland and Nigeria in 2013, this study shows how women's position within the family allows them to detect early signs of radicalisation, to recognise unusual behaviours or signs of impending violence and to change the radical mind-set of family members. This NGO later developed its Mothers' School Model which is the first-ever family-centred counter-radicalisation platform (Schlaffer and Kropiunigg, 2016).

However, existing studies on these topics are still limited. Despite differing viewpoints as to whether women indeed have a "unique" role in preventing and countering violent extremism (P/CVE) (Fink *et al.*, 2016), most experts agree that women can offer diverse perspectives on problem solving and provide different approaches that can complement counter-terrorism efforts (Haynie and de Jonge Oudraat, 2017). This can be particularly useful in de-radicalisation processes and in anti-extremism and anti-violence campaigns. Counter-narratives against jihadist propaganda can be disseminated more effectively among families and communities by women. Thus, more efforts have to be made to empower women and to leverage their ability to recognise critical signs and challenge extremist narratives in domestic, educational and social environments. When it comes to hard measures against terrorism, female security officials can be mission-critical by having access to populations and sites that men do not, by improving the perception the local communities have towards law enforcement and, in turn, by enhancing the ability of the latter to provide security.

Examples of women's involvements in terrorist activities, as in the 2015 San Bernardino attack, convey how women are influential in whatever capacity they may serve. It is therefore critical to recognise their potential, assess their capabilities and involve them in both terrorism prevention and resolution. Such necessity is already recognised in various UN Security Council resolutions (UN/SC/R 2013, 2014), which ask to ensure effective implementation of comprehensive, integrated legislation and P/CVE strategies. Addressing the role of women and girls is an essential part of those efforts. This encourages Member States to develop strategies, through empowering women, to counter violent extremist narratives that can incite terrorist acts and to address the conditions conducive to the spread of violent extremism.

The same happens with attempts of individual countries to strengthen counter-terrorism efforts. Many countries, in cooperation with non-governmental organisations, support networks and programmes to promote the role of women in countering violent extremism. There are already a few good examples of P/CVE initiatives, such as Mothers for Life in Germany, The Women and Extremism (WaE) programme in the United Kingdom, Austrian Women Without Borders (WWB) and its global SAVE – Sisters Against Violent Extremism campaign, Stop-Jihadism campaign in France, etc.[9] They consult women, involve them in programme design and implementation, carry out gender-specific programmes, have programmes specifically aimed at women, ensure gender indicators in programme monitoring and evaluation, and promote gender equality. In addition, recent recommendations on how to incorporate women into national counter-terrorism strategies include using the potential of women to prevent or mitigate the radicalisation of family and community members, promoting women's participation in military and law enforcement roles to improve security operations and maximising intelligence gathering, and promoting women's participation in security efforts.

Thus, any national level approach that addresses the role of women in terrorism should be similar to other strategies that equally honour the concepts of law enforcement, crime and punishment along with the criminological study of causation, management and prevention, all the while embracing a viable model for diversion and rehabilitation. This measured approach – one that recognises the reality and the consequences of women as both potential perpetrators and potential pacifiers – is vital for the safety and security of a world plagued with the threat of militant jihadism.

Conclusion

Modern terrorism is not the exclusive purview of men, nor can it be so for the efforts to eradicate it. Jihadist organisations recognise the importance of women. They deploy them to motivate and recruit new members, both male and female, to provide supporting roles and logistics for the actions, and to serve as active members. Women have proved to be especially effective as recruiters and contributors to IS propaganda efforts, the most effective jihadist propaganda ever witnessed. It succeeded in attracting more foreign fighters and domestic supporters from all around the world than any past efforts to do so by other terrorist organisations.

Many female sympathisers of the jihadist ideology see the possibility of empowerment of women in the current jihadist propaganda, and especially in creating a new generation of female jihadists that will bring more women to the global jihadist scene. Calls on women to prepare themselves to play an active and not just a passive role in jihad additionally spread such thoughts. Some terrorist organisations, notably those headed by IS, show signs of an intent to distance themselves from other jihadist interpretations on the subject of combatant women and female martyrs, even if this provoked negative reactions from the religiously conservative Muslim audience. Active roles for women are still not officially fully accepted by all jihadist organisations due to their dubious compliance with Islamic law. Nevertheless, women's expectations of playing active roles in jihad are supported when it comes to gaining an advantage over enemies or in extreme cases of lack of male cadres and desperation. It is expected that jihadist organisations will continue to interpret the classical legal doctrine in a way that allows them to deploy women in the capacity the groups will need: as fighters, suicide bombers or passive supporters. However, public support and celebration of the first two activities will remain low.

With the aim of retaining support from more conservative circles, jihadist organisations will officially continue to give more publicity to women as female supporters of jihadist husbands and mothers of the future jihadists than as female fighters and suicide bombers. This leads to the conclusion that in the future activities of jihadist organisations there will be more differences between the publicly pronounced policies and the real operations that take place in the field. However, by greatly expanding undisputed active roles for women in jihad, the post-IS era will likely introduce the combination of both roles. Female jihadism will hence most probably transform from a limited and occasional phenomenon into a new normal.

IS female sympathisers, by being empowered with larger and more significant functions, seem to become important actors on the global jihadist scene. They will be more involved in encouraging male jihadists to take action, in supporting them as planners and companions and in keeping jihadist networks alive during men's detention. By instilling in their children the spirit of the Islamic State and the moral obligation to revive it, jihadist women will hold the key to the success of the jihadist agenda in future, "or could be the reason for its failure" as warned by Yusuf al-'Uyayri, the founding leader of al-Qaeda in the Arabian Peninsula (killed in 2003), who strongly believed in women's prominent role in the affairs of the *umma* today (Lahoud, 2014: 787).

Women currently play a mixture of passive and active roles in contemporary jihad. After they return to their home countries, they are more likely to play extended roles whose spectrum is yet to be known. Therefore, the limit of the extent to which women can further the jihadist cause is still hard to anticipate. Counter-terrorism efforts can neither misjudge nor ignore the threat the female jihadists pose. Nor they can risk the advantages and better results that women's participation in various counterterrorism fields can bring.

Notes

1 *Muhajirat* is the Arabic word for the "women who made *hijra*." It denotes the women who migrated from the "lands of infidels" to the "Caliphate" of IS.
2 In the first five months of 2017, 23% of the total terrorist plots in Europe involved women. It is a significant increase over 2014 and 2015 when the numbers had been only 13% and 5% respectively.
3 The term "feminisation of jihad" was first used by Dr. Alexei Malashenko in a panel discussion on martyrdom and jihad held in Washington D.C. on 1 March 2004 (Brill Olcott and Haggani, 2004). He is the former chair of the Carnegie Moscow Center's Religion, Society, and Security Program. The recent rising trend in deploying women in jihad has validated his term.
4 Written in 1993, Muhammad Khayr Haykal's three-volume Arabic work "Jihad and Fighting According to the Shar'ia Policy" presents a detailed discussion of jihad and killing in various Islamic legal perspectives.
5 This Manifesto was purportedly developed by the media wing of al-Khanssaa Brigade, an all-female policing unit of IS operating in Raqqa, as a recruitment tool. It was translated

into English and analysed by Charlie Winter and published by the Quilliam Foundation in February 2015.

6 *Mahram* is any male relative whom it is unlawful for a woman to marry, such as her brother or father.

7 Anwar al-Awlaki was an American-born Muslim scholar and cleric who acted as a spokesperson for al-Qaeda in the Arabian Peninsula before he was killed in a drone strike in Yemen on 30 September 2011.

8 The IS Caliphate regards anyone who reaches 15 as "adult"; hence one who has legal capacity.

9 For more about these programmes see De Leede *et al.* (2017) which studied how women become radicalised and how to empower them to prevent radicalisation.

References

AIVD. (2017). 'Jihadist Women, A Threat Not to Be Underestimated'. The Hague: General Intelligence and Security Service. [Online]. Available at: https://english.aivd.nl/publications/publications/2017/12/14/publication-jihadist-women-a-threat-not-to-be-underestimated [accessed 10 March 2018].

Al-Anfal (2018). *'Iftitahiyya al-'adad al-ththamin 'ashr: al-ghars al-mubaraka'*. *Al-Anfal*, Shawwal 1439 [AH], 18, 2.

Allen, P. (2016). 'France's First All-Female ISIS Terror Cell Held in Notre Dame Probe Were Plotting to Blow up Paris Train Station'. *The Sun*, [online] 9 September 2016. Available at: https://www.thesun.co.uk/news/1754152/teen-girl-gunned-down-after-stabbing-cop-in-notre-dame-probe-was-isis-fanatic-plotting-to-attack-main-train-station-in-paris/ [accessed 30 April 2018].

Barret, R. (2017). 'Beyond the Caliphate: Foreign Fighters and the Threat of Returnees'. *The Soufan Center*. [Online]. Available at: http://thesoufancenter.org/wp-content/uploads/2017/11/Beyond-the-Caliphate-Foreign-Fighters-and-the-Threat-of-Returnees-TSC-Report-October-2017-v3.pdf [accessed 15 March 2018].

BBC. 2018 'Mother and Daughter Jailed for Terror plot' *BBC*, [online] 15 June 2018. Available at: https://www.bbc.co.uk/news/uk-44496433 [accessed 3 May 2018].

Bloom, M. (2014). 'Female Suicide Bombers are Not a New Phenomenon'. *The Washington Post*, [online] 6 August 2014. Available at: https://www.washingtonpost.com/news/monkey-cage/wp/2014/08/06/female-suicide-bombers-are-not-a-new-phenomenon/?utm_term=.88c9078f3e2a [accessed 22 June 2018].

Brill Olcott, M. and Haqqani, H. (2004). *A Panel Discussion on Martyrdom and Jihad*. [Online]. Available at: https://carnegieendowment.org/2004/03/01/martyrdom-and-jihad-event-684 [accessed 22 August 2018].

Cook, D. (2005). 'Women Fighting in Jihad?'. *Studies in Conflict & Terrorism*, 28, 375-384.

Cook, J. and Vale, G. (2018). 'From Daesh to "Diaspora" Tracing the Women and Minors of Islamic State'. *ICSR*. [Online]. Available at: https://icsr.info/wp-content/uploads/2018/07/ICSR-Report-From-Daesh-to-%E2%80%98Diaspora%E2%80%99-Tracing-the-Women-and-Minors-of-Islamic-State.pdf [accessed 21 June 2018].

Dearden, L. (2016). 'My Son Collects Grenades Now: Person Claiming to be Sally Jones Claims British Boy in ISIS Execution Video 'Not Her Son'. *Independent*, [online] 3 September 2016. Available at: https://www.independent.co.uk/news/uk/home-news/british-boy-isis-execution-video-not-sally-jones-son-jihadi-bride-uk-joe-dixon-a7223921.html [accessed 3 May 2018].

De Leede S., Haupfleisch, R., Korolkova, K., Natter, M. (2017). 'Radicalization and Violent Extremism – Focus on Women: How Women Become Radicalized and How to Empower Them to Prevent Radicalization'. *Study for the Committee on Women's Right and Gender Equality* (FEMM). [Online]. Available at: http://www.europarl.europa.eu/RegData/etudes/STUD/2017/596838/IPOL_STU(2017)596838_EN.pdf [accessed 21 March 2018].

Deutsche Welle. (2017). 'German Authorities Target Islamist Women's Network'. *Deutsche Welle*, [online] 27 December 2017. Available at: https://www.dw.com/en/german-authorities-target-islamist-womens-network/a-41939883 [accessed 3 May 2018].

EUROPOL. (2017) *European Union Terrorism Situation and Trend Report 2017*. EUROPOL. [Online]. Available at https://www.europol.europa.eu/activities-services/main-reports/eu-terrorism-situation-and-trend-report-te-sat-2017 [accessed 21 March 2018].

Fink, N.C., Zeiger S. and Bhulai, R. (ed.) (2016). 'A Man's World? Exploring the Roles of Women in Countering Terrorism and Violent Extremism'. *Hedayah and The Global Center on Cooperative Security*. [Online]. Available at: https://wiisglobal.org/wp-content/uploads/2016/07/AMansWorld_FULL.pdf [accessed 21 August 2018].

Gartenstein-Ross, D., Hagerty, V., MacNair, L. (2018). 'The Emigrant Sisters Return: The Growing Role of the Islamic State's Women'. *War on the Rock's: Texas National Security Network*. [Online]. Available at: https://warontherocks.com/2018/04/the-emigrant-sisters-return-the-growing-role-of-the-islamic-states-women/ [accessed 15 March 2018].

HAMAS. (1988). *The Covenant of the Islamic Resistance Movement*. [Online]. Available at: http://avalon.law.yale.edu/20th_century/hamas.asp [accessed 15 March 2018].

Haynie, G.J. and de Jonge Oudraat, C. (2017). 'Women, Gender, and Terrorism:

Understanding Cultural and Organizational Differences'. *Women in International Security.* [Online]. Available at: https://wiisglobal.org/wp-content/uploads/2014/02/4th-WIIS-Policy-Brief-v2-5-1-17.pdf [accessed 17 August 2018].

INSITE (2008). "The Women of Jihad". *Insite Blog on Terrorism and Extremism.* [Online]. Available at: https://news.siteintelgroup.com/blog/index.php/contributors/21-jihad/225-the-women-of-jihad [accessed 30 April 2018].

Lahoud, N. (2014). 'The Neglected Sex: The Jihadis' Exclusion of Women from Jihad'. *Terrorism and Political Violence,* 26(5), 780-802.

Lahoud, N. (2017). 'Can Women Be Soldiers of the Islamic State?'. *Survival,* 59(1), 61-78.

Maza, C. (2018). *Women of ISIS Demand Equal Rights to Wage Violent Jihad, Claim to Be Girls With The Souls of Men, According to Letter. Newsweek,* [online] 2 July 2018. Available at: https://www.newsweek.com/women-isis-demand-equal-rights-wage-violent-jihad-claim-be-girls-souls-men-800710 [accessed 30 April 2018].

Mekhennet, S. and Warrick, J. (2017). 'The Jihadist Plan to Use Women to Launch the Next Incarnation of ISIS'. *The Washington Post,* [online] 26 November 2017. Available at: https://www.washingtonpost.com/world/national-security/the-jihadist-plan-to-use-women-to-launch-the-next-incarnation-of-isis/2017/11/26/e81435b4-ca29-11e7-8321-481fd63f174d_story.html?noredirect=on&utm_term=.78656bc31c02 [accessed 3 May 2018].

Perešin, A. (2015). 'Fatal Attraction: Western Muslimas and ISIS'. *Perspectives on Terrorism,* [online] 9(3). Available at: http://www.terrorismanalysts.com/pt/index.php/pot/article/view/427 [accessed 15 August 2018].

Perešin, A. and Cervone, A. (2015). 'The Western Muhajirat of ISIS'. *Studies in Conflict & Terrorism,* 38(7), 495-509.

Pieters, J. (2018). 'ISIS trained Dutch, Belgian Women to Commit Attacks: Report'. *The New York Times,* [online] 26 January 2018. Available at: https://nltimes.nl/2018/01/26/isis-trained-dutch-belgian-women-commit-attacks-report [accessed 30 April 2018].

Rohmah, A. (2018). 'A Shortcut to Heaven: How Women and Children Became Suicide Bombers in Indonesia'. *The Defense Post,* [online] 22 May 2018. Available at: https://thedefensepost.com/2018/05/22/indonesia-women-children-suicide-bombers/ [accessed 30 April 2018].

Saul, H. (2015). 'ISIS Wedding Certificate Shows Jihadi Bride Demanding Right to be A Suicide Bomber as Condition of Getting Married'. *Independent,* [online] 14 May 2015. Available at: https://www.independent.co.uk/news/world/middle-east/isis-wedding-certificate-shows-jihadi-bride-demanding-right-to-be-a-suicide-bomber-as-condition-of-10250346.html [accessed 22 April 2018].

Schlaffer, E. and Kropiunigg, U. (2016). 'A New Security Architecture: Mothers Included', in N. Chowdhury Fink, S. Zeiger and R. Bhulai (eds), *A Man's World? Exploring the Roles of Women in Countering Terrorism and Violent Extremism*. Abu Dhabi: Hedayah and the Global Center on Cooperative Security, pp. 63-67.

Slobodna Dalmacija (2016). 'Majka najtraženijeg džihadista iz BIH: On je junak, da imam još deset sinova, svi bi išli u džihad!'. *Slobodna Dalmacija*, [online] 4 July 2016. Available at http://www.slobodnadalmacija.hr/novosti/bih/clanak/id/318321/majka-najtrazenijeg-dzihadista-iz-bih-on-je-junak-da-imam-jos-deset-sinova-svi-bi-isli-u-dzihad [accessed 3 May 2018].

Svirski, M. (2018). 'Advice for Jihadi Brides Brought to You by Al-Qaeda'. *Clarion Project*. [Online]. Available at: https://clarionproject.org/advice-jihadi-brides-brought-al-qaeda/ [accessed 22 June 2018].

UN/SC/R. (2013). UN Security Council Resolution No: 2129 [online]. Available at: http://www.un.org/en/ga/search/view_doc.asp?symbol=S/RES/2129%282013%29 [accessed 21 March 2018].

UN/SC/R. (2014). UN Security Council Resolution No: 2178 [online]. Available at: http://www.un.org/en/ga/search/view_doc.asp?symbol=S/RES/2178%20%282014%29 [accessed 21 March 2018].

Warner, J. and Matfess, H. (2017). *Exploding Stereotypes: The Unexpected Operational and Demographic Characteristics of Boko Haram's Suicide Bombers*. New York: United States Military Academy Combating Terrorism Centre at West Point. [Online]. Available at: https://ctc.usma.edu/app/uploads/2017/08/Exploding-Stereotypes-1.pdf [accessed 15 March 2018].

Winter, C. (2015). *Women of the Islamic State: A Manifesto on Women by the Al-Khanssaa Brigade*. London: Quilliam Foundation. [Online]. Available at: https://therinjfoundation.files.wordpress.com/2015/01/women-of-the-islamic-state3.pdf [accessed 15 March 2018].

Winter, C. and Margolin, D. (2017). 'The Mujahidat Dilemma: Female Combatants and the Islamic State'. *CTC Sentinel*, [online] Volume 10(7). Available at: https://ctc.usma.edu/app/uploads/2017/08/CTC-Sentinel_Vol10Iss7-9.pdf [accessed 5 March 2018].

CHAPTER 6

The More Things Change, the More They Stay the Same: The Post-Caliphate Jihadist *Modus Operandi* in Europe

Teun van Dongen

Introduction

From the moment it became clear that European citizens were travelling to Syria to join jihadist groups in their fight against the Assad regime, government and intelligence officials sounded dire warnings about what would happen when these foreign fighters returned. What terrible damage could such returnees do with the training and combat experience they had gained during their time with IS or other jihadist organisations? Such worries only became more pressing once IS began to yield territory to its opponents. With the Caliphate in tatters and the organisation on the run, Julian King, the EU Commissioner for the Security Union, feared that "[r]e-taking the Islamic State stronghold in northern Iraq can lead to a scenario in which violent militants would return to Europe" ("'Mosul offensive may see violent ISIS militants going back to Europe' – EU security commissioner," 2016). EU Counter-Terrorism Coordinator Gilles de Kerchove joined King in voicing these concerns, claiming that the loss of Raqqa would make IS decide to send foreign fighters home to commit attacks against the West (Vallance, 2016), adding later that "[t]hese people are trained to use explosives and firearms and they have been indoctrinated by the jihadist ideology" (Macguire, 2016).

But to what extent is this fear justified? Is it indeed true that, in the words of one analyst, "[o]ne of the most urgent threats to counterterrorism is now the re-entry of jihad fighters, trained in and hardened by combat experience and able to execute complex and coordinated terrorist attacks in their countries of origin" (Boncio, 2017)? Or do we also need to entertain other, less dramatic possibilities? In order to answer these questions, this chapter will make a projection of the impact of the collapse of the Caliphate on the *modus operandi* of jihadist terrorist attacks in Europe in the near future. The first section of this chapter will use the most relevant operational characteristic of foreign fighters, the terrorist expertise they gained during their time with IS, to make an educated guess about the nature of the attacks they are going to commit. The second section will assess whether the collapse of the Caliphate released a wave of potential perpetrators who are willing and able to commit such attacks. The conclusion will tie these two sections together by combining the probability and the likelihood of the type of attack that returnees are likely to commit.

The Likely *Modus Operandi* of Foreign Fighters

One of the most important reasons why foreign fighters are considered dangerous upon their return to their home countries is their expertise, which they acquired through training and combat experience with IS. The Dutch intelligence service AIVD, for instance, is concerned about the capabilities of foreign fighters with training and experience, and stresses that women and even children have received such training as well. And indeed, as the AIVD's report *Terugkeerders in Beeld (Returnees: A Closer Look)* suggests, it is safe to assume that the vast majority of people who spent more than a few weeks in the Caliphate as members of IS have received some form of weapons training (AIVD, 2017: 4–6).

From what we know about the experiences of foreign fighters, they all went through a registration process shortly after they arrived in IS territory. Their names, ages, nationalities, educational levels and knowledge of Islam were put in files. At this point it was also assessed whether a recruit might be a suitable candidate for a role in an attack plot against the West. According to Harry Sarfo, a German former IS member, the IS unit that plans the attacks against the West was particularly interested in people with a criminal record, as they might have some skills (e.g. acquiring weapons and false documents) that would help them to successfully plan and carry out the terrorist attack (Callimachi, 2016).

The majority of the new recruits, however, were trained to prepare them for a role as a fighter for IS in the Caliphate. Their training may not have been as specialised as that of the recruits who were singled out as perpetrators of terrorist attacks in the West, but they still went through, in most cases, some two to three months of training. The first parts of these training programmes in particular involved much religious indoctrination, which was important as a means to provide the recruits with the justification for the brutalities they would go on to commit (Hassan, 2015). Later on, the recruits received training in the use of Kalashnikovs, rocket propelled grenades (RPGs) and hand grenades. They have also been trained to withstand physical hardship (hunger, cold, fatigue). Near the completion of their training, they stood guard or performed other tasks short of full deployment in combat (Weggemans et al., 2016: 47–48).

Some fighters will, when facing charges, claim that they have been performing support roles in the Caliphate. Some will say they tended to the wounded, whereas others will try to make the court believe they were only involved in spreading propaganda. It should be noted, though, that the pressure on IS members to contribute to the fighting is considerable. In fact, IS commanders can easily interpret unwillingness to engage the enemy in combat as a form of betrayal. The norm is that IS fighters should fight, and it goes without saying that IS has few qualms about the punishments it metes out to those who violate the norms. This means that many recruits will have fought, if not because they actually wanted to, but because they wanted to escape the IS's brutal punishments (Weggemans et al., 2016: 50).

Having established that foreign fighters underwent training and saw combat, we arrive at the question what that means for the threat foreign fighters pose once they are back in Europe. Some have argued, not entirely unconvincingly, that the expertise that foreign fighters gained by fighting for IS may not be that useful for someone who wants to commit a terrorist attack in the West. It is true that waging irregular warfare in Syria and Iraq is not the same thing as committing a terrorist attack in North America or Europe. As Daniel Byman and Leonard Shapiro point out, "conducting surveillance, building an underground network, operating clandestinely, and other skills useful for conducting terrorist attacks— especially terrorist attacks in hyper-vigilant Western countries—are not always part of the curriculum" that IS provides to new recruits (Byman and Shapiro, 2014: 20). Moreover, a foreign fighter for IS will work with weapons and materials that are not, or at least not as easily, available in the West, which means that a jihadist terrorist in the West will need to find out where to get the right materials or substitutes (Kenney, 2010: 922).

Also, some authors claim that the Internet now serves as a virtual training camp. They reason that the wealth of information that is available online and that is promoted by groups like IS and al-Qaeda to instruct potential jihadist terrorists in the West supplants the need for travel to terrorist organisations to acquire terrorist skills (UN Office on Drugs and Crime (UN ODC) Report 2012: 8; Weimann, 2006: 119–123). As a result, "stay-at home terrorists" can be just as dangerous as terrorists who have been to training camps and who have seen combat as fighters for a jihadist group.

Interestingly though, the available research on terrorist *modus operandi* does not line up with the assessments of those who want to downplay the importance of terrorist training. It suggests that the *modus operandi* of trained jihadist terrorists is different from those of other terrorists in several related and worrying respects. Their attacks are more complex, they are more likely to use Improvised Explosive Devices (IEDs) and their attacks tend to have higher casualty rates.

More Complex Attacks

An analysis of jihadist terrorist attacks and foiled plots in Europe in the period 2004-2011 has shown that the attacks and plots perpetrated by those who went to a training camp are decidedly more complex than those perpetrated by the untrained. Trained perpetrators were more likely to commit simultaneous attacks, build their own weapons (usually IEDs) and adjust their weapons in order to conceal them from security personnel and intended victims (Van Dongen, 2012). The most common example of the latter tactic is an IED that has to fit in a backpack or a suitcase.

This analysis about the complexity of terrorist attacks was published in 2012, so it does not cover the period after the onset of the civil war in Syria, but the findings appear to apply to more recent attacks as well. The attacks after 2012 by trained perpetrators, such as the ones in Paris (November 2015), Brussels (March 2016) and Manchester (May 2017) display (some of) these three indicators of complexity. This lends credence to the notion that attacks by trained perpetrators are more elaborate schemes that require more effort in the preparatory stages. The foreign fighter is a trained terrorist, so his attacks will probably be more complex than those of his untrained counterparts.

More IED Attacks

A recent analysis of all jihadist terrorist attacks in the West in the period 2004-2017 shows that trained jihadist terrorists are considerably more likely to use IEDs than untrained terrorists. Of the twelve attacks committed by perpetrators who received training in terrorist training camps run by al-Qaeda, IS or another terrorist organisation, nine, or 75%, involved the use of IEDs. This percentage is much lower for untrained perpetrators: of the 70 attacks by untrained perpetrators, only eleven, or 16%, involved the use of IEDs. This suggests that the IED is the weapon of choice of the organisations that provide terrorist training, probably because they have the necessary bomb making expertise and because it allows their trainees to attack many people at once (Van Dongen, forthcoming).

Possibly because of these advantages of the IED, even trained perpetrators show little inclination to choose a more innovative *modus operandi*. Over the years, various analysts and policy makers have made suggestions about innovative attack modes. The CBRN (chemical, biological, radiological and nuclear) attack was a matter of "if, not when" (Yeo, 2015), and jihadists would start forest fires (Fighel, 2009) and attack livestock and the food supply in Western countries (Jayaharo, n.d.). Some would even undergo surgery to insert IEDs in their bodies (Saletan, 2011), and the technologically minded among them would launch cyber attacks to paralyse the banking systems or the electricity supplies of their target countries (Albahar, 2017; for a poignant critique of the cyber terrorism hype, see Singer, 2012). These fears, some of which were uttered more than a decade ago, never materialised. As the attacks by IS-trained perpetrators were so far fairly conventional and as there is little evidence that IS fighters are being trained in surgery or hacking, the returning foreign fighters are most likely to stick to the familiar script when preparing a terrorist attack. It is true that IS has made extensive use of drones in fighting off the enemies of the Caliphate, but drones are of much more use on the battlefield, where IS can deploy large numbers of them simultaneously, than it is in the execution of terrorist attacks, which tend to be much smaller operations.

Higher Casualty Rates
Trained perpetrators are likely to have been trained in the construction of IEDs, which means that they have the capabilities to construct and use one of the most deadly weapons available to a terrorist. This being the case, it can be expected that trained foreign fighters will commit attacks with higher casualty rates. In fact, they have done so already. The perpetrators of the attacks in Paris in November 2015, in Brussels in 2016 and in Manchester in 2017 were all trained, so it is no surprise that the casualty rate of their attacks was higher than that of the attacks without foreign fighter participation (Vidino et al., 2017: 60–61). Similarly, Hegghammer found that jihadist attacks entirely or partially perpetrated by foreign fighters were more likely to result in lethalities, and Hegghammer and

Sageman each found that plots that are entirely or partially prepared by foreign fighters are more likely to reach the execution stage than plots that are prepared by perpetrators who never visited a training camp (Hegghammer, 2013: 11; Sageman, 2009).

Assuming that returnees will act in the same way as other trained and experienced jihadist terrorists, one can surmise from the previous discussion that the returnees who engage in terrorist attacks against their home countries will likely commit complex, deadly IED attacks. In this sense, they are different from untrained perpetrators, who generally commit less complex attacks, are less likely to use IEDs and commit less deadly attacks. There are, however, also some aspects that attacks by trained terrorists have in common with attacks by untrained terrorists.

Proximity
Studies into various kinds of terrorism have established that terrorists like to strike close to home. Becker, for instance, examined 84 lone actor-terrorist attacks in the period 1940-2012 and found that the majority of the perpetrators attacked targets they knew from their everyday routine, for instance because they went by them every day on their way to work (Becker, 2014: 967–969). In a similar vein, Gill, Horgan and Corner show that some two thirds of the 235 members of the Provisional Irish Republican Army (Provisional IRA) who carried out IED attacks and shootings during the Northern Ireland conflict, struck within four miles of their homes. They also found that few Provisional IRA fighters travelled more than fifteen miles to get to their targets (Gill et al., 2017: 7–8). Like the lone actor-terrorists from Becker's research, they were aware of the obvious advantages of targets close to home: the perpetrator can move more easily around the target without raising suspicion, which may help the preparation as well as the execution.

Although these two studies concern other forms of terrorism, a quick glance at the record of jihadist terrorism in Europe shows a similar pattern. Jihadist terrorists, too, are unlikely to travel long distances to attack their targets. The Paris attacks of November 2015 constitute a rare instance of a jihadist attack in Europe in which the perpetrators did not attack in the country where they lived at the time of the attack. To the best knowledge of the current author, there have been only two other jihadist terrorist attacks in which the target was not located in the country where the perpetrator lived: in December 2010 Taimour Abdulwahab al-Abdaly travelled from his home in Luton to Stockholm to commit a suicide bombing, and in February 2017 Abdullah Reda al-Hamamy, who lived in the United Arab Emirates, travelled to Paris to commit a knife attack near the Louvre. A recent study confirms this pattern by demonstrating that the vast majority of the jihadist attacks in Europe between 2014 and 2016 was committed in the countries of which the perpetrators were citizens or where they lived as immigrants (Vidino et al., 2017: 53–54).

What this shows is that a European country is most likely to be attacked by its own jihadist terrorists, regardless of whether they have received training or fought with IS. Jihadists that are better trained and more experienced, too, display a strong preference for attacks in familiar locations, usually in the country, and sometimes even in the city, where they live. The man who committed a suicide bombing in Manchester lived in Manchester, and the two brothers who committed a shooting at the offices of the satirical magazine Charlie Hebdo in Paris lived in Paris. Similarly, the perpetrators of the 2016 bombings in Brussels lived in Brussels.

Soft Targets
Another similarity between trained and untrained perpetrators is that they prefer soft targets. Like the preference for targets close to home, this suggests a certain tendency to give feasibility precedence over other considerations. In a recent assessment, Hemmingby calculates that the vast majority (more than 85%) of the jihadist terrorist plots in Europe in the period between 1994 and 2016 were aimed against targets that had few or no protective measures around them (Hemmingby, 2017: 30). Hemmingby does not clearly identify which attacks he considers have been committed against soft and hard targets, yet it appears that perpetrators with training and expertise also prefer soft targets. It is true that there were some security measures around the offices of Charlie Hebdo, but the bombings by the trained perpetrators in Madrid (2004), London (2005), Paris (2015), Brussels (2016) and Manchester (2017) were all directed against soft targets. As argued above, their training and expertise allow such perpetrators to attack larger groups of people at once, but there is little reason to assume that they are more likely than their untrained counterparts to attempt an attack against a hardened target, like a head of state or a heavily secured government building.

Drawing on the brief reviews of the five attack characteristics above (complexity, casualty rate, IED use, target selection and proximity), one could attempt to formulate a basic template for the kind of attack that returnees are likely to commit, should they decide to plot a terrorist attack: the returnee is likely to succeed in building powerful, deadly IEDs for simultaneous attacks against soft targets close to where s/he (mostly he) lives. This is an attack profile that closely resembles the 'classic' IED attack that was introduced to Europe during the first wave of al-Qaeda attacks almost fifteen years ago. This profile suggests that there is a modest degree of predictability for attack plans by returnees, but the downside is that there is every reason to consider a returnee terrorist more dangerous than an independent, self-made plotter.

Alternative Paths for Foreign Fighters

The foreign fighter who returns to his home country to use his expertise in a terrorist attack is obviously the darkest scenario for Western intelligence agencies. As demonstrated above, there is some ground for these concerns, as trained terrorists are indeed more dangerous than untrained terrorists. However, the fact that a perpetrator has considerable operational capabilities does not automatically mean that s/he poses a threat to his/her home country. A lot can happen to a wo/man, especially when s/he is a foreign fighter for IS. The following are the most probable paths that foreign fighters can take other than committing an attack in Europe.

Incapacitation
According to one estimate, at least some 7,000 of the total of 40,000 foreign fighters died on the battlefield.[1] Admittedly, confirming the death of a foreign fighter is not an easy task. For instance, some jihadists, including Abdelhamid Abaaoud, the ringleader of the cell that committed the November 2015 attacks in Paris, faked their deaths in an attempt to pull the wool over the eyes of the authorities (Castillo and Cruickshank, 2015). Nonetheless, given the intensity of the fighting in Syria and Iraq and the fact that many inexperienced recruits have been used as mere cannon fodder (UN CTED, 2018: 7), it is quite plausible that a sizeable part of the European foreign fighter contingent is no longer alive. Also, some 5,400 others are currently detained (Cragin, 2017); 600 of them are held in prisons run by the Kurdish Syrian Democratic Forces (SDF) (Savage, 2018), while most others are imprisoned in their home countries (Mekhennet and Warrick, 2018). There is no telling what these returnees will do after they are released from prison, but at least in the short term they are unlikely to commit terrorist attacks against their home countries.

Staying in Iraq and Syria
IS is down, but not out. The group is currently regrouping in the desert and in mountainous areas to create bases from which to commit terrorist attacks, sometimes under a different name (Daragahi, 2018). Members of other units shaved off their beards to blend in with the local population, giving rise to concerns that they are going to act as sleeper cells. This strategy does not have the same allure as the Caliphate, but the death toll of the terrorist attacks in Baghdad and other major cities shows that IS is beginning to find its feet in its previous incarnation, that of a terrorist organisation. Indeed, one should consider the transformation of IS from a proto-dictatorship back to an insurgent group as a strategic retreat rather than as a full-on defeat. This being the case, some foreign fighters will stay with the group to do what they have been doing over the last years, which is waging violent jihad. One should remember that many foreign fighters want to build an alternative to their lives in what they see as their godless home countries (Barrett, 2017: 14). At least some of them will believe they can do more to help their cause by fighting themselves to death than by returning home to commit a terrorist attack (Landay, 2017). Some foreign fighters who are still at large can decide to return home and plan an attack there, but some others will certainly choose to use their operational capabilities to help IS in Syria and Iraq.

Transfer to Other Places
During its heyday IS has spent much time building branches in areas far away from the Caliphate, notably in Afghanistan and Libya. These foreign branches might well – and to some extent they already do – have much to gain from the collapse of the Caliphate. Although the stream of financial and technical support from IS might dry up, some foreign fighters have been able to flee the battlefield in Syria and Iraq to join the IS branches in other countries. For instance, it is reported that some 80 foreign fighters moved to the Philippines to join Abu Sayyaf Group, an IS affiliated jihadist group (Tracing Islamic State's Foreign Fighters, 2017). Similarly, the IS branch in Afghanistan attracted several francophone foreign fighters (French Fighters Appear with IS in Afghanistan, 2017). There is no real way of knowing where they will go next, but such transfers to other combat zones do not suggest a strong urge to commit terrorist attacks in Europe.

Disillusionment
From quite early on in the Syrian civil war, there have been foreign fighters who became disillusioned with the organisations they joined. They felt that their participation in the group did not hold up to their idealised expectations about jihad. In some cases, this is because life as an IS fighter lacked the heroism they were hoping for, whereas others could not stomach waging war on fellow Muslims. Yet others broke with IS because they believe the group violated Islamic rules and principles, for instance by engaging in corruption (Neumann, 2015). Such disillusionment, though, does not always suggest a new-found regard for human life or a sudden rediscovery of the merits of liberal democracy. The case of the Kosovar foreign fighter Fitim Lladrovici is instructive in this respect. He did not feel there was anything untoward about the massacres and the sexual slavery that characterised IS's rule in Syria and Iraq, but he was deeply offended by the organisation's negligence in fulfilling its financial obligations to the widows of IS fighters who died on the battlefield. Also, he felt that IS was not providing adequate healthcare to the wives of the IS fighters. He was so angry about this that he refused to fight for IS any longer and left the organisation (Speckhard et al., 2018: 12). Nevertheless, even in cases like that of Lladrovici, one can be reasonably sure that those who are truly done with IS will not be involved in terrorist plots in Europe after their return.

Turning Back
Returning from a war zone to the mundane reality of everyday life at home in Europe may not be easy. Certainly some foreign fighters will still crave action after they get back, but this does not mean that committing a terrorist attack will be their first option. Remarkably, some returnees who were still loyal to IS and wanted some action went back to the battlefield instead of trying to plan a terrorist attack in their home countries (Hecker, 2018: 33–35; Speckhard et al., 2018: 2–3). Given the low number of people who went to Syria and Iraq to join IS in recent years, the return to the battlefield is not the most likely scenario. As Syria and Iraq are now decidedly harder to reach and as IS is on the strategic retreat, IS veterans will perhaps travel from their home countries to other IS branches to fight. Whether this is actually going to happen remains to be seen. Nevertheless, the cases of the returnees who went back to IS make it clear that a returnee's urge to fight does not always have to translate into a terrorist attack in Europe.

Career Move

Perhaps a returnee still feels committed to IS and wants to do something in his home country to further the cause. Does this mean that returnees in this category are likely to commit terrorist attacks in Europe? Perhaps, but even here there are other possibilities. Rather than engaging in terrorist plots, returnees might take on different roles. Their combat experience and the fact that they have lived in the Caliphate enhance their status in jihadist networks. It is, hence, quite plausible that such returnees will act as recruiters and inspirers rather than as attack plotters. They may also act as conduits by helping new recruits get in touch with organisations that can provide terrorist training (Meleagrou-Hitchens et al., 2018: 71).

Remaining Passive

Finally, some returnees may still subscribe to IS's worldview and may still be supportive of the group's project. They may also, however, simply be too burned out to engage in an attack. Years of fighting and constant danger are demanding even for trained soldiers and will certainly take their toll on many foreign fighters who are less experienced than soldiers who served in regular armies. Also, they may succumb to pressure from family members to stay away from any terrorist activities (Boncio, 2017; Reed et al., 2017: 5–6). It may be noteworthy in this respect that hundreds of foreign fighters have returned to Europe.

In 2015, when the Islamic State was at its peak, Thomas Hegghammer and Petter Nesser calculated a "blowback rate" of 0.0028%, meaning that up to that point only one in every 360 foreign fighters from the battlefield in Syria and Iraq had been involved in terrorist plots in their home countries (Hegghammer and Nesser, 2015: 20). This impression finds confirmation in a more recent estimate, which puts the blowback rate at 0.002%. According to this study there have been twelve returnee plotters out of the roughly 6,000 Western foreign fighters (Vidino et al., 2017: 60–61). Moreover, although the intelligence agencies and security officials warned of a stream of foreign fighters going back to their home countries after the decline of the Caliphate, this prediction so far has failed to materialise. Some foreign fighters do not want to go home, and those who already have may not have any attack plans in mind. Returned foreign fighters can be quite dangerous once they decide to plot a terrorist attack, but it is too simple to describe them, as politicians and intelligence officials routinely do, as ticking time bombs. The attack in the home country is only one of many possible scenarios, as the discussion above illustrates. Furthermore, if we consider the total number of Europeans among all foreign fighters and then subtract all those who have taken (or were forced to take) one of the other paths outlined above, the remaining number is probably low.

Conclusion

The developments in the global jihadist movement between 2012 and 2015 were dramatic, but they have not done much to change the *modus operandi* of jihadist terrorists in Europe. Recent analyses of the jihadist *modus operandi* convincingly claim that the rise of IS did not have a significant impact on the nature of the terrorist attacks committed on European soil. Hemmingby (2017: 36) observes that the jihadists who attacked Europe "are conventional and imitative when it comes to their targeting preferences – in contrast to suggestions implying that IS has shown innovation in this area." Nesser et al. (2016: 3) make a similar point in their analysis of the jihadist terrorist threat to Europe: "For all the talk of a new threat we argue that, apart from scope, less is new than most assume."

So the rise of the Caliphate has not changed much about the jihadist *modus operandi* in Europe. But what, then, about the next major development in the global jihadist movement? What about the collapse of the Caliphate? Will the impact of this shift in the terrorist threat have a limited impact on the *modus operandi* of jihadist terrorists in Europe as well? At this point, we can only speculate, but it is quite possible that the answer is yes, at least in the short term.

In conventional risk assessment methods, possible threat scenarios are weighed on their probability and their impact (National Network of Safety and Security Analysts, 2016: 26, 182). This means that there are, roughly speaking, four threat categories: low impact/low probability, low impact/high probability, high probability/low impact and high probability/high impact. Jihadist terrorist attacks in Europe by the perpetrators who attended training camps and/or who gained battlefield experience would qualify as low probability/high impact scenarios. The attacks are quite rare, but when they do occur they cause many deaths.

Understandably, after the emergence of IS there has been a fear in Europe about the increasing number of jihadists and the possibility that they will commit attacks with a large impact. In terms of the risk assessment categories, government officials and intelligence agencies believe that a terrorist attack by a trained and experienced jihadist is becoming a high probability/high impact scenario, where previously it had been a low probability/high impact scenario. The literature review on terrorist *modus operandi* in this paper shows that the training and combat experience of the returnees are likely to contribute to the complexity and deadliness of their terrorist attacks. At the same time, it demonstrates that it is far from certain that such attacks are becoming more likely in the post-Caliphate period, particularly given the various paths that foreign fighters may take other than plotting an attack in Europe. Only a small segment of the foreign fighters seems to get involved in the planning and execution of a terrorist attack on European soil.

Thus, a skilfully executed deadly IED attack against a soft target close to the perpetrator's home – the most important elements of the plausible *modus operandi* of a returned foreign fighter – is probably a low probability/high impact scenario, just as it was before the emergence of IS as a proto-state in Syria and Iraq. Such attacks always made up only a small portion of all terrorist attacks and plots in Europe. It is likely to remain this way, even now that foreign fighters are trickling back into Europe.

There are, of course, things that need to be monitored in order to be sure that the threat of professional IED attacks does not increase. For the short term, this chapter argues, there are reasons to believe that the collapse of the Caliphate will not fundamentally change the *modus operandi* of jihadists in Europe, but this does not mean that the current *modus operandi* is somehow written in stone. If some returnees are successful in playing new roles as recruiters or facilitators, there may be serious reasons to expect that professional IED attacks will become more likely. After all, such returnees do have a network that allows them to act as a conduit to new recruits who want to receive training. This may lead to an increase in the number of those who are willing and able to commit a deadly IED attack in Europe. The development of jihadist networks in Europe in this regard must be watched carefully. Intelligence services should also watch the next move of those who went to other jihadist groups and those who stayed in Syria and Iraq. These foreign fighters chose not to go to Europe for now, but they may come back to Europe at a later stage to carry out attacks or to act as recruiters. A third possibility is that one of the IS branches in another part of the world – Libya is currently a prime candidate (Saal, 2017; Varvelli in this volume) – could become a new centre to provide training for jihadists who want to commit a terrorist attack in the West. A hub of this kind could obviously lead to a professionalisation of jihadist terrorists in Europe.

In assessing such possibilities it is important not to automatically assume too easily that the worst case scenario is the most plausible one, which is what appears to have happened in assessing the impact of the Caliphate's rise and of its collapse. Realistic assessments will get us further than kneejerk resorts to our deepest fears. Therefore, when evaluating the threat of terrorist attacks to Europe, one should stay open to the possibility that trends and developments in the global jihadist movement may not work out as badly as they might. The jihadist threat is likely to stay with us for the time being and will plague many countries in Europe and elsewhere. We will, hence, have our fair share of policy dilemmas and conundrums in the near future. Nevertheless, it would be a mistake to believe that the jihadist threat will always manifest itself in its most dangerous form. The terrorist attacks in Europe by trained and experienced jihadists have long been a low probability/high impact scenario, and are likely to remain just that, with or without the Caliphate.

Notes

1 The data of this estimate were derived from the 79 countries that release information about their foreign fighters, but there are foreign fighters from 120 countries in Syria and Iraq, so the overall number of foreign fighters who were killed in battle is likely to be much higher.

References

AIVD. (2017). *Terugkeerders in Beeld.* The Hague: Algemene Inlichtingen- en Veiligheidsdienst.

Albahar, M. (2017). 'Cyber Attacks and Terrorism: A Twenty-First Century Conundrum'. *Science and Engineering Ethics*, 1–14.

Barrett, R. (2017). *Beyond the Caliphate: Foreign Fighters and the Threat of Returnees.* Soufan Center and the Global Strategy Network.

Becker, M. (2014). 'Explaining Lone Wolf Target Selection in the United States'. *Studies in Conflict & Terrorism* 37(11): 959–78.

Boncio, A. (2017) *The Islamic State's Crisis and Returning Foreign Fighters: The Case of Italy.* Working Paper. Milan: Instituto per gli Studi di Politica Internazionale (ISPI).

Byman, D., and Shapiro, J. (2014). *Be Afraid. Be a Little Afraid: The Threat of Terrorism from Western Foreign Fighters in Syria and Iraq.* Policy Papers. Washington, DC: Brookings Institute.

Callimachi, R. (2016). 'How a Secret Branch of ISIS Built a Global Network of Killers'. *The New York Times*. Available at https://www.nytimes.com/2016/08/04/world/middleeast/isis-german-recruit-interview.html [accessed 26 September 2018].

Castillo, M., and Cruickshank, P. (2015). 'Who Was Abdelhamid Abaaoud, Suspected Ringleader of Paris Attack?' *CNN*. Available at: https://edition.cnn.com/2015/11/16/europe/paris-terror-attack-mastermind-abdelhamid-abaaoud/index.html [accessed 26 September 2018].

Cragin, K. (2017). 'Foreign Fighter 'Hot Potato''. *Lawfare*. Available at https://www.lawfareblog.com/foreign-fighter-hot-potato [accessed 26 September 2018].

Daragahi, B. (2018). 'The New Face of ISIS in Iraq Calls Itself the White Flags'. *Buzzfeed News*. Available at https://www.buzzfeednews.com/article/borzoudaragahi/isis-iraq-white-flags-syria-new-name#.er7o7AZA8X [accessed 26 September 2018].

Fighel, J. (2009). 'The "Forest Jihad"'. *Studies in Conflict & Terrorism* 32(9), 802–810.

"French Fighters Appear with ISIS in Afghanistan." (2017). *NDTV*. Available at https://www.ndtv.com/world-news/french-fighters-appear-with-isis-in-afghanistan-1785903 [accessed 26 September 2018].

Gill, P., Horgan, J., and Corner, E. (2017). 'The Rational Foraging Terrorist: Analysing the Distances Travelled to Commit Terrorist Violence'. *Terrorism and Political Violence*. Available at https://www.tandfonline.com/doi/abs/10.1080/09546553.2017.1297707 [accessed 26 September 2018].

Hassan, H. (2015). 'The Secret World of ISIS Training Camps'. *The Guardian*. Avaiable at https://www.theguardian.com/world/2015/jan/25/inside-isis-training-camps [accessed 26 September 2018].

Hecker, M. (2018). *137 Shades of Terrorism: French Jihadists before the Courts*. Focus Stratégique. Paris: Institut français des relations internationales (IFRI).

Hegghammer, T. (2013). 'Should I Stay or Should I Go? Explaining Variation in Western Jihadists' Choice between Domestic and Foreign Fighting'. *American Political Science Review* 107(1), 1–15.

Hegghammer, T., and Nesser, P. (2015). 'Assessing the Islamic State's Commitment to Attacking the West'. *Perspectives on Terrorism* 9(4), 14–30.

Hemmingby, C. (2017). 'Exploring the Continuum of Lethality: Militant Islamists' Targeting Preferences in Europe'. *Perspectives on Terrorism* 11(5), 25–41.

Jayaharo, B.M. (n.d.). *Agroterrorism: A Threat to US Animal Agriculture*. University Park: PennState Extension. Available at https://extension.psu.edu/agroterrorism-a-threat-to-us-animal-agriculture [accessed 26 September 2018].

Kenney, M. (2010). '"Dumb" yet Deadly: Local Knowledge and Poor Tradecraft among Islamist Militants in Britain and Spain'. *Studies in Conflict & Terrorism* 33(10), 911–32.

Landay, J. (2017). 'Many Foreign Fighters Likely to Stay in Syria, Iraq: U.S. Official'. *Reuters*. Available at https://www.reuters.com/article/us-mideast-crisis-usa-baghdadi/many-foreign-fighters-likely-to-stay-in-syria-iraq-u-s-official-idUSKBN1A61ZJ [accessed 26 September 2018].

Macguire, E. (2016). 'ISIS Fighters Returning from Iraq, Syria May Unleash Europe Attacks: Cops'. *ABC News*. Available at https://www.nbcnews.com/storyline/isis-terror/isis-fighters-returning-iraq-syria-may-unleash-europe-attacks-cops-n691106 [accessed 26 September 2018].

Mekhennet, S., and Warrick, J., (2018). 'ISIS behind Bars'. *Washington Post*. Available at https://www.washingtonpost.com/graphics/2018/world/europe-isis-prisons/?noredirect=on&utm_term=.3ad68075c430 [accessed 26 September 2018].

Meleagrou-Hitchens, A., Hughes, S., and Clifford, B. (2018). *The Travelers: American Jihadists in Syria and Iraq*. Washington, DC: Program on Extremism.

'"Mosul Offensive May See Violent ISIS Militants Going Back to Europe" – EU Security Commissioner'. (2016). *RT*. Available at https://www.rt.com/news/363125-isis-mosul-militants-europe/ [accessed 26 September 2018].

National Network of Safety and Security Analysts. (2016). *National Risk Profile 2016: An All Hazard Overview of Potential Disasters and Threats in the Netherlands*. Bilthoven: Rijksinstituut voor Volksgezondheid en Milieu (RIVM).

Nesser, P., Stenersen, A., and Oftedal, E. (2016). 'Jihadi Terrorism in Europe: The IS-Effect'. *Perspectives on Terrorism* 10(6), 3–24.

Neumann, P. (2015). *Victims, Perpetrators, Assets: The Narratives of Islamic State Defectors*. London: International Centre for the Study of Radicalisation and Political Violence (ICSR).

Reed, A., Pohl, J., and Jegerings, M. (2017). *The Four Dimensions of the Foreign Fighter Threat: Making Sense of an Evolving Phenomenon*. The Hague: International Centre for Counter-Terrorism (ICCT).

Saal, J. (2017). *The Islamic State's Libyan External Operations Hub: The Picture so Far*. CTC Sentinel 10(11), 19–23.

Sageman, M. (2009). 'Confronting Al-Qaeda: Understanding the Threat in Afghanistan'. *Perspectives on Terrorism* 3(4), 1–22.

Saletan, W. (2011). 'Sew-inside Bombers'. *Slate*. Available at http://www.slate.com/articles/health_and_science/human_nature/2011/07/sewinside_bombers.html?via=gdpr-consent [accessed 26 September 2018].

Savage, C. (2018). 'As ISIS Fighters Fill Prisons in Syria, Their Home Nations Look Away'. *New York Times*. Available at https://www.nytimes.com/2018/07/18/world/middleeast/islamic-state-detainees-syria-prisons.html [accessed 26 September 2018].

Singer, P.W. (2012). 'The Cyber Terror Bogeyman'. *Brookings* (blog). Available at https://www.brookings.edu/articles/the-cyber-terror-bogeyman/ [accessed 26 September 2018].

Speckhard, A., Shajkovci, A., and Yayla, A. S. (2018). 'Defected from ISIS or Simply Returned, and for How Long? – Challenges for the West in Dealing with Returning Foreign Fighters'. *Homeland Security Affairs* 14, 1–21.

'Tracing Islamic State's Foreign Fighters: Over 40,000 People Who Joined Caliphate Are Unaccounted For'. (2017). *First Post*. Available at https://www.firstpost.com/world/tracing-islamic-states-foreign-fighters-over-40000-people-who-joined-caliphate-are-unaccounted-for-4261341.html [accessed 26 September 2018].

UN CTED (UN Counter-Terrorism Committee Executive Directorate). (2018). *The Challenge of Returning and Relocating Foreign Fighters: Research Perspectives*. UN Security Council, Counter-Terrorism Committee, Executive Directorate.

UN ODC (UN Office on Drugs and Crime). (2012). *The Use of the Internet for Terrorist Purposes*. Vienna: United Nations.

Vallance, C. (2016). 'Collapse of IS Will Lead to Attacks, Say EU Officials'. *BBC News* Available at https://www.bbc.com/news/world-europe-37691490 [accessed 26 September 2018].

Van Dongen, T. (2012). *Jihadistisch Terroristische Aanslagen in de EU, 2004-2011: Onderzoek naar Complexiteit, Daderkarakteristieken en de Relatie Daartussen*. The Hague: The Hague Centre for Strategic Studies (HCSS).

Van Dongen, T. (forthcoming). 'Linking Perpetrator Characteristics to Jihadist Modus Operandi: An Explorative Study', in S. Knittel and Z. Goldberg (eds.), *Handbook of Perpetrator Studies*, New York: Routledge.

Vidino, L., F. M., and Entenmann, E. (2017). *Fear Thy Neighbour: Radicalization and Jihadist Attacks in the West*. Milan: ICCT, ISPI and George Washington University.

Weggemans, D., R. Peters, E. Bakker, and R. de Bont. (2016) *Bestemming Syrië: een Exploratieve Studie naar de Leefsituatie van Nederlandse 'Uitreizigers' in Syrië*. The Hague: Leiden University and University of Amsterdam.

Weimann, G. (2006). 'Virtual Training Camps: Terrorists' Use of the Internet', in J.J.F. Forest (ed.), *Teaching Terror: Strategic and Tactical Learning in the Terrorist World*, 110–32. New Delhi: Viva Books.

Yeo, W. (2015). *The Growing Threat of CBRN Weapons*. RSIS Commentary. Singapore: RSIS.

CHAPTER 7
Jihadists in Belgian Prisons

Johan Leman

Among the causes for radicalisation, the literature distinguishes geopolitical-historical, social and personal factors (Beelman et al., 2018). Personal factors may be, among others, problematic personal characteristics (Besta et al., 2015; Campbell and Volhardt, 2014; Pauwels and Heylen, 2017) that can be complemented by such social ones as intra-family conflicts or the absence of integration on the labour market. It is mainly youngsters among 18 and 25 years old who correspond to that profile and may end up in prison and become or are already radicalised. One may say that the step to delinquent behaviour, in their case, is already a form of radicalisation. With their deviant and delinquent behaviour they already challenge society or an important part of its norms. However, there exists not only jihadist radicalisation. There is also extreme right and extreme left radicalisation; and there is delinquency as such.

Imprisonment and Jihadisation

When I asked the question "What is the profile of radicalised prisoners in Belgian prisons?", the psychologist Nico Braspenning and the psychologist-criminologist Astrid Boelaert, who are both the coordinators of the Belgian "Central Psycho-Social Service Extremism,"[1] distinguished various profiles, even of men older than 60, and also of women (Braspenning and Boelaert 2018). As the most common profile, they find young men, married or unmarried, who via processes inside as well as outside prison, find a route to becoming still more sympathising with violent jihadism, or who empower this route. They themselves never saw people in prison who went to fight after leaving prison. They see prisoners "in" jail who seem to have radicalised, or who seem to have radicalised "more" (cf. "seeing their canal empowered"). They, however, also see prisoners who entered prison as (strongly) radicalised (for example condemned for terrorist crimes), but seem to have "deradicalised" there, or at least no longer behave in an activist way (i.e. disengagement).

They ask to pay attention to the fact that the age category between 18 and 25 among young men has always been a sensitive age with regard to several forms of general criminality. Their overrepresentation in the penitentiary population illustrates this fact.[2] To my question whether jihadists are becoming younger and younger as of 2018, they answered that they also observe this; but they cannot totally verify it in their function since they have no access to the files of people younger than 18. Such access is a specific mission for the juvenile court and this is not a federal competence in Belgium, but a competence of either the Flemish or the French Community.

Karim El Khmilichi (2018),[3] the director of St.-Gilles prison in the Brussels region, puts the challenge with which he is confronted in this way: "for primarily radicalising youngsters attracted to delinquent behaviour, prison may become an in-between space where radicalisation may become jihadisation or where jihadisation may receive a more clear form. It may become explicitly formatted as jihadisation."[4] The opposition between the youngster and society can become confirmed and empowered. When older prisoners, in the event that some of them are perceived as charismatic, present to the youngster the possibility of a jihadist "noble" self-image, the young man may feel touched and open himself to it. In this sense, one may say that radicalisation comes first, and then Islamisation may become intermingled with it. But it would be misleading to state that jihadisation is mainly spread via prisons. Nevertheless, once someone is deprived of freedom, he may become more easily exposed to the jihadist propaganda. What follows is a possibility that the youngster may meet people who have a longer and more developed career in delinquency and he takes over some of their practices and/or enters in a network.

There is in fact more jihadisation outside than inside prisons. However, prisons are more dangerous because they are places where one may meet people who have passed some barriers. It is more likely that they will normalise the behaviour, insights and practices of true criminals. "Prison is one of the places of Islamisation of an already existing radicalisation, but also of the constitution of possible networks among people already condemned for criminal association. The official figures in France inform us that among 68,000 prisoners, more than 1,500 have been identified as sympathisers of IS in Syria. Many violent jihadists who conducted attacks in France stayed more or less for a long time in prison, namely Mohamed Merah, Fabien Clain, Mehdi Nemmouche, the Kouachi brothers and Amedy Coulibaly" (Khosrokhovar, 2018: 237).

Devalorisation of the West

El Khmilichi (2018) observes that there is a complementary element that one should not underestimate; namely, candidate jihadists do not hold the moral and religious value of the West in high esteem. In fact, what is typical in the West is that the foundation of spiritual authority is questioned. Spiritual authority is shifted from religious institutions to science and/or to the market (Stedman Jones, 2010; De Ridder, 2018). To the religious believers who still look for spirituality in a "sacred book", Western society tells that such an attitude and value system no longer has any place in public space and should be privatised. We all know, however, that most human beings do not participate in "science" and are in fact not really interested in it. But secular authorities and dominant public opinion in the West, even if the latter remains ethnically Christian, push as much as possible to the private sphere what still remains based on biblical (or Qur'anic) spirituality. Institutional religions continue to offer important services, such as education and health care in the public space. But these services are however treated from a consumption perspective. Thus, a Western person may have recourse to it or not. For most Westerners, and surely for those who are not interested in "science" or who do not develop a strong personal private spirituality, it is the "market" and "consumerism" that build the new spirituality. At least, this is what many youngsters experience.

For the young criminal with an immigrant background, the moral and religious spirituality he recognises or projects in non-Western societies does not match with the one that is experienced in a Western society. But at the same time he has only very limited or no access to what he thinks to be the Western spirituality: materialism and consumerism. He feels it as unfairness. Why cannot he participate just as his peers to the Western spirituality of consumerism? He thinks he has the right to undo this unfairness, even if it can only happen via criminal acts. When he is put in prison afterwards, it is a shock. When obliged to remain in prison, he feels it as a new injustice. Prison may thus radicalise him still more. At a second moment, this radicalisation may be filled by some jihadist ideological content, recently even with content that remains confined to extremely poor one-liner content. We can thus nowadays witness an "instant ideologisation." This is different from the Fouad Belkacem type of jihadisation that we saw between 2012 and 2015.

Short versus Long Stay in Prison

Karim El Khmilichi emphasises that one should make a distinction between those who are imprisoned for a short time (4 to 6 months) and those imprisoned for a longer time. In reflecting on the prevention of radicalisation, one should surely also keenly take short-term prisoners into account. Most of the time, the youngsters who stay in prison for a short period of time are not jihadists, but they are very vulnerable to jihadism. They may have the idea that their imprisonment is unfair and start resenting society. It is a dangerous moment and precisely at that moment not much is done with them. They are rather abandoned to themselves and to "other co-prisoners." The feeling of injustice may become a source of jihadist radicalisation for them. Others who have already become jihadist sympathisers may become their influencers and fill the radicalisation process with jihadist ideas.

For four to six months, these youngsters may feel that they are being reduced to their ethnic identity or to being only a number. Such reduction may create a stigma that can become a source or starting point for Islamist radicalisation. This is a reason why moral and religious counsellors have an important role to play in prisons for this category of prisoners. They should discuss citizenship values with these short-stay young prisoners. It concerns questions such as: What is *laïcité*? Is sacredness really absent in our society? Do we live in a society without values? One should also discuss their professional future with them. One may work on identity. One should not wait for a judgment by a judge coming only after 4 to 6 months. Moreover, prison warders should be better trained as their conversations with the young prisoners can positively contribute to the prevention measures against radicalisation and to their later reintegration into society.

The question is then: is it better to bring them together in small separate pavilions with educators? Discussing the reception of youngsters in general,

Braspenning and Boelaert (2018) follow El Khmilichi's reasoning and propose to keep youngsters in small separate pavilions. They, however, warn that in such a formula there may also be young strong informal leaders among them who already have a serious criminal past. The criminal records of such leaders are often not shared in advance with the adult prisons because their cases are dealt with juvenile courts. Thus, such information can be lacking for the managers of adult prisons. They also say that it always may be interesting to have some quiet older prisoners among the youngsters. In this case, the profiles of young and senior prisoners must match to each other. What is critical is that the youngsters should be avoided to come into contact with serious criminals or jihadist influencers during their stay in prison. Therefore, in order separate pavilions to be an effective solution in preventing radicalisation of young prisoners, the authorities should design them in a way that both a well-balanced composition of the prisoners and the pedagogy they apply have positive effects on these young people who would serve their short-term sentence. Some youngsters wait for 4 to 6 months before they hear a first judgment about their future. Nothing happens with them during that period. Prisons are also much too large. If nothing positive happens with them, "negative" leaders, with some charisma are more likely to become their mentors.

Evidence of a Co-Prisoner of Fouad Belkacem

The following evidence of a co-prisoner of Fouad Belkacem, the leader of the influential jihadist recruiter of Sharia4Belgium illustrates quite well how a jihadist leader assumes this role in prison:

> I was in prison in Merksplas, near Antwerp, when Fouad Belkacem was imprisoned. He was in the same pavilion. So we could meet at the inner court when we could leave our cells. He was a quiet person, very kind. He was silent. Very often he sat on the ground, surely in summer. Once I sat next to him during a visit, when his children visited him. Sometimes I could make some jokes with him. 'Tell me, what did you do? Are not you a Belgian, born here in Belgium? Why then are you here?' He never answered in an aggressive way.
>
> If your question is if I understand that young people may radicalise in prison, my answer is: sure, I understand it perfectly. First, you feel

abandoned. You are in a no man's land. If you have no money, you cannot even brush your teeth. You cannot buy toothpaste. You don't receive soap. Food is very elementary. If you want something else with it, you have to pay for it. Drink is water from the tap. Secondly, there is not really legal security. It all depends on what direction and chiefs decide. There is much arbitrariness. You feel that so often. Thirdly, they treat you very often in an unfair, crazy way. Fourthly, young Belgian Moroccans do not enjoy the sympathy of the other non-Moroccan prisoners. They do not receive much money from outside. So they look for some grip elsewhere. The Muslim counsellor did not come so often. The Protestant counsellor was really ok. The Catholic counsellor was not bad at all. But Islam was quite absent. Fifthly, many of the young prisoners are small criminals. They do not see much future for themselves. I saw a youngster who crapped always in his pants. No one took care of him. Sixthly, among equals you understand one another in such a situation. Your sympathy and loyalty increase vis-à-vis the ones who signify something positive to you. Fouad Belkacem had become a person of reference in our small pavilion. He gave a feeling of stability.

How did these youngsters around him feel about themselves? For them, society did not inspire them as something just and correct. It was not that difficult to convince them that this was not only the case in prison, but also outside. O yes, they know that they did something wrong, but their impression was that they now understand why they did wrong things, what they did not see before being put in prison. For these kinds of young people Fouad brought quietness. He gave them an identity and a future, a hope." (Personal communication of a former prisoner to Johan Leman, 2018).

Isolating Hardliner Jihadists in Prisons

In August 2018 in Belgium, 23 hardliner jihad sympathisers (nine Dutch-speaking in Hasselt and 14 French-speaking ones in Ittre) were put together and separated from all others in a so-called "D-Rad:Ex" section.[5] Some of them never left for Syria, but strongly incited others to do so. They are jihadists who radiate some leadership and charisma and who try to influence other prisoners for their ideas. The authorities do not want them to recruit others. For the moment and for some of them, there are no indications that they want to change their convictions or behaviour. When they become free, they will most probably adhere again to

Salafist jihadism. This confines us to two possibilities about their future: Some of them will probably leave again for jihad, while others, who would become older, still will not change their ideas but will probably disengage. The risk for the latter second case is that some of them may influence younger people for the jihadist cause.

Once hardliner jihadists are brought into D-Rad:Ex, they are not condemned to remain there for the rest of their stay in prison. If someone feels himself deradicalised, he can propose to the local director of the prison that he be transferred to another prison. The local director can ask, with the required arguments, for a re-evaluation.

Concluding Considerations

In Belgium and probably in many other countries, the prison system should be reformed if the real concern is the prevention of jihadism in the future. Youngsters who are imprisoned for reasons where jihadism is completely absent should be separated from the genuine jihadists. There should be more investment in the reintegration in society of these youngsters, with the support of educators and social workers and in small groups, hence avoiding the criminal leaders among them orienting them again to delinquency. It is also a defendable option to separate hardliners from the others, for the reasons developed by the interviewed psychologist and criminologist. Religious and philosophical counsellors have an important place in prisons. Nevertheless, they should invest less in doctrines but more in a sense of citizenship, as the quintessence of the counselling efforts.

Notes

1   I had a good talk with both professionals about radicalised prisoners in Belgian prisons. Under their supervision they have about 200 files from the Dutch side of Belgian prisons, covering the period between 2015 and July 2018, actual prisoners included. Currently they closely follow around 80 files. In Belgium, there are also files written in French, which are followed by other professionals.

2   "On a sample of 1,200 individuals who left between 2012 and 2015 from Western countries to join Syria and Iraq, 14% are younger than 18 years old, 27% are between 18 and 21, 26% between 22 and 25, 17% between 26 and 29, 9% between 30 and 35 and 7% are 36 and more (Perliger and Milton 2016). If one qualifies "youngsters" as the category of age from

14 to 25 years old, they then represent 67% of the total. This is more than two thirds" (Khosrokhavar, 2018: 101).
3   I interviewed him in July 2018 on many important issues about Belgian prisons. His observations are similar to those of Khosrokhavar. Khosrokhavar writes about second, third and even fourth generations in some poor marginal city districts: "Prison has an important meaning, it is a place of socialisation and of adoption of a counter culture, but also the place where hatred of society becomes obstinate and where the link between various imprisoned guys leads to the creation of networks that may become activated in jihadism" (Khosrokhavar, 2018:238). El Khmilichi observes it in this way: "What Belgium and France have in common is that there are ghettos outside and inside the prisons. The prisons in St-Gilles and Forest, both in Brussels, are good for 15 to 20 per cent of the prison population in Belgium."
4   This leads us to Khosrokhavar's conclusion: "The real problem is the articulation between radicalisation of Islam and Islamisation of radicalism" (Khosrokhavar, 2018:9).
5   For more on the detailed presentation of isolation measures in Belgian prisons see Vervaet, 2017.

References

Beelmann, A., Jahnke, S. & C. Neudecker (2018). 'Radikalisierung und Extremismusprävention,' in Beelmann, A. (ed.), *Toleranz and Radikalisierung in Zeiten Sozialer Diversität: Beiträge aus Psychologie und Sozialwissenschaften*. Darmstad: Wochenshau Wissenschaft Verlag.

Besta, T., Szulc, M. & Jeskiewicz, M. (2015). 'Political Extremism, Group Membership and Personality Traits: Who Accepts Violence?' *Revista de Psycologia Social*, 30(3), 563-585.

Braspenning, N. and Boelaert, A. (2018). Interviewed by Johan Leman. Personal Interview. 23 August 2018.

Campbell, M. & J. R. Volhardt. (2014). 'Fighting the Good Fight: The Relationship Between Belief in Evil and Support for Violent Policies.' *Personality and Social Psychology Bulletin*, 40(1), 16-33.

De Ridder, W. (2018). 'On the 'Absence of Spirit': The Legacy of the Abstinence from Revolution in Belgium', in Moggach, D. & G. Stedman Jones (eds.), *The 1848 Revolutions and European Political Thought*. London: Queen Mary University of London, pp. 185-215.

El Khmilichi, K. (2018). Interviewed by Johan Leman. Personal Interview. 13 July 2018.

Khosrokhavar, F. (2018). *Le nouveau jihad en Occident*. Paris: Robert Laffont.

Pauwels, L. J. R. & Heylen, B. (2017). 'Perceived Group Threat, Perceived Injustice, and Self-Reported Right-Wing Violence: An Integrative Approach to the Explanation of Right-

Wing Violence'. *Journal of Interpersonal Violence*, [online]. Available at: https://doi.org/1 0.1177/0886260517713711[accessed 5 July 2018].

Perliger, A. and Milton, D. (2016). *From Cradle to Grave: The Lifecycle of Foreign Fighters in Iraq and Syria*. New York: United States Military Academy Combating Terrorism Centre at West Point. [Online]. Available at: https://ctc.usma.edu/from-cradle-to-grave-the-lifecycle-of-foreign-fighters-in-iraq-and-syria/ [accessed 7 July 2018].

Stedman, J. G. (2010) 'Religion and the Origins of Socialism,' in Katznelson, I. & Stedman J. G. (eds), *Religion and the Political Imagination*. Cambridge: Cambridge University Press, pp. 171–189.

Vervaet, L. (2017). "Les regimes d'isolement dans les prisons belges.' [Online]. Available at: http://supermax.be/les-regimes-disolement-dans-les-prisons-belges-extraits-du-rapport-2017-de-lobservatoire-internationale-des-prisons-oip-belgique/ [accessed 15 July 2018].

CHAPTER 8

Urban Terrorist Sanctuaries in Europe: The Case of Molenbeek

Adolfo Gatti

Introduction

Sanctuaries, or safe havens, have always played an important role in the activities of groups living underneath, or in direct opposition to, the Weberian state. Since the time of piracy, violent non-state actors have sought out places where they could be harboured away from the eyes of the authorities and where they could prepare their next moves. Theoretically, if one takes hold of an actor's safe haven, then that actor has nowhere to stay. However, when the sanctuary no longer has a specific geographic form, or even a physical one, then targeting it and denying access to it become more difficult. As globalisation is seemingly reshaping the relevance of states as international actors, so is the concept of sanctuary moving from a simple state-centric view to a more complex context-specific one. Rather than occupying a specific geographic part of a state where the legitimate government cannot enforce its authority, safe havens are now understood to occupy social spaces where several sources of authority fight for control (Campana et al, 2011: 402). Under this framework, the literature on terrorist safe havens suggests several observable factors to indicate whether an area can indeed be defined as a safe haven. Besides these "prescriptive traits," the literature also provides "descriptive traits" to identify what underlying conditions are necessary for an area to become a safe haven.

Recent terrorist attacks carried out by domestic actors in Europe bring forth the question of whether terrorist safe havens are possible within the continent's urban environments. What makes these areas useful to terrorist groups? How do you recognise them and how could they possibly develop in mature western democracies? This chapter begins by providing insight on the concept of a terrorist sanctuary and on its relevance in contemporary international security. From this literature review, it then divides previously identified safe haven characteristics into two categories: prescriptive traits and descriptive traits. The former are then used to demonstrate that the environment represented by the Brussels neighbourhood of Molenbeek up to 2017, in which the Paris and Brussels attacks were planned and launched, does indeed fit the criteria while the latter are used to inform the discussion on why such an area developed in the centre of Europe. Ultimately, the role Molenbeek played in the Paris and Brussels attacks is proof that, contrary to the conventional view on the matter, terrorist safe havens can exist in European cities and have several recognisable factors that can be found in many of the continent's urban environments.

"Terrorist Sanctuary": An Evolving Concept

As terrorist sanctuaries become a more central concern in defence policy making, how they are defined now becomes increasingly relevant. Indeed, the way one defines a terrorist sanctuary informs the way one would propose to address the issue. Sanctuaries are simply defined as areas where the establishment or the exercise of formal control is impeded in various degrees. Some suggest that they do not simply provide refuge from authorities. They are rather safe operational environments where a group is able to maintain a structure that can support its subversive activities (Innes, 2007: 16). Al-Qaeda's current leader al-Zawahiri once clearly stated the need for a physical base where his jihadist movement could learn combat, politics, and administration (Bale, 2007: 139). The current academic literature on the subject defines sanctuaries as areas that provide specific reliable opportunities for several types of operations such as organisation, planning, fundraising, communication, recruitment, training (Campana et al, 2011: 396-399), use a secure logistics network for travel, money transfer, weapons smuggling (Kittner, 2007: 308), and establish a base for operations (Korteweg, 2008). The policy debate has moved from understanding safe havens purely within state-structures to viewing them within failing states. Yet, the above traits may also be found in cities or neighbourhoods in developed nations. Thus, the deconstruction of previous state-centric notions of terrorist sanctuaries through a social-contextual approach gives us an opportunity better to understand the presence of terrorist sanctuaries not only in the ungoverned or poorly governed geographical spaces, but also in areas at the heart of modern urban democratic societies.

During the Cold War, the concept of "safe haven" was applied to the states harbouring armed groups, either through open protection or by acquiescence. Safe havens existed because the harbouring state had either a limited capacity to prevent it or a policy supportive of it. The latter was often motivated by strategic considerations vis-à-vis other states, ideological compatibility with the group being harboured, or desire to influence it. Already in July 1985, Ronald Reagan was applying the concept to terrorist organisations: "We must act together, or unilaterally if necessary, to ensure that terrorists have no sanctuary anywhere" (Reagan, 1985). Even before 9/11, members of the Clinton Administration were developing policies to prevent a Bin Laden sanctuary in Afghanistan (Lizza, 2015).

As the Bush Administration's "War on Terror" unfolded, the conceptual evolution of "sanctuary" merely passed from harbouring states to weak or failing states, where the only variable was the extent of government control over its territory and the eventual vacuum left open for terrorist groups to fill (Campana et al., 2011: 398). The 9/11 Commission identified weak states as ideal breeding grounds for harbouring terrorist groups as they provided the ability for recruitment, fundraising and reliable logistics and communication network (Innes, 2008: 255). As summarised by the then Office of the Coordinator for Counter-Terrorism at the US Department of State, the Bush administration described safe havens as terrorist sanctuaries within weak states: they have a geographic footprint, are primarily a rural phenomenon mostly on frontiers, have a low population density, and provide resources for terrorist organisations to grow and operate (Innes, 2008: 257). Later, academics such as Cristiana Kittner and Rem Korteweg adopted this framework, but added the following necessary conditions for the development of a sanctuary: a weak political governance, a history of corruption and violence, specific geographic features that can help to provide secrecy (Kittner, 2007), the presence of ethnic or religious communities, economic opportunities, economic underdevelopment and exterior influences (Korteweg, 2008). Korteweg goes so far as to claim that "lack of central governmental control over an area is a *sine qua non* for [sanctuary] creation" (Korteweg, 2008: 65).

The above notions of sanctuary are all concentrated around the idea that the Westphalian state is collapsing or deficient in a geographic enclave where terrorists can find refuge. The difficulty in using the terms "sanctuary" and "safe haven" interchangeably is that safety is not the only thing that terrorist groups look for, and it may divert the analysis away from the aims that a specific group might want to achieve when settling in or establishing a sanctuary (Innes, 2008: 262). In particular, the 9/11 Commission characterises safe havens as having to be remote from any recognised governmental authority or population centres. While the commission viewed remoteness as physical isolation, this concept holds a need for solitude and alienation similar to the personal sense of alienation that immigrant groups may feel when living in different cultures, such as in Western Europe (Innes, 2008: 263). Although remoteness from the "battle space" is often viewed as a necessary characteristic for safe havens (physical depth), this may manifest itself also in the form of solitude and alienation (cognitive depth) often felt by immigrant communities living in social isolation (Innes, 2007: 17). Hence, the importance of the state's reach is not about its extent, physical and geographical, but rather its depth through the social framework.

In an attempt to reframe the concept, Campana and Ducol provide the new element of "social space" to the literature. They contend that, within the ungoverned areas in weak or rogue states, there are different levels of social spaces ("framework in which interactions between local actors take place") that can be contested and occupied by various groups (Campana et al., 2011: 402). Hence, in what was previously conceived as ungoverned territory, there actually may exist several forms of social spaces governed by actors other than the state (Clunan, 2010). While the authors envisaged this framework for rogue states, the idea of contested social spaces may be used to describe the reality of some urban areas in Western democracies.

Another factor to keep in mind when thinking of the conceptual change of terrorist sanctuaries is that terrorist groups have learned to operate and to leverage globalisation. Like many other non-state actors in different sectors, illicit groups have used the global decrease in physical and virtual barriers as means to expand their operations internationally and to create bases in various corners of the world. International terrorist groups now rely on more than just a single contiguous sanctuary in order to provide cover for whichever endeavour they are set to bring forth (Innes, 2007: 17). For instance, the movements such as IS are described as "de-territorialised" phenomena because of the de-contextualisation of identity and social relations represented by "multi-national" or "foreign" fighters (Zakeri, 2016: 39).

Considering the criticism of the weak-state approach and instead viewing "safe havens" through a social space lens, one can then propose that sanctuaries may similarly develop in environments where there are several competing and overlapping sources of political authority (Campana et al, 2011: 399). Moreover, any environment where the authority of the state and institutional trust is eroding may become fertile ground for terrorist groups to operate safely and in secrecy. Therefore, any urban setting with isolated social groups may be vulnerable to infiltrations. In order to classify them as terrorist sanctuaries, such areas need to provide terrorist groups with the ability to run their illicit activities safely – with the need for secrecy rather than safety dictated by the goals the group wants to achieve (Innes, 2007: 19).

In defining urban terrorist sanctuaries, we should consider the necessary characteristics identified in the failing-state framework, but adapt them to the contextual differences highlighted in the "social space" approach. It is essential here to distinguish between "prescriptive" traits and "descriptive" traits. Both kinds appear simultaneously in the lists of previous analyses. The former are the required factors to define a certain area as a safe haven. They hence help to ascertain whether an area is indeed a sanctuary. The latter, on the other hand, refer to the commonalities observed among known sanctuaries. They point to how these areas have emerged in the past. Therefore, both are useful for a comprehensive understanding of the phenomenon of safe havens. Considering the current literature on the subject, we can identify the following elements for each type of trait:

Prescriptive traits: A terrorist safe haven/sanctuary must provide the means to serve a terrorist group's specific objectives. In order to successfully qualify an area as a safe haven, one should ask to what extent the following operations are satisfactorily provided in that area: 1) organisation and planning, 2) fundraising, 3) communication, 4) recruitment, 5) training, and 6) secure logistical network.

Descriptive traits: The following are the current subject literature's necessary conditions for the development of safe havens. While these are mostly applied to state and failing state contexts, one should examine to what extent they are applicable to urban terrorist sanctuaries. Terrorist sanctuaries 1) exist within state structures; 2) have specific geographic features that can provide secrecy; 3) are primarily rural phenomena mostly on frontiers and with low population density; 4) have weak governance; 5) have a presence of ethnic or religious communities; 6) have a history of corruption, violence or weapons; 7) are economically underdeveloped yet could provide economic opportunities; and 8) are remote or isolated from governmental authority.

The following section will analyse the role played by the Brussels district of Molenbeek leading up to and during the Paris and Brussels terror attacks of 2015 and 2016. When comparing it to the aforementioned prescriptive traits this district in the heart of Europe clearly satisfied, at least up to 2017, the criteria for being labelled a terrorist sanctuary. In order to understand how such a case, presumably not unique in Europe, has developed, the final part of the analysis will discuss how this safe haven compares to the previously recognised descriptive traits of safe havens in the hopes of informing future policymaking.

Molenbeek: A Jihadist Safe Haven at the Heart of Europe

The Paris attacks in November 2015 and the Brussels attacks in March 2016 were both planned in Brussels. "At least fourteen people tied to both attacks were either Belgian or lived in Brussels" (Cohen, 2016). Two of the three cars used in the French capital were registered in Belgium (Cruickshank, 2016). Rather than fleeing after the March 2016 attacks, one of the drivers, Mohamed Abrini who was raised in Molenbeek, hid in the city for 20 days before being arrested. Salah Abdeslam, the Belgian-born French citizen involved in the Paris attacks, hid in Brussels for almost four months before being captured in Molenbeek (Cohen, 2016). Adbelhamid Abaaoud and Chakib Akrouh, two of the Paris gunmen, also grew up in Molenbeek just as Ali Oulkadi and Abraimi Lazez who are suspected of having helped Salah escape after the Paris attacks (Parlapiano et al., 2016). The terrorist connections to this Brussels neighbourhood, and to the city itself, go beyond these two momentous attacks. Amedy Coulibaly, who was involved in the Charlie Hebdo attack, and Mehdi Nemmouche, the Frenchman who shot four people at the Brussels Jewish Museum in 2014, are believed to have bought weapons there (Parlapiano et al., 2016). Ayoub el Khazzani, the Moroccan man who attempted an attack on the Brussels-Paris high speed train in August 2015, stayed in his sister's apartment in the district (Cohen, 2016). These and more connections point to a pattern that depicts the area as a preferred hotspot for terrorists, or perhaps as a safe haven.

Using the framework developed in the previous section, one could test whether each prescriptive trait may be applied to the situation in Molenbeek as of 2017. Once confirming that the Brussels neighbourhood (and the city itself) indeed qualifies as a terrorist sanctuary, one can then search for the causes that led an area in the middle of a fully developed European democracy to turn into what many think to be possible only within failing states. By testing the descriptive traits identified in older conceptualisations of terrorist safe havens on Molenbeek, one can link the relevant factors to the European urban setting, and accordingly develop alternative explanations.

Organisation and Planning

Time and security are crucial to properly planning and organising a terrorist action. Terrorists must be confident that in their sanctuary they are able to organise themselves for successful operations. Molenbeek, according to the Belgian police, provided the terrorist cell with all the safety and secrecy needed to organise and plan the attacks in Paris (Lefebvre, 2017). Not only were the plans hatched there, but they were also launched and coordinated from this cell in the city.[1] After the attack on French soil, the cell did not disband or flee from Belgium. They knew that there they could find cover to continue plotting operations in Europe. As in other terrorist acts in Europe, the group was most likely in contact with and received the green light from the IS leadership, but it was the returned foreign fighters who planned the attack using local recruits (European Union Terrorism Situation and Trend Report 2016: 6).

Fundraising

While fundraising is critical for a terrorist group's ability to operate, the importance of its magnitude is relative to the terrorist group's aims. Most terrorist operations in Europe have been self-financed because of their usually cheap nature. Though there have been some examples of transfers as well, using *hawala*, a more secret and cost-effective system of global money or value transfer used by jihadists, has been less common possibly because of its confidential nature (Nesser, 2017). Despite this, the Paris attacks provided the first known example of *hawala* in Europe: The Abaaoud network used it to transfer money to the attackers (Nesser, 2016a: 16). Rather than just receiving money, a safe haven should be able to provide different forms of self-financing, especially when it engages in international operations. In fact, several members of the cell in Molenbeek have been radicalised and sent to the conflict zone in Syria through the Zerkani network: a network led by Moroccan-born Khalid Zerkani who has radicalised street criminals and who raised money for foreign fighters' trips (Van Vlierden, 2016b). Theoretically, practising Muslims should not be allowed to steal; but this Molenbeek-based network convinced its members to commit petty crimes in the name of "*ghanima*," or the spoils of war (Van Vlierden, 2016b). Leading his network as a gang, Zerkani was nicknamed Papa Noel (a reference to Santa Claus) because of his cash handouts. He was known to have paid up to €4,000 for foreign fighters' travel expenses (Van Ostaeyen, 2016: 9). Abdelhamid Abaaoud, Chakib Akrouh and Najim Laachraoui (the returnee who blew himself up in the March 2016 attack and the suspected bomb maker for both attacks) were all part of this jihadist network and there learned how to "fundraise." Moreover, Brussels and Molenbeek were hosts of other examples of direct fundraising for IS. Fatima Aberkan, the mother of a foreign fighter, played an important role in convincing young people to raise funds for the cause (Van Ostaeyen, 2016: 10). Similarly, Jean-Louis Denis, a Brussels resident suspected of being a recruiter of foreign fighters, managed to radicalise people and raise funds through fake charity initiatives (Van Ostaeyen, 2016: 8). The jihadist terrorist plots in Europe have been increasingly financed from abroad and decreasingly from the criminal nexus – 23% of plots in 2014-2016 versus 38% before 2014 (Nesser, 2016a: 16). This ability to raise money locally in Brussels seems to go against this general trend. It indicates the considerable advantage provided by the safe haven.

Communication
In order to consider a specific area as a safe haven, terrorist groups must be able to communicate both with their operatives and with their target audience. Since the time of Groupe Islamique Armé (GIA) of Algeria in the 1990s, of al-Qaeda in the 2000s and of IS today, terrorist networks in Europe have consistently kept in contact with groups in their respective conflict zones (Nesser, 2016b). These individuals are important both for operational purposes and for inspiration. The great majority of independent organisers (do-it-yourself or solo terrorists) have been in direct or indirect contact with terrorist influencers (Nesser, 2016b). Through its already established connections, social and criminal, Molenbeek created a natural structure where networks were easily taken advantage of (Samouris et al, 2017). For instance, the coordination of the Paris attacks happened in Brussels under the leadership of Mohammed Belkaid who, together with Najim Laachraoui, kept in contact with the groups on the ground (Cruickshank, 2016).

The digital dimension of terrorist communications is key to their operational and marketing success. Many of the jihadist plotters in Europe who received instructions online were communicating with Belgian and French fighters (Nesser, 2016a: 9). Likewise, many of those who decided to join IS were radicalised and recruited through social media. Some conspiracy theory websites have been portraying an image of the Islamic State as the perfect place for building a new life (Leman, 2017). While the Zerkani network used its pre-existing criminal modes of communication, the Antwerp-based Sharia4Belgium, the other major jihadist network in the country, used open media such as rallies and YouTube videos to radicalise young Muslims until it was finally declared a terrorist organisation. It is expected that, despite law enforcement's increased efforts, terrorist organisations will continue to enjoy considerable operational freedom on the Internet (Hegghammer, 2016: 158). On the ground, the use of modern encryption programmes allows them to operate discretely to the point that, even if captured, their communications may be unreachable to investigators (Cruickshank, 2016).

Recruitment
The ability to recruit in their safe havens is important for the very existence of illicit organisations as fresh recruits are needed to replace those who perish. Molenbeek, Brussels, and the country of Belgium have been rich breeding grounds for jihadist recruitment. Most of the people involved in the Paris attacks either were from or had lived in Brussels, and by January 2017 Belgium as a whole had produced 576 foreign fighters (Van Ostaeyen, 2017).

In the past five years, there have been three major jihadi recruitment networks in Belgium: the Antwerp-based Sharia 4 Belgium (S4B), the Brussels-based Zerkani network, and again another Brussels-based *Resto du Tawhid* network. Known also as the Denis network, the last acted as a bridge between the other two. S4B is a 2010 neo-Salafist offshoot of the Islam4UK movement, which denounces democracy and promotes shari'a law in the West benefitting from the cover provided by freedom of speech (Van Vlierden, 2016a: 51). In 2012, the Belgian authorities began pushing back on S4B. Yet the network was able to send its members to Syria and Iraq, which later led a Belgian court in 2015 to officially designate it as a terrorist group (Higgins, 2015a). While the S4B movement attracted young Muslims on the basis of its strong ideological message and drew from all social backgrounds (Van Ostaeyen, 2017), the criminal context of the Zerkani network (based in Molenbeek) appealed more to those who look for adventure (Van Vlierden, 2017). The latter mostly attracted unemployed young people who had a criminal background rather than an Islamic one and "Islamised" them through a radical religious ideology (Van Ostaeyen, 2016: 10). Somewhere in between is the *Resto du Tawhid* network led by Jean-Louis Denis who posed as the head of a Muslim food charity in the Brussels North railway station in order to attract and radicalise dissatisfied Muslims (Van Vlierden, 2016b).

Surprisingly the recruitment did not occur in mosques (Lefebvre, 2017: 6), but rather in cafés, open areas (Leman, 2017), and next to sports activities specifically organised for that purpose (Van Vlierden, 2016a: 53). Prisons are also a potential pool for recruitment and networking (Basra et al, 2016: 30-32). Even though Muslims make up only about 6% of the Belgian population, 20% to 30% of Belgium's 11,000 inmates have a Muslim background (Williams et al, 2016).

Brussels Metropolitan Area	Brussels City 69	Molenbeek 42	Schaerbeek 22	Laeken 16
Antwerp Metropolitan Area	Antwerp City 45	Borgerhout 18	Antwerpen 2060 14	Deurne 10
Other Cities	Vilvoorde 29	Mechelen 17	Verviers 10	Unknown 284

Figure 1: The number of known Belgian foreign fighters per region (Van Ostaeyen, 2017)

Sharia 4 Belgium 92	Zerkani Network 58	Denis Network 33	Denis + Zerkani 19	Denis + S4B 6

Figure 2: The number of known Belgian foreign fighters per network (Van Ostaeyen, 2017)

Approximately 75% of the Belgians who managed to reach the war zone joined IS (Van Vlierden, 2016a: 49). While foreign fighters do not necessarily go to Syria and Iraq with the intention of targeting the West (Van Ostaeyen et al, 2014), they may represent a serious terrorism threat as returnees (as in the Paris and Brussels attacks) and as foreign fighters themselves. While just a small minority of foreign fighters move on to international terrorism (Nesser, 2016b), their presence there may be a source of inspiration for other individuals in their country of origin. These may look to either join them or perform domestic terrorist acts. Moreover, virtually no terrorist cell forms in the absence of an "entrepreneur" or a charismatic figure who radicalises and leads the other members (Nesser, 2016b). Returning foreign fighters may become tomorrow's entrepreneurs, bringing with them combat experience and the network they developed abroad (Nesser, 2016a: 19). Finally, analysing the recurring components of plot formation, the factor that jumps out is the almost omnipresent foreign fighting experience or link to a conflict zone of at least one member of the cell (Nesser, 2016b).

Considering the link between the past foreign fighter recruitment and the potential risks for future terrorism, we can assume that Molenbeek and Belgium may continue to be a breeding ground for jihadist causes. Unless the country effectively stops being a space that allows security and secrecy for terrorist recruitment, the risk will remain high.

Training
Training is required to successfully bring about a desired terrorist operation. It is thus a key factor for a terrorist organisation to efficiently run itself. Training must be carried out safely outside the enemies' reach. Belgium and Molenbeek, in this sense, did not seem to have provided the combat training that the more conventional safe havens allow for. The attackers used automatic weapons in Paris and Brussels but most of the perpetrators had been to war zones. Nonetheless, the underground scene, particularly the criminal networks in Molenbeek, could provide the necessary skills needed to perform terrorist attacks. A criminal past, for instance, can provide technical skills, such as finding access to weapons and forging documents, which may prove more useful than those learned in conflict (Basra et al, 2016: 32). Moreover, their previous criminal background must have already given them "the psychological 'skill' of familiarity with violence" (Basra et al, 2016: 33). In any case, much of the theoretical training can be accessible online and today terrorist cells are more likely to receive instructions through the Internet (Nesser, 2016b).

Secure Logistical Network
A safe haven, by definition, must provide the ability to move securely within, as well as to and from, the area. Moreover, being able safely to procure weaponry, money, and all other necessary material for planning and the successful execution of an attack is a key component of a terrorist sanctuary. Molenbeek and Belgium have offered safe passage for all of the above. Although increasing, information sharing between police forces within the Schengen area is still experiencing lags in time and effectiveness (Samouris et al, 2017). The members of the Brussels cells have

been able to move people from Molenbeek and other Belgian neighbourhoods to Syria and back with relative ease (Pop, 2016). In fact, it has been estimated that around one third of those who left have successfully returned, with many performing the trip more than once (European Union Terrorism Situation and Trend Report 2016: 27). Taking advantage of overstretched law enforcement capabilities, some groups used refugee streams to transfer operatives (Schmid, 2016: 4). The Molenbeek-based Zerkani network has specialised in forging documentation for its members before putting them in contact with smugglers operating on the Turkish-Syrian border (Van Ostaeyen, 2016: 9). Moreover, many of the neighbourhood's inhabitants plan to stay there only for short periods of time before moving to other areas, further complicating surveillance efforts (Leman, 2017). Finally, Brussels is considered to be an easy place to buy illegal firearms, even heavy ones, at the black market and terrorist actors have made use of this advantage (Clerix, 2015). The members of the Zerkani network who were the perpetrators of the Paris and Brussels attacks were able to use their Molenbeek connections to procure weapons, chemicals for bomb building, cars, and safe houses (Van Ostaeyen, 2016: 10).

The above explanations have so far shown how the Paris and Brussels attackers used Molenbeek, and Brussels as well, as their base of operations for their activities (Twining, 2016). This small district served as a base for planning, organising, launching, coordinating, and supporting the attacks in safety and secrecy. What is particularly noteworthy about the Molenbeek sanctuary is that it presented the first European case since 1995 of the same jihadist cell striking twice (Hegghammer, 2016: 157), adding "regrouping" to its potential set of advantages. This occurred despite the fact that the continent's counter-terrorism forces were at their historical peak for capabilities and experience (Hegghammer, 2016: 157). Unfortunately, these last two major attacks were not the only examples in which terrorist operatives have used the neighbourhood as a sanctuary. This suggests that it may happen again if the underlying causes remain unaddressed.

Molenbeek: A New Type of Sanctuary

The literature on safe havens identifies the aforementioned *descriptive traits* as the underlying necessary conditions for an area to develop into a terrorist safe haven. However, these factors are merely observed as characteristics of areas that fit into the previous conceptualisations which excluded Europe's urban environments.

Hence, while trying to apply them to Molenbeek, some of the traits will be confirmed while others will be adapted to give a new conception. In so doing, some features of liberal political systems will be questioned to see whether they may explain the existence of terrorist sanctuaries in developed democracies of Europe.

State Structure and Extent of Governmental Authority
The traditional view on the subject contends that terrorist sanctuaries exist within state structures. This trait highlights the state-centric approach used to conceptualise safe havens in the early 2000s. The assumption is that safe havens are either sponsored by state authorities or exist where the authority of the state does not reach. However, the "social space" approach urges that what is more significant is the depth of a state's authority rather than its breadth. In the Molenbeek case, the safe haven existed in an area where the state had full reach, but not enough depth. In concrete terms, this means that if a state knows where to exert its authority it would have the means to do so. The Molenbeek case tells that the Belgian state has faced several obstacles, as discussed below, which did not allow it to know where and how to operate properly. Moreover, it tells that terrorist hubs can emerge anywhere where there are critical masses of extremism authority figures under different circumstances; not just in suburbs like Molenbeek, but also in universities, capitals, small towns, and even in functioning welfare states (Nesser, 2016b).

Urban terrorist safe havens are not physically remote or isolated. Rather, they have a degree of social remoteness and isolation from the governmental authority or from the established system. This is a key factor for a successful safe haven as it provides an automatic separation between the inhabitants of the sanctuary and law enforcement. Failed integration creates hospitable conditions for terrorism as it reinforces a dichotomous mentality of "us versus them" (Bale, 2017). The difference in youth unemployment between Molenbeek and the rest of Brussels already puts the district's future on a different path from that of its neighbouring districts (Williams et al., 2016). From a structural point of view, the high volume of turnover in the area, around 7,000 new residents per year, turns it into something of a transition city: "you arrive in Molenbeek and if you succeed you leave; but, if you fail, you stay with the stigma of being a loser" (Leman, 2017).

Molenbeek's isolation is also felt from the system of law enforcement. The district's mayor claims that the police force knows the neighbourhood and its residents; but does not have the resources to maintain surveillance of all the terrorist suspects (Higgins, 2015b). Besides, initiatives aimed at combating radicalisation often lack the necessary human capital such as knowledge of Arabic (Higgins, 2015b). Building trust among the community and institutions is key both for human intelligence collection and for radicalisation prevention (Nesser, 2017). Furthermore, cultural isolation helps to create diaspora-specific subcultures where informal norms rule over formal ones. The North African community of Molenbeek does not relate with other communities in the neighbourhood and it follows norms based on family values (European Institute of Peace, 2016). Strong family ties and friendships form the basis of a culture of omertà, the Italian word to describe the silence around Mafia crimes (i.e. I do not see, I do not hear, I do not talk) (Van Vlierden, 2017). Ultimately, isolated communities' inherent conservatism may face tensions with local norms which, in turn, help the community view extremists merely as being anti-establishment (Samouris et al, 2017). Something that directly affects a community's isolation and, at the same time, is strengthened by it is the local "native" population's hate for the immigrant community. Indeed, an important driver towards radicalisation seems to be "the feeling of rejection as non-indigenous citizens, as Muslims, or as a combination of both" (Van Vlierden, 2016a: 57).

Geography: Centrality, Population, and Secrecy
Geography is the key to strategic success when choosing a place from which to launch terrorist operations. Molenbeek, and Belgium as a whole, have several geographic advantages that make it an attractive area for terrorists. First and foremost, it is in the Schengen area which allows visa free travel and border free commerce for its operatives. Second, it is strategically located between France, Germany, the Netherlands and the UK. Also, the country's geographic separation along language lines provides a convenient set up for launching operations in different directions from within a very close area. Brussels, only one hour and half from Paris by high-speed train, is viewed by IS as operationally part of France, whereas Antwerp is seen as part of the Netherlands, but with contacts in the UK (Leman, 2015). Brussels and Molenbeek served as hubs for attacks in France from as early as the 1990s, during the Algerian Civil War (Van Vlierden, 2017). Furthermore, Europe's proximity to the Middle East makes it easily accessible from the relative conflict zones.

An urban terrorist sanctuary is obviously not a rural phenomenon, is not necessarily on frontiers, and neither does it entail low population density. It, in fact, exists partly because of its metropolitan location. Molenbeek is in the centre of a country and therefore is not a frontier space. It is in the middle of Brussels' metropolitan area and therefore it is not rural. About three quarters of the foreign fighters who left Belgium originate from Brussels, Antwerp or from other urban areas between the two. This is also the case at the European level. More than 90% of all European foreign fighters come from metropolitan areas (Van Vlierden, 2016a: 50). When it comes to population density, the opposite of what seems to be an advantage for conventional safe havens seems true. High population is indeed a crucial component of an urban terrorist sanctuary. In a demographically dense area, it is common to meet people that one does not know, thus it is easier to employ "hive terrorism" – a tactic that allows the perpetrator to strategically attack and hide immediately afterwards in the large crowd of bystanders or to escape from the location altogether (Kholer, 2016: 97). Thanks to the high population density and the residents' frequent intra-district house moves, the whole jihadist activity in Molenbeek and in Brussels has been kept clandestine and hidden from most of the area's inhabitants (Leman, 2015).

Weak Governance and Underdevelopment
Illicit actors operate where the state cannot stop them successfully. As discussed above, a terrorist sanctuary is a place where terrorist groups feel safe and are allowed to operate because of the impotence of the legitimate authority. Hence, conventional terrorist sanctuaries were established where the lesser degree of government control was exploited by the terrorist group. Belgium, and particularly the region of Brussels, has been suffering from such weak political, bureaucratic, and security governance.

The Belgian federal government's division into three language groups is dysfunctional, particularly for the city of Brussels, which is geographically within Flanders, but speaks French like the rest of southern Belgium. Information sharing between local and federal agencies is lagging behind due to this difference (Higgins, 2015b). As an example of this divided system, Brussels has six police forces, each reporting to a different mayor, lacking a coordinating chef mayor. When asked about the reasons for which the Abdeslam brothers were not arrested before the attack despite having been on a list of 80 dangerous people handed to her, the Mayor of Molenbeek answered that this was a federal issue, but unfortunately for her the Interior Minister is a secessionist (Higgins, 2015b). Furthermore, with three Parliaments and a new information gathering centre (L'Organe de Coordination et d'Analyse de la Menace – OCAM) that is under the joint authority of the Ministry of Justice and the Ministry of Interior

(Coolsaet et al., 2007: 14), Belgium's bureaucracy is unsurprisingly inefficient and riddled with turf wars (Lefebvre, 2017). The stratification of counter-terrorism responsibilities within the country's political structure is seen as a crucial obstacle as it enhances inefficiencies already present in the decentralised system (Economist Intelligence Unit, 2016).

In response to what seemed to be a problem of overwhelmed capacity rather than analytical failure of Europe's law enforcement (Nesser, 2016b), European governments are stepping up their information sharing through Europol's European Counter Terrorism Centre (ECTC). They consequently signed a permanent cooperation protocol between Belgium and France. Nonetheless, national authorities continue to handle their respective foreign fighter and terrorist legal cases themselves (Samouris et al., 2017).

The risk of radicalisation exists even in better economic conditions as ideology may play a role at all social levels. Nevertheless, structural factors, such as economic factors, may affect the pool of potential recruits (Nesser, 2016b). A particular urban area with a large portion of the population with grievances may be beneficial to terrorists both in recruiting (Hegghammer, 2016: 158) and in maintaining anonymity among a population that depends on informal sources of income (Leman, 2017). "Molenbeek is the second-poorest commune of Belgium, with 57 per cent of the population living in poverty" (Lynch, 2016). The unemployment rate is around 30%, much higher than Belgium's overall 8.5% rate (Pop, 2016). More significantly, the proportion of people between the ages of 15 and 29 is 27% compared with Brussels' average of 19% (Williams et al, 2016). Given that the only empirically valid distinctive characteristic of a typical jihadist terrorist profile is that he is a young male (Nesser, 2016b), this is a key factor for the jihadist networks' success here.

The refugee situation may worsen the problem as European states fail to integrate immigrants into society and into the job market (Hegghammer, 2016: 159). Among Molenbeek's residents, there is a belief that violent radicalisation is caused by lack of opportunities. Many young residents do not see education as value added for their chances in the labour market (European Institute of Peace, 2016). They may have a point as the country's education policy has resulted in a *de facto* segregated system which is particularly evident in Molenbeek (Williams et al, 2016). When formal economic channels do not provide opportunities, one may turn to informal ones. This includes criminal channels. Similarly, when one's chances for social recognition are low, turning to militant Salafism may make him a hero in the eyes of his peers in Molenbeek (Leman, 2015).

Presence of Specific Ethnic/Religious Communities
Ethnic and religious communities may create tight-knit subcultures that run on their own rules before those of others (e.g. those of the state) and that are suspicious of the local authorities. Terrorist networks may want to embed and camouflage within these communities in order to take advantage of the governmental dysfunctions they may provide and to increase the culture of mutual distrust between the diasporas and the authorities. 81% of Molenbeek's residents are of foreign origin, and 41% are of Muslim background (Lynch, 2016). If you are of Moroccan origins and want to hide (all the Belgium-related Paris attackers were of Moroccan descent), then you would connect with your diaspora in lower Molenbeek, where 50% of the inhabitants are of northern Moroccan provenience (Leman, 2015).

The presence of a religious community may have similar effects to the presence of an ethnic one, with the important addition that a common religion allows deeper ideological ties among its members. In the case of Islam, a member of a Muslim diaspora may feel an attachment to the *umma* (the global Muslim community) and therefore may feel involved when a violent conflict in any Muslim country erupts. This is supported by the fact that jihadist terrorist plots and attacks against Europeans increase when Western countries intervene in Middle Eastern conflict zones, something that feeds perfectly into the jihadist narratives (Nesser, 2016b). In Molenbeek, many of the clerics have been sent there by Saudi Arabia or other Gulf states and follow the Wahhabi doctrine which is a very conservative version of Islam practised mainly in Saudi Arabia (Lynch, 2016). The lack of local imams and community leaders discredits attempts to counter recruiters' narratives in mosques (Schmid et al, 2015: 41). Moreover, the recent religiously targeted policies, such as the face veil ban, can be easily interpreted as being repressive (Van Ostaeyen et al., 2014).

Although Belgium itself could be considered a "hotbed of Islamic extremism" in Europe (Van Vlierden, 2016a: 49), this does not necessarily translate to a hotbed of terrorism. While religion does play an important role in the radicalisation of jihadist terrorists, the great majority of Muslims who have a sense of grievance against Europe are not violent. Many seek out radical preachers without becoming terrorists. Besides, non-ideological youngsters can also join jihadist terrorist groups (Nesser, 2016b). Hence, there must be more than just the mere presence of a religious community at play in order for an area to become a safe haven. Although the ethnic/religious factor may make it a target for radicalising agents, the history of the networks seems to be more relevant. This is shown by the disproportionately high numbers of foreign fighters recruited between the cities of Antwerp and Brussels compared to other Belgian regions with a high presence of Muslim communities (Van Vlierden, 2016a: 51). Indeed, there seems to be no meaningful proportional link between extremism and terrorist plot activity (Nesser, 2017).

History of Violence
Besides providing potential recruits, having a history of violence makes the local community more amenable to being associated with future violence. This allows terrorist groups to keep operating in their midst.

Belgium has been a transit country for several terrorist groups in the last decades such as Action Directe (the French left-wing armed group), the Red Army Faction (former Western Germany left-wing militant group), ETA (the separatist Basque group), and IRA (the Irish republican paramilitary group) (Clerix, 2015). It was also the case for some Islamic terrorist groups such as the GIA and the GICM (Moroccan Islamic Combatant Group) (Van Ostaeyen, 2016: 7). There are several instances that link Molenbeek in particular to previous cycles of jihadist terrorism. For example, one of the attackers of the 2004 Madrid train bombings lived in the Brussels neighbourhood (Cohen, 2016). The al-Qaeda hit team that on 9 September 2001 assassinated Ahmad Shah Massoud, the Afghan military leader who was fighting against the Taliban, lived and plotted the assassination in Molenbeek (Lefebvre, 2017: 3). There is a generational element to the jihadist threat to Europe. From the GIA, to the Afghan veterans, to the London preachers, and then finally to Belgium, veterans from previous jihadist groups came out of jail and influenced future ones behind the scenes or as recruiters (Nesser, 2016a: 7). While the S4B evolved from the London ideologues, the Zerkani network had links with the French-speaking jihadist circles (Van Vlierden, 2016b). Besides the experience with violence introduced by a previous generation of jihadists, returning foreign fighters will add their own familiarity with combat to the collective conscience of their places of origin. As in the past, noble war stories and a new network developed on the battlefield may effectively create a fifth column back home, but this time contacts would not need to occur face-to-face (Bale, 2017).

The existence of previous networks in Antwerp and Brussels was a key factor for successful recruiting. The members of the Molenbeek circle used to be petty criminals, but later turned to terrorism. This may be an indicator that their previous experience with criminality and clandestine activity lowered the threshold when it came to their willingness to use violence and increased their chances of successfully evading law enforcement. Indeed, this is one of the major reasons why jihadist recruiters prey on "misfits" or the people who have a history of conflict with the system (Nesser, 2017).

Liberal Democracy and Terrorist Sanctuaries

Terrorist sanctuaries can exist underneath state authority rather than out of its reach. Certain characteristics of liberal democracies can be paradoxically conducive to the formation and use of urban terrorist safe havens. In Europe, terrorists seem to benefit from factors that are inherent in a liberal democratic rule. For instance, the rule of law and the principle of freedom of speech that govern Western democracies have created hurdles for the prosecution of jihadists. Jihadist recruiters do not always necessarily break the law. They do have a right to express extremist views as long as they do not exhort others to engage in violence. Even if they do, it is hard to prove (Van Vlierden, 2017). Under the protection of freedom of speech, the London jihadist community, guided by Omar Bakri, was able to operate and inspire other European jihadists for several years (Nesser, 2017). While there has been a reaction by authorities on this front, particularly in the cyber realm, law enforcement may often run into the conundrum of whether to leave their communications and propaganda as bait to identify radicals or to take them down to lower their media effect.

Another issue that is more specific to Belgium is that the prison sentences have been ineffectively curbing extremism, allowing radical individuals still to get back in action or to support new networks. This was, for instance, the case of Abdelkader Hakimi who served eight years for being the leader of the GICM and joined the conflict in Syria after his release. As another legal issue, on the other hand, it is harder to prove whether a returned foreign fighter has committed crimes in Syria. Membership of a terrorist group alone may not be seen as a crime, or it is seen at most as a minor crime (Nesser, 2016b). Another relevant factor of liberal democratic rule vis-à-vis urban sanctuaries is the generous welfare system of northern Europe. Economically speaking, people who do want to integrate have very little incentive to do so as they still have a right to social assistance even if they are indefinitely unemployed (Van Ostaeyen, 2017).

Conclusion

Terrorist safe havens can exist in European urban environments. The Paris and Brussels attacks reveal that a terrorist cell successfully used a European metropolitan district in Brussels, the "capital of Europe," as a secure base for its operations. From there, its members were able to launch their activities and evade law enforcement. While other areas in Belgium were also used by terrorist groups, the case of Molenbeek clearly demonstrates that a European urban area can fully act as a terrorist sanctuary. In and from Molenbeek, the perpetrators could safely perform all the activities required for their organisation and planning, their fundraising, their communication, their recruitment, their training, and their use of a secure logistics network for travel, money transfer and weapons smuggling. Moreover, by acknowledging the contextual change from rural ungoverned space to urban autonomous "social space," one finds that all other descriptive traits fit the new picture. This new conception of safe haven, furthermore, showcases how certain elements of European liberal democratic systems can in fact add a layer of protection for the illicit activities of terrorist actors.

Existing underneath the extension of a government's authority rather than next to it, the terrorist urban safe haven in Europe may be vulnerable to the reaction of the state. This may suggest that such urban safe havens are destined, sooner or later, to dissolve as the government control deepens. Nevertheless, it is important to remember that terrorists' ability and freedom of activity in these areas have developed because of the specific descriptive traits discussed above. They will hence not disappear until those underlying conditions are successfully and efficiently addressed. The international efforts in bombing, raiding and surveilling terrorist sanctuaries in different failing states around the world may have curbed the illicit groups' activities there, but not fully impeded them. This may be the case for the Belgian government's short-term "repressive policies". They have slowed down the terrorist activity in Molenbeek; but whether they were really able to eliminate the possibility of it recurring in future is yet to be seen. Now that all eyes are on this neighbourhood of Brussels, it is possible that jihadist cells may be waiting, as in the past, before using it again as a base of operation or silently expanding to other areas with similar conditions. The past cycles of European jihadist movements warn that new terrorist entrepreneurs may perhaps find the same ripe conditions in the district, or in similar ones, in the future.

Notes

1   The police believe it was Mohammed Belkaid, an Algerian IS operative who had previously resided in Sweden, who kept in phone contact from Molenbeek itself with the death team throughout the Parisian night of violence (Van Ostaeyen, 2016: 11).

References

Al-'Ubaydi, M., Lahoud, N., Milton, D. and Price, B (2014). 'The Group That Calls Itself a State: Understanding the Evolution and Challenges of the Islamic State'. *The Combating Terrorism Center at West Point*, [online]. Available at: https://www.ctc.usma.edu/v2/wp-content/uploads/2014/12/CTC-The-Group-That-Calls-Itself-A-State-December20141.pdf. [accessed 12 March 2017].

Bale, J. (2017). 'Radicalization and Terrorism in Europe'. Interviewed by Adolfo Gatti. Telephone interview. 3 April 2017.

Bale, J. M. (2007). 'Hiding in Plain Sight in Londonistan', in M. A. Innes (ed), *Denial of Sanctuary: Understanding Safe Havens*. Westport, CT: Praeger Security International, pp. 139-151.

Basra, R. and Neumann P. R. (2016). 'Criminal Pasts, Terrorist Futures: European Jihadists and the New Crime-Terror Nexus'. *Perspectives on Terrorism*, [online] Volume 10(6). Available at: http://www.terrorismanalysts.com/pt/index.php/pot/article/view/554. [accessed 29 May 2017].

Botelho, G., Cruickshank, P. and Almasy, S. (2016). 'Paris Terror Suspect Mohamed Abrini Arrested in Belgium'. *CNN*, [online]. Available at: http://www.cnn.com/2016/04/08/europe/brussels-attack-arrests/ [accessed 2 April 2017].

Campana, A. and Ducol, B. (2011). 'Rethinking Terrorist Safe Havens: Beyond a State-Centric Approach'. *Civil Wars,* [online] Volume 13(4). Available at: http://www.tandfonline.com/doi/abs/10.1080/13698249.2011.629868. [accessed 26 January 2017].

Clerix, K. (2015). 'Why Are Terrorists Drawn to Belgium?'. *The Guardian*, [online]. Available at: https://www.theguardian.com/commentisfree/2015/nov/17/terrorists-belgium-paris-attacks [accessed 2 April 2017].

Clunan, A. L. and Trinkunas, H.A. (2010). 'Conceptualizing Ungoverned Spaces', in A. L. Clunan and H. A. Trinkunas (eds), *Ungoverned Spaces: Alternatives to State Authority in an Era of Softened Sovereignty*. Stanford: Stanford University Press, pp. 17–33 [accessed 26 January 2017].

Cohen, R. (2016). 'The Islamic State of Molenbeek'. *NY Times*, [online]. Available at: https://www.nytimes.com/2016/04/12/opinion/the-islamic-state-of-molenbeek.html [accessed 29 May 2017].

Consilium.Europa.com, (2003). *A Secure Europe in a Better World*. [online] European Security Strategy. Available at: https://www.consilium.europa.eu/uedocs/cmsUpload/78367.pdf [accessed 26 January 2017].

Coolsaet, R. and Struye De Swielande, T. (2007). 'Belgium And Counterterrorism Policy In The Jihadi Era (1986-2007)'. *Brussels: Academia for Egmont*, [online]. Available at: http://www.egmontinstitute.be/wp-content/uploads/2013/09/ep15.pdf [accessed 29 April 2017].

Cruickshank, P. (2016). 'The inside Story of the Paris and Brussels Attacks.' *CNN*, [online]. Available at: http://www.cnn.com/2016/03/30/europe/inside-paris-brussels-terror-attacks/ [accessed 29 May 2017].

Economist Intelligence Unit, (2016). *Belgium politics: Quick View – Counter-terrorism efforts ramped up*. [online]. Available at: http://go.galegroup.com/ps/i.do?p=ITOF&u=mlin_m_tufts&id=GALE%7CA472191881&v=2.1&it=r&sid=summon&ugroup=outside&authCount=1 [accessed 29 April 2017].

EIP – European Institute of Peace, (2016). *What Does Molenbeek Think?* [online]. Available at: http://www.eip.org/en/news-events/what-does-molenbeek-think-%E2%80%93-new-eip-survey-reveals-drivers-violent-extremism [accessed 23 March 2017].

EuroPol, (2016). *European Union Terrorism Situation and Trend Report 2016*. [online]. Available at: https://www.europol.europa.eu/activities-services/main-reports/european-union-terrorism-situation-and-trend-report-te-sat-2016 [accessed 2 January 2017].

Hegghammer, T. (2016). 'The Future of Jihadism in Europe: A Pessimistic View'. *Perspectives on Terrorism*, [online] Volume 10(6). Available at: http://www.terrorismanalysts.com/pt/index.php/pot/article/view/566/1122 [accessed 24 March 2017].

Higgins, A. (2015). 'Head of Belgian Group Said to Recruit Fighters for Syria Gets 12-Year Term.' *New York Times*, [online]. Available at: https://www.nytimes.com/2015/02/12/world/europe/fouad-belkacem-sharia4belgium-verdict-trial-belgium.html [accessed 29 May 2017].

Higgins, A. (2015). 'Terrorism Response Puts Belgium in a Harsh Light.' *New York Times*, [online]. Available at: https://www.nytimes.com/2015/11/25/world/europe/its-capital-frozen-belgium-surveys-past-failures-and-squabbles.html?_r=0 [accessed 29 May 2017].

Innes, M. A. (2007). 'Cracks in the System', in M. A. Innes (ed), *Denial of Sanctuary: Understanding Safe Havens*. Westport, CT: Praeger Security International, pp. 1-20.

Innes, M. A. (2008). 'Deconstructing Political Orthodoxies on Insurgent and Terrorist Sanctuaries'. *Studies in Conflict & Terrorism*, [online] Volume 31(3). Available at: http://dx.doi.org.ezproxy.library.tufts.edu/10.1080/10576100701879646 [accessed 26 January 2017].

Jackson, R. (2007). 'Critical Reflections on Counter-Sanctuary Discourse', in M. A. Innes (ed), *Denial of Sanctuary: Understanding Safe Havens*. Westport, CT: Praeger Security International, pp. 139-151.

Jacoby, J. (2016). 'Why There Are Muslim Ghettos in Belgium, but Not in the US.' *The Boston Globe*, [online]. Available at: https://www.bostonglobe.com/opinion/columns/2016/03/27/why-there-are-muslim-ghettoes-belgium-but-not-united-states/zek1CSRRoepWhLmSCiPWKK/story.html [accessed 2 April 2017].

Jones, S. 'Obama: If We Send 50K Troops Into Syria, What Do We Do When Terrorists Attack From Yemen? Or Libya?' *CNS News*, [online]. Available at: https://www.cnsnews.com/news/article/susan-jones/obama-if-we-send-50k-troops-syria-what-do-we-do-when-terrorists-attack [accessed 27 January 2017].

Kittner, C. C. B. (2007). 'The Role of Safe Havens in Islamist Terrorism'. *Terrorism and Political Violence*, [online] Volume 9(3). Available at: http://dx.doi.org/10.1080/09546550701246791 [accessed 26 January 2017].

Kohler, D. (2016). 'Right-Wing Extremism and Terrorism in Europe: Current Developments and Issues for the Future'. *Prism: A Journal of the Center for Complex Operations*, [online] Volume 6(2). Available at: http://cco.ndu.edu/PRISM/PRISM-Volume-6-no-2/Article/839011/right-wing-extremism-and-terrorism-in-europe-current-developments-and-issues-fo/ [accessed 29 May 2017].

Korteweg, R. (2008). 'Black Holes: On Terrorist Sanctuaries and Governmental Weakness'. *Civil Wars*, [online] Volume 10(1). Available at: http://dx.doi.org.ezproxy.library.tufts.edu/10.1080/13698240701835482 [accessed 26 January 2017].

Lefebvre, S. (2017). '"The Belgians Just Aren't Up to It": Belgian Intelligence and Contemporary Terrorism'. *International Journal of Intelligence and Counter Intelligence*, [online] Volume 30(1) Available at: http://dx.doi.org/10.1080/08850607.2016.1230699 [accessed 29 April 2017].

Leman, J. (2015). 'Is Molenbeek Europe's Jihadi Central? It's Not That Simple'. *The Guardian*, [online]. Available at: https://www.theguardian.com/commentisfree/2015/nov/17/molenbeek-jihadi-isis-belgian-paris-attacks-belgium#img-1 [accessed 28 March 2017].

Leman, J. (2017). 'Molenbeek as a Safe Haven'. Interview by Adolfo Gatti. Personal interview. 11 April 2017.

Lizza, R. (2015). 'Isis, Terrorist Sanctuaries, and the Lessons of 9/11'. *The New Yorker*, [online]. Available at: http://www.newyorker.com/news/daily-comment/isis-terrorist-sanctuaries-and-the-lessons-of-911 [accessed 26 January 2017].

Lynch, J. (2016). 'Here's Why so Many of Europe's Terrorist Attacks Come through This One Brussels Neighborhood'. *The Washington Post*, [online]. Available at: https://www.washingtonpost.com/news/monkey-cage/wp/2016/04/05/heres-why-so-many-ofeuropes-terror-attacks-come-through-this-one-brussels-neighborhood/?utm_term=. e4b169d0a237 [accessed 2 April 2017].

Nesser, P. (2016). 'Jihadi Terrorism in Europe: The IS-Effect'. *Perspectives on Terrorism*, [online] Volume 10(6). Available at: http://www.terrorismanalysts.com/pt/index.php/pot/article/view/553/1096 [accessed 21 March 2017].

Nesser, P. (2016). *Terrorism in Europe*. [online] New America. Available at: https://www.c-span.org/video/?409224-1/petter-nesser-discusses-terrorism-europe [accessed 21 March 2017].

Nesser, P. (2017). 'Terrorist Entrepreneurs and Sanctuaries in Europe'. Interviewed by Adolfo Gatti. Video conference interview. 22 March 2017.

Parlapiano, A., Andrews, W., Park, H., Buchanan, L. and Almukhtar, S. (2016). 'Unraveling the Connections Among the Paris Attackers'. *New York Times*, [online]. Available at: https://www.nytimes.com/interactive/2015/11/15/world/europe/manhunt-for-paris-attackers.html?_r=0 [accessed 29 May 2017].

Pop, V. (2016). 'Islamic State Terror Cell Found Refuge in Brussels District; Molenbeek Has Come to Symbolize Belgium's Failure to Integrate Its Muslim Population'. *Wall Street Journal*, [online]. Available at: https://www.wsj.com/articles/islamic-state-terror-cell-found-refuge-in-brussels-district-1458694455 [accessed 29 May 2017].

Reagan, R. (1985). *Remarks at the Annual Convention of the American Bar Association*. [online] The American Presidency Project. Available at: http://www.presidency.ucsb.edu/ws/?pid=38854 [accessed 27 January 2017].

Samouris, A. and Arnaoutidis, P. (2017). 'European Cooperation Against Terrorism'. Interviewed by Adolfo Gatti. Personal interview. 11 April 2017.

Schmid, A. P. and Tinnes, T. (2015). 'Foreign (Terrorist) Fighters with IS: A European Perspective'. *The International Centre for Counter-Terrorism – The Hague*, [online] Volume 6 (8). Available at: https://icct.nl/publication/foreign-terrorist-fighters-with-is-a-european-perspective/ [accessed 23 March 2017].

Schmid, A.P. (2016). 'Links between Terrorism and Migration: An Exploration'. *The International Centre for Counter-Terrorism – The Hague*, [online] Volume 7(4). Available at: https://icct.nl/publication/links-between-terrorism-and-migration-an-exploration/ [accessed 23 March 2017].

Twining, D. (2016). 'Europe Must Adapt to a Dangerous World'. *YaleGlobal*, [online]. Available at: http://yaleglobal.yale.edu/content/europe-must-adapt-dangerous-world [accessed 28 May 2017].

Van Ostaeyen, P. (2016). 'Belgian Radical Networks and the Road to the Brussels Attacks'. *CTC Sentinel*, [online] Volume 9(6). Available at: https://www.ctc.usma.edu/posts/belgian-radical-networks-and-the-road-to-the-brussels-attacks [accessed 23 March 2017].

Van Ostaeyen, P. (2017). 'Belgian Safe Havens and Foreign Fighters'. Interviewed by Adolfo Gatti. Personal interview. 15 April 2017.

Van Ostaeyen, P. and Zaougui, C., E. (2014). 'Overblown Fears of Foreign Fighters: Don't Fear Jihadists Returning From Syria'. *New York Times*, [online]. Available at: https://www.nytimes.com/2014/07/30/opinion/dont-fear-jihadists-returning-from-syria.html?_r=0 [accessed 23 March 2017].

Van Vlierden, G. (2016). 'Molenbeek and Beyond. The Brussels Antwerp Axis as Hotbed of Belgian Jihad'. *ISPI Report*, [online]. Available at: http://www.ispionline.it/it/EBook/Rapporto_Hotbeds_2016/Cap.3.pdf [accessed 23 March 2017].

Van Vlierden, G. (2016). 'The Zerkani Network: Belgium's Most Dangerous Jihadist Group'. *The Jamestown Foundation*, [online]. Available at: https://jamestown.org/program/hot-issue-the-zerkani-network-belgiums-most-dangerous-jihadist-group/ [accessed 23 March 2017].

Van Vlierden, G. (2017). 'Belgian Terrorist Networks'. Interviewed by Adolfo Gatti. Personal interview. 15 April 2017.

Vidino, L. (2017). 'European Terrorism'. Interviewed by Adolfo Gatti. Telephone interview. 26 March 2017.

Williams, A., Hinck, K., Karklis, L., Schaul, K. and Stamm, S. (2016). 'How Two Brussels Neighborhoods Became 'a Breeding Ground' for Terror.' *The Washington Post*, [online]. Available at: https://www.washingtonpost.com/graphics/world/brussels-molenbeek-demographics/ [accessed 2 April 2017].

Zakeri, M. (2016). 'De-territorialized Phenomenon: ISIS As a Hybrid Criminal Terrorist Organization'. *Hemispheres*, [online] Volume 31(1). Available at: http://search.proquest.com/openview/599e2fa346cbf04b48f3db8d02b8857a/1.pdf?pq-origsite=gscholar&cbl=856346 [accessed 26 January 2017].

CHAPTER 9

Migrant Smuggling Networks and Jihadist Terrorism

Johan Leman and Stef Janssens

Introduction

For an understanding of the future of violent jihadism and the structure it may take, it is important to examine how it may be financed. One possible source may be Smuggling of Migrants (SoM). The business permits the creation of financial capital, in the centre (in the Middle East) as well as in territorialised cells inside the "global jihad." It also permits networking and transfer of militant jihadists. The criminal money obtained in this business may become one of the techniques for financing jihadist terrorism in the future. This should not be surprising, since this technique was and remains practised by other organisations in the past (Leman and Janssens, 2015: 95-98).[1]

Richard Labévière (2018a) distinguishes four important financial sources for future terrorist jihadism: financial reserves kept in bank accounts (principally in Switzerland and the US), charity organisations, money collections in places of worship, and criminal money. He cites antique art trafficking as an example of criminal money. He (2018b) estimates that IS still has 3 billion US dollars in financial bank reserves to finance its operations. For him, this money is used not so much to finance possible attacks, but to organise propaganda and to financially support families that have lost a "soldier." This remains, in fact, a possible use in the future.

In Belgium, we see that criminal money to finance terrorism is generally raised from drug trafficking. SoM remarkably permits various strategies for the jihadists:

providing financial capital to use for global or local objectives, territorialising human and social capital, networking or transferring money among (candidate) terrorists. This chapter analyses such cases from seven Belgian files. It should be noted that SoM is in fact a wider phenomenon about migration movements. It is unfair to consider it simply as a terror related business. Nevertheless, its illegality makes room for jihadist terrorism as well. We should be aware of this fact. The aim is thus not to overestimate the jihadist use of SoM nor to underestimate its future potential for jihadist mobilisation.

The empirical materials used here consist of judicial files that have been treated by the courts in Belgium under the label of SoM and/or Trafficking of Human Beings. They were obtained through the reports on human trafficking by the former Belgian Centre for Equal Opportunities and Opposition Against Racism (e.g. CEOOR, 2009, 2012) and by those of its successor Myria-Federal Migration Centre (e.g. Myria, 2017). The latter was established to particularly analyse migration, to defend the rights of foreigners and to combat human smuggling and trafficking. The seven files that concern jihadism are from the years between 2005 and 2016. They indeed constitute a minority in the total number of SoM and human trafficking files.

Three Scenarios

Our analysis of these seven cases reveals mainly three scenarios with regard to militant jihadism: SoM to create financial capital for jihadism, SoM to facilitate networking, and SoM to make transfer of jihadists possible. As an example of the first scenario, we will examine an Indo-Pakistani network. For networking and central enrichment, we will analyse a Punjabi and an Afghan network. For the third scenario where various interests may come together, we will examine an Iraqi and a Syrian network. The Indo-Pakistani, Punjabi and Afghan networks are related to the Taliban and al-Qaeda, whereas the Iraqi and Syrian networks discussed here are related to Islamic State. The analysis will conclude with what may be seen as a case of manipulated networking.

Financing Jihadism
The Indo-Pakistani file indicates possible "territorialised" financing of future terrorism. There are connections between criminal organisations in the countries of provenance (al-Qaeda and Taliban) and some jihadist networks in Western

countries of destination. Two techniques are discernible in realising the aim. The first aims at producing financial capital via the system of sham marriages:

> 20,000 € was charged for a sham marriage ... According to the file, the money courier collected daily between 100,000 and 200,000 € and carried those amounts to other cities in other countries, in particular to Paris. After his arrest, the US requested his extradition for money laundering in connection with terrorism. In addition, a financial and money laundering investigation was requested (Leman and Janssens, 2015: 126).

The second technique, used by another network, is making money through SoM investments in the carwash business. In a Pakistani carwash dossier, Indo-Pakistani workers were economically exploited over the 2005-2007 period. The victims were smuggled with false documents, and delivered by a collaborator at the Afghan embassy in Brussels. The criminal organisation in question used criminal constructions to set up carrousels with different companies and frontmen. The managers of this criminal organisation were known by the police for organised crime. They made use of different cash couriers and a *hawala* mediator to transfer the money.[2] The cash courier operated from a restaurant organised by a so-called Afghan social-cultural organisation. A remarkable conversation was found in the phone tap between the suspects. They were talking about 13 people, that all had a link to al-Qaeda and had been intercepted in a tram. Another indication in the direction of a probable connection with jihadism is that one of the straw men they used was revealed to be an ex-Taliban fighter who had acquired Belgian nationality.

What is typical for both Indo-Pakistani cases is that a direct link with terrorism has never been clearly proven; but that there were strong indications of a more than casual connection with terrorism and of the creation of financial capital that might be used for actions in Western Europe and in the countries of provenance.

In another, this time Iraqi, network, violence is very present and the smugglers do not hide their sympathy for jihadist martyrs. The files contain indications of contacts with terrorists. The provenance of the smugglers is Kirkuk, where there was a war in that period. In 2010, IS was not present in Kirkuk. However, some statements revealed during the interrogations are interesting for understanding the links between some Iraqi smugglers and the Islamic State. It would later be confirmed in files from 2015 on. This Iraqi network can be considered as a precursor of the profile in a later Syrian network that we shall see.

In the Iraqi file of 2009-2010 concerned, a criminal organisation smuggled Afghans, Iraqis, Iranians, Turks and Vietnamese with trucks and refrigerators to the UK and to Scandinavia in some cases. Once the migrants arrived in the UK and debts were paid, financial benefits matching the benefits made in the UK were paid in Iraq, after oral agreement given by the *hawala* mediator in the UK to his colleague in Iraq. The system did not permit even minimal tracing of money transferred from the UK to Iraq. No money moved between the two countries. In this case, we do not see territorialisation of financial benefits within Europe. From a phone tap, the benefits of the last three weeks for the chief of the organisation appeared to be £134,705. In this file, two ofamong the accused smugglers did not have a problem in showing their sympathy for or their relations with, the terror attacks in Iraq. One of the smugglers said, "I have received the money from my mother for eight months already. My father died as a martyr. My mother receives a salary for his martyrdom and she sends me part of it". When confronted with proof of his smuggling practices, another smuggler declared twice that he would kill Christians once back in Iraq: "Once I am free again, I will go back to Iraq. No problem! I am even disposed to return already now. I am a Muslim and there, we will kill some Christians, for the money".

Networking
In an Indian Punjabi SoM file from 2005, in which the rented house occupied by the smugglers was investigated, a newspaper article about the bomb attacks in the London Underground was found in the dustbin. During a search in the Netherlands conducted at the house of an Indian suspect who organised financial business and who was involved in money laundering, the Dutch police found a document on a table in which almost all terrorist organisations of the world were listed. More traces were not discovered with respect to this person. The same network had contacts at the Indian embassy and at Kolkata airport. What is the implication, then? The detectives in their official report made the comment that the SoM circuits are an excellent way of travelling for terrorists through which all legal control possibilities (e.g. ID cards) can be avoided. In this case, it is not clear if we are confronted with money transfers or with transfers of persons, and for which kind of use. Networking, however, may be suspected to be present.

Transferring Jihadists
In an Afghan network there is a clear link between a case of SoM and an illegal transport of terrorists, namely al-Qaeda fighters. It concerns a file of 2012. An

Afghan criminal organisation organised the transport of Afghans, Pakistanis and Iranians into the UK. There were also smuggling routes into the US and Canada. The convicted Pashtun smugglers were the Belgian partners of an international smuggling network. They had contact with service providers and smugglers in Italy, France, Greece, Russia, Afghanistan, Iraq, Iran, Pakistan and the UK. There was also a link with the top of the Afghan army. The chief was the son of an Afghan general who used his family relations to menace the families of the victims. Smugglers as well as smuggled clients feared him. If the confessions of the smugglers are correct, the criminal profits were sent to his father, the general in the army in Afghanistan, who was also involved in money laundering.

A financial investigation was possible due to good collaboration between Belgian justice and Western Union on money transfers between the UK and Belgium. The wiretapping revealed the role of a *hawala* mediator and of the money laundering in a carwash in London. The wiretapping also gave some indications on the transport of al-Qaeda terrorists. On the phone, the smugglers discussed a smuggled Afghan whose brother was imprisoned in Guantanamo. They wanted to give him special treatment in the name of Islamic charity with a free smuggling transport to the UK as a gift. The smugglers agreed on the phone that his transport to the UK could only be carried out when there was no risk of police intervention.

Two Complex Syrian Networks

The recent files since 2015 indicate that some Iraqi smugglers bring IS fighters over to some countries in Western Europe. Here they operate mainly in a Syrian smuggling context. It is no surprise that there may be links between the Syrian smuggling networks and IS. The objective may be to earn money for themselves, to territorialise some financial capital in Europe, to transfer fighters, or to infiltrate in networks. What may make it more complex is that the Assad regime in Syria and its allies, Russia and Hezbollah, may also have an interest in the business. We have two related cases of 2015 which point to the fact that a Syrian-Iraqi smuggling network is linked with Islamic State.

The First Syrian SoM Case: Connection to IS
The 2017 Myria annual report documents an international network that smuggled people from Syria, Iraq and Iran to the UK. In the wiretap, 1,290

smuggled victims were traced during at least 56 days of smuggling. Up to 10 to 15 people could be smuggled per crossing. Most leaders were living in England and coordinated their operations with the smugglers from Belgium, France and the Netherlands. They had contacts with other smugglers and document suppliers in Germany, Hungary, Bulgaria, Austria, Czech Republic, Slovakia, Greece, Italy, Serbia, Turkey and Iraq. The money was centralised in the UK but there were also money transfers to Italy, Greece and Turkey. The illegal assets of the smuggling network amounted to (at least) €3,125,000 over a period of 9 months. This was calculated on the basis of at least 125 proven crossings of 10 people, with a smuggling price of €2,500 per person. They used a *hawala* banker and money remittance agencies for their financing

One of the victims was a 15-year old Palestinian boy from Damascus who travelled in one year from Lebanon to Belgium and made declarations on the Libya route where different warlords and jihadist groups are active. The smugglers were a military group with anti-aircraft weapons to shoot down airplanes. The boy had been smuggled in a 10 metre long sinking boat with 270 other people. The child victim was offered smuggling victim status and told his full story to the police:

> The journey into the desert lasted seven days. There were twelve cars driving in convoy. The escorts were armed and had anti-aircraft weaponry. We were with up to fifty people in the pick-up with a large rope around us so that we would not fall out. Sometimes people fell off the truck, and they were simply shot dead by the smugglers and buried in the desert. Everyone feared for their lives. They then just carried on driving. When we arrived in Libya, we were dropped off with other traffickers, and we stayed in Ajdabiya, the first city in Libya you arrive at when coming from Egypt. We stayed there for three days in tents. After that, we were taken to a farm. From there we went in trucks to Benghazi on the coast. On the way, we came across a roadblock, and everyone had to get out. We were taken to a prison. The prison is called Rajma. We stayed in this prison for 6 months and I was mistreated, tortured with electric shocks on my hands and teeth, and beaten on my head. Since then I have had constant headaches. I was tortured because I am a Palestinian from Damascus (Syria) and a stateless person without rights. After six months, they released me, and I did some work for two months to earn money. From Benghazi I went to Tripoli, which is also on the coast. In Tripoli, I paid €1,000 to go by boat to Italy. I found the people who organise

these boat crossings through the man I worked for in Benghazi. He was actually also a smuggler whom I met in prison. On this boat crossing, only a few children had life jackets on. I cannot swim well, so I also asked for a life jacket, but I had to pay €1,000 for it. I did not have that money. We were picked up en route by Italians with a large boat and we were taken to a camp. … If I had known all this in advance, I would never have started the journey. My mother sold all her jewellery to give me a future in England. I confirm that I was informed about the possibility of being declared an 'injured party', and about the associated rights. I declare myself to be an injured party and also consider myself to be a victim of human smuggling (Myria, 2017).

The two leaders of the smugglers from the West European smuggling network the boy was talking about were IS-supporters. They were operating in the UK. One of them was an Arab-speaking Iraqi smuggler from Bagdad with a Belgian permit to stay. After his arrest, he threatened another smuggler (the money manager) with decapitation in the name of IS if he did not redraw his declarations. When the police analysed his computer, they found 270 deleted photos linked with IS. The second leader is a Syrian smuggler with a British permit tof stay living in London. Another Iraqi smuggler declared him to be an IS supporter to the police and said that he also supplied Syrian clients directly to the IS smuggling leader in Belgium. He also declared that the Syrian IS leader of smuggling owns carwashes and restaurants in London.

This is an obvious case where IS fighters were themselves involved in SoM organisers. They were involved either for their own personal benefit, or as part of a reorganisation of IS structures (in Libya or elsewhere in Africa in this case) or to put all these interests together in one business project. One may expect that such people will never hesitate to bring candidate terrorists over to Europe, when they are asked to do so in the future.

The Second Syrian SoM Case: Possible Intelligence/Political Manipulation
In another Syrian smuggling file of 2015-2016, we see a Syrian smuggler who has relations with foreign fighters; but at the same time he cooperates with a member of the Syrian embassy in Paris and with Hezbollah sympathisers in Belgium and Syria. His profile is very ambivalent. While he presents himself as a foreign fighter, in his Facebook page he is a sympathiser of Putin in military uniform. One seems to be confronted with a guy with a double agenda, or even someone

who works for Syrian intelligence. In Belgium, however, his case is treated as an ordinary SoM case.

In this file, people were smuggled from Syria via Turkey, Greece and Belgium to the UK and Sweden. The Syrian smugglers came from Damascus and Aleppo and operated in Belgium, France, Greece and Turkey. The Belgian investigation was based on an analysis of messages on social media between the smugglers and their clients. The police could detect 291 WhatsApp messages on smuggling transports. It resulted in a calculation of criminal profits of a minimum €1,124,000.

The investigation started with the arrest of a smuggler at Brussels Airport. This smuggler was known by the police for different smuggling investigations but also for an investigation by the Belgian State Security. The smuggler had already taken suspicious pictures of buildings and was linked with foreign fighters. When he was arrested, the smuggler destroyed his smartphone before the police could download his pictures.

The Syrian smuggler played a dual role. In his first interrogation, he declared to the police that he was a supporter of Assad. Afterwards, he admitted to the police that he supported and knew a lot of foreign fighters and that his brother was also a foreign fighter. His accomplices, however, pretend that he has another brother who is fighting in the Syrian army. This smuggler also cooperates with Hezbollah-related smugglers in Belgium and Syria where they are recruiting clients to be smuggled. The latter have an import-export company that is involved in smuggling to Belgium and Germany.

Another defendant in this case is a Syrian collaborator of the Syrian embassy in Paris who delivered documents and was running a safe house. He had temporal diplomatic immunity. Because the French authorities arrested him at the wrong moment, he could not be convicted. The court, then, ordered the destruction of the part of the investigation that was linked to him.

This is a very unclear case. Is a middleman of the Syrian regime manipulating the foreign fighters here? What is the role of the Iran supported Hezbollah in this smuggling network? Does the collaborator from the Syrian embassy in Paris indicate a possibility of political manipulations? These questions are yet to be answered.

Conclusion: Will SoM be Instrumental for Future Jihadism?

From the seven files we presented one may conclude that SoM has already been used in the past to create financial capital and to provide networking for jihadists. Sometimes it was also used to bring over some candidate terrorists. As already said, it is not only jihadists who operate SoM. There are also files known of other terrorist groups using SoM. The question is whether this strategy will be exploited more in the future by jihadists than is currently the case.

In the meantime, what authorities can do is to improve their strategies in combating SoM. It may be good practice to improve the international cooperation in financial investigations, also on *hawala* money transfers (FATF, 2011:44). In the UK, where the SoM leaders centralised most of their criminal money until mid-2018, there are still no executed seizures of the money laundered. Improvements are also possible for investigations on social media. Here, victim declarations are important.

Another strategic move could be informing the directors of prisons in advance when an IS sympathiser smuggler is jailed. All information about a smuggler available in the SoM files which indicate IS sympathy should be effectively communicated to prison administration. Normally, IS supporters have to be monitored in prison after a conviction or registration for terror. However, the smugglers are very often not officially registered as IS supporters when indications in this sense are found in the margins of their files. We should not neglect the possibility that smugglers, even if they are jailed not for jihadist terrorism but for SoM, may become influencers for radicalisation among the prisoners. Smugglers sympathising with IS who are not accused of terrorism should also be investigated as possible recruiters in the context of radicalisation and in a strategy of prevention. They may be important informants in understanding the strategies of jihadists in the future, both for their global objectives and territorialisation.

Notes

1 Belgian judicial files document that SoM has sometimes been practised by such other terrorist groups as the PKK of Turkey and the Kosovo Liberation Army. For the latter's practice of SoM see Europol (2011:20).
2 In the *hawala* system, "money is handed over via brokers who guarantee the transfer in the country of destination" (Leman and Janssens, 2015:120). It happens in an anonymous,

efficient way, without paper trail, and without the intervention of a bank. For more explanation see El-Qorchi (2002), Schaeffer (2008: 11-17) and Martin (2009:923).

References

CEOOR (Centre for Equal Opportunities and Opposition to Racism). (2009). *In a Haze of Legality: Annual Report on Trafficking and Smuggling of Human Beings* (translated from Dutch/French). Brussels: CEOOR.

CEOOR (Centre for Equal Opportunities and Opposition to Racism). (2012). *Building Trust: Annual Report on Trafficking and Smuggling of Human Beings* (translated from Dutch/French). Brussels: CEOOR.

El-Qorchi, M. (2002). '*Hawala*', *Finance and Development* 39 (4). Available at: http://www.gdrc.org/icm/hawala.html [accessed 3 July 2008].

Europol. (2011). *Trafficking in Human Beings in the European Union*. The Hague: Europol Public Information Office.

FATF (Financial Action Task Force) Report. (2011). *Money Laundering Risks Arising from Trafficking in Human Beings and Smuggling of Migrants*. Paris: FATF/OECD.

Labévière, R. (2018a). 'Les nouveaux enjeux de la lutte contre le financement du Terrorisme'. La Référence, [online] 31 April 2018. Available at: http://www.lareference-paris.com/80 [accessed 2 September 2018].

Labévière, R. (2018b). *Paris oeuvre à unir le monde contre le financement du terrorisme* (La Référence, [online] 24 April 2018. Available at: http://www.lareference-paris.com/124 [accessed 2 September 2018].

Leman, J. and S. Janssens. (2015). *Human Trafficking and Migrant Smuggling in Southeast Europe and Russia*. Palgrave Macmillan.

Martin, M. (2009). 'Hundi/Hawala: The Problem of Definition'. *Modern Asian Studies*, 43(4): 909-937.

Myria. (2017). *Jaarrapport Mensenhandel-Mensensmokkel Online*. Brussels: Myria.

Schaeffer, E. C. (2008). 'Remittances and Reputations in Hawala Money-Transfer Systems: Self-Enforcing Exchange on an International Scale'. *The Journal of Private Enterprise*, 24(1): 1-17.

CHAPTER 10

Prospects for Counter-Theology against Militant Jihadism

Serafettin Pektas

Introduction

Territorial victory against the IS's Caliphate did not eradicate the organisation, nor did it end its ideological appeal. The previous chapters in this volume carefully scrutinised various aspects of jihadist transformation and attempted to identify future scenarios. This chapter has a different yet complementary concern. It rather looks at the Muslim critiques of jihadist militancy, evaluates their counter-arguments and tries to provide some future reflections on their counter-religious strategy. IS's propaganda has mainly targeted and appealed to Sunni Muslims. The following analysis accordingly focuses on Sunni counter-responses. To make the analysis sharper and more viable, it considers four leading Sunni institutions from the four Sunni-majority countries: *al-Azhar al-Sharif* (Azhar) in Egypt, *Diyanet İşleri Başkanlığı* (Diyanet) in Turkey, *Nahdatul Ulama* (NU) in Indonesia and *al-Rabita al-Muhammadiyya lil-'Ulama'* (RMU) in Morocco. Each country and institution has a particular significance for the political history of the Sunni world.

Founded in 760, Azhar is the oldest surviving Sunni academy, and perhaps the most prominent and global Sunni authority. Founded in 1926, NU is arguably the largest Sunni organisation with a following of about 90 million in the most populous Muslim nation. It was established by the traditional Indonesian ulama as a response to the emergence of the modernist/reformist agenda of its competitor Muhammadiyah at home and abroad to the emergence of the

Saudi state with a puritanist agenda and the emergence of Turkey with a secular agenda. Diyanet was founded in 1924 just after the abolition of the Ottoman Caliphate and religious bureaucracy. It was originally created as a religious state apparatus to manage religious services in the newly established secular Turkey. For the last 15 years, it has become indisputably the highest religious authority and a convenient tool to govern the religious sphere in the hands of successive political Islamist governments. Although originally established in 1960 by the traditional Qarawiyyin-linked ulama, RMU was substantially transformed into a consulting body following the post-2004 reforms that aimed to restructure the religious field as a response to increasing extremism and terror in the country. Its institutional design and privileged position suggest that the monarchy intends it to be the leading and most progressive institution in Morocco's religious establishment (Bruce, 2015; Wainscott, 2017).

Each institution recently adopted a particular mission to deconstruct the jihadist discourse and to face contemporary jihadist militancy. This chapter first synoptically analyses these institutions' Sunni critiques of jihadist organisations and later critically evaluates their counter-theological strategies. Secondly, it explores how these institutions cooperate or negotiate with their respective political authorities and how this would affect their religious authority and their fight against Islamic extremism. In so doing, it also reflects on future possibilities.

Muslim Critiques of Jihadist Militancy

A very common and frequent Muslim critique is the complaint that the atrocities of jihadist militants "tarnish the image of Islam." Almost all leading Sunni groups and scholars accuse IS and similar organisations of having defamed Islam's "lofty" and "noble" teachings. They are blamed for having discredited the peace message of Islam whose very name means "peace." Countering Islamist militancy thus becomes a primary religious duty in their view in order to save the image of Islam. From this accusation ensue other further critiques that frame their counter-arguments. First, they question the sincerity of jihadists. Although the latter often emphasise that they fight for the sake of God's cause, they are viewed as those who abuse religious feelings and teachings for their political and self interest. They are those who do the most harm to Islam. A repeated argument is that statistically Muslim victims of bombings and massacres perpetrated by the jihadists outnumber non-Muslims, and it is the Muslims themselves who suffer most. The jihadist militants thus cannot be honest in their claim of saving and upholding Islam, given that their actions usually hurt Muslim believers and estrange many from Islamic ideals. Secondly, they therefore hold jihadists responsible for the accelerating Islamophobia, hate crimes and the perceived or real discrimination Muslim citizens face, particularly in Western countries. The extremism of jihadist militancy, they reason, is often responded to by the far-right, anti-Islamic extremism. Thirdly, the extremists damage Islam because they fail to understand that Islam indeed principally supports peace and safety. The messages and statements of the four institutions indicate, sooner or later, that Islam encourages reconciliation, co-existence, stability and security. An emphasis here is that not just Islam but also other belief systems do not justify terrorism. Like others, Islam values human life. They also argue that Islamic history has had a relatively better record of handling minorities.

In lamenting that the image of Islam is seriously eclipsed by the jihadist insurgency, the Muslim critiques often question the militants' declared objectives and intentions. They identify a clear contrast between what they want to achieve and what they end up with. The contradiction is explained with an attempt to define who these violent people and organisations really are. How they are defined, in turn, frames what kind of counter-religious strategy they seek or employ. It should, however, be noted that various depictions often appear simultaneously in their analyses. Jihadists are described as "bad" or "ignorant" Muslims that are unaware or disregardful of the universal message of Islam. Azhar, for instance, refused to declare the jihadist militants as infidels. Following a fatwa in an Azhar event in December 2014 by the Nigerian Mufti who called members of IS apostates, an Azhar statement rejected such call. The statement claimed that they are indeed Muslims, although their actions do not represent Islamic values. "No believer can be declared an apostate, regardless of his sins," it reads (cited in Fouad, 2015). On another occasion, *Shaykh al-Azhar* indicated that IS militants "practise corruption on earth." They should hence receive similar punishment (i.e. execution) ordained in Islamic law for such violent insurgences. They are, however, "grave sinners" but not infidels (cited in Saker, 2017). Against criticisms that consider this stance as appeasing, Azhar's counter-argument states that its theological and institutional position does not allow them to make such a declaration: Sunni orthodoxy dictates that anyone who believes in God and resurrection cannot be infidel and IS people believe in both. Azhar is not an authority for such a denunciation; hence this is not its business. Such a denunciation would put Azhar on the same footing as IS (cited in Mustafa, 2014).

Although not as explicit as Azhar, others are also reluctant to declare Islamist militants apostates. Diyanet and RMU, for instance, do not directly discuss the Muslimness of IS. Their reluctance rests heavily upon their wish not to vindicate the excommunicatory stance of jihadist organisations. They criticise their exclusivist outlook with reference to the traditional Sunni principle that anyone who worships God by turning their face to *al-Kaʻba* cannot be excommunicated. Declaring IS or others as infidels would hence negate this principle, they reason. This is why these people appear in Sunni counter-discourse as malevolent "heretics", whose interpretations evidently deviate from Muslim orthodoxy. Diyanet, for instance, accuses IS ideologues of "lacking the proper methodology" (*usulsüzlük*) in applying Islamic fundamentals in a given context. In its view, they rather pursue an "eclectic pragmatism" where normative sources are read selectively for practical purposes (Diyanet, 2016: 6-7). RMU has launched a book series called "Islam and Contemporary Context" to directly "dismantle the extremist discourse." These books blame IS for failing to consider the "higher objectives of Islamic legislation" (*maqasid al-shariʻa*) and accordingly end up with "misguided paths and evil deviations."[1] Many Azhar statements similarly accuse the jihadists of being deviant from orthodox Islam, misreading normative Islamic texts and spreading heretical extremist ideas. They are held responsible for the contemporary "misinterpretation" of Qur'anic concepts, prophetic tradition and Islamic history. For al-Tayyib, their ideology violates and is in clear contrast to teachings of Islam; thus it is already regarded as heretical (al-Tayyib, 2014a). Likewise, Ahmad Mustofa Bisri, NU's spiritual leader, stated in an interview (cited in Cochrane, 2015) that the message of the extremist groups "spread of a shallow understanding of Islam" whose interpretations are "grievously mistaken." He stated that "according to the Sunni view of Islam, every aspect and expression of religion should be imbued with love and compassion, and foster the perfection of human nature." The representatives of these leading Sunni organisations complain about the heresy brought by the contemporary jihadist movement whose followers "distort" Islamic ideals, Qur'anic concepts and prophetic practice. As we shall see, they differ in explaining the nature and causes of jihadist distortion. Yet they agree that the Islamist militants are indeed religiously heretical people.

On the other hand, they usually describe followers of jihadist organisations, especially IS, as those who are deceived by "foreign powers" to maintain their political, financial and sectarian interests. They however differ in identifying these foreign powers and their aims. NU and RMU put more blame on Middle Eastern countries, namely S. Arabia and Iran, while Diyanet and Azhar primarily blame Western colonial struggle for the global acceleration of violent extremism. The difference arises from how each organisation explains the relationship between violence and Islam as well as how textual and contextual factors interacted in the emergence of the global jihadist movement.

Many question the role of ideology or, to express it better, which Islamic elements are effective in making some believers more prone to violent extremism. Some equate theology and ideology; therefore they blame Islamic theology itself or its certain teachings. For more learned observers, on the other hand, it is particularly Salafism – or its jihadist branch (*al-salafiyya al-jihadiyya*) – that is responsible.[2] Salafism, they observe, is playing an integrating role between the contextual (both structural problems and those of human agency) and textual causes. The Salafist claim of complete and utter certainty accompanied by a simplistic and highly polarising outlook often appeals to those vulnerable, depressed and perplexed believers.

Sunni Discourse on Violence

Sunni discourse, exemplified by the foregoing organisations, does not categorically reject the use of violence. They indeed follow the traditional (Sunni) Islamic teaching that war is a human reality and violence is (and should be) employed when necessary but in a limited way to restore peace and reconciliation. The Sunni understanding hence promotes the idea of just war. With regard to military jihad, it therefore makes room for "defensive jihad" instead of "offensive jihad." While the latter interprets the duty of military jihad as a personal and unconditional responsibility, the former holds that military action is a collective duty that is only authorised by a legitimate political organisation.[3] The difference between the two marks the difference between the traditional Sunni doctrine of war and the contemporary jihadist doctrine of militancy. It also marks the difference between the "global jihadist" ideology introduced by al-Qaeda and the "classical jihadist" ideology embraced by leading Saudi militants who fought in Afghanistan, Chechnya, Bosnia and later in Iraq (Hegghammer, 2010). The Sunni critiques are well aware that the jihadist militants refer to certain teachings present in normative Islamic sources to justify terror. In response, they remind one that each religious ruling should be considered with regard to its *ratio legis* (*'illa*). That is to say: a ruling is concomitant with its underlying legal reasoning, they either both exist or disappear; therefore a past ruling cannot be randomly used (GPADHI, 2017: 2; al-Tayyib, 2014b: 10). The jihadists are hence viewed as those who have non-contextualised, narrow expertise on Qur'an and Sunna while usually lacking a sophisticated and broader scope of traditional religious knowledge and discursive flexibility (Spannaus, 2018: 93-94; Diyanet, 2015: 8). The latter is considered to be the prerogative of the Sunni ulama. Jihadist distortion is also attributed to their failure to understand *maqasid al-shari'a* (GPADHI, 2017; Diyanet, 2016; 'Abbadi, 2016a).

Counter-Arguments: Explaining Textual and Contextual Factors

Sunni critiques agree that militant jihadism is a complex phenomenon where both contextual and textual factors interact. Yet they differ in identifying their respective explanatory power. *Shaykh al-Azhar* calls the religious dimension "*inhiraf al-fikriyya*" or religious/conceptual deviation. He attributes this deviation to what he labels "the heritage of extremism and fanaticism in the Islamic thought" (al-Tayyib, 2014a). He associates this heritage with the early Kharijite movement and their excommunicatory (*takfir*) mentality, which plays a critical role in today's jihadist misreading. However, this is not the real cause, in his view, of the violence witnessed in the region. Although this extremist heritage implies a "direct" religious cause, the reality is masked under this "religious cloak" (al-Tayyib, 2014b: 8). The political actors instrumentalise this deviation for the sake of their interests. On the one hand, the "disunity" among Arabs/Muslims ensuing from national, sectarian or jurisprudential differences provokes such a deviation: "Nothing proved detrimental to Muslims as the intellectual divisions and sectarian alignments resulting in inevitable polarisations and exclusions" (MCE Statements, 2017: 14). On the other hand, (pro-Israeli) Western powers often exploit the regional disunity and provoke religious extremist deviation to maintain their geostrategic gains (al-Tayyib, 2015a). In a public speech in the wake of the Paris attacks in November 2015, al-Tayyib (2015b: 55) asserted "terrorism is an intellectual and psychological disease which uses religion as a front. It has no link to authentic Islam." Its causes are often linked to "social, economic and political doctrines," or "biased double standards policies and the greed of international and national interests as well as arms race and market" (al-Tayyib, 2016a: 13). The Azhar leadership tends to explain Islamic violent extremism with the assumption that the political and sectarian polarisation in the Middle East opens space for the resurgence and reshaping of the heritage of religious extremism and militancy, which in turn makes it more amenable to foreign manipulation. Most of Azhar's scholarly energy is, accordingly, allotted to challenging the distortions and misconceptions brought about by this religious deviation and to curing the disunity among Muslims. The emphasis is hence on promoting "*sahih al-din wa wasatiyyatuhu*" or correct/authentic teachings of religion and its principle of moderation (Azhar website).

Diyanet similarly draws parallels between Kharijites and today's jihadism. However, it sharply describes the latter as a "brand new phenomenon" that is "nominally Salafist, actually nihilist" (Diyanet, 2015: 12; 2016: 21). As a "domestic" contextual factor, Diyanet notes that the rise of extremist ideas among Muslims corresponds to a "search for authenticity" which results from their "inability to properly relate faith with lived reality and renew and update the relation in between" (Diyanet, 2015: 11). Its next report on IS, however, puts far more emphasis on "foreign" contextual factors. This might be due to the political context where conspiracy theories became a prominent feature of political discourse, especially after the coup attempt in July 2016. Diyanet (2016) rejects the idea that organisations like IS "in any way stem from Islam's own dynamics," arguing that such an idea puts Muslims in a "defensive mood" which creates more obstacles than solutions. They are rather the product of "modern political, economic, and social injustices, international power struggles, and ensuing conditions" or of "alienation", "marginalisation" and "discrimination" felt or experienced by Muslims in the West and the "failure of [European] integration policies". The extremist/terrorist organisations "exploit Islamic values for their own political and ideological agenda" and their religious distortions are to be viewed "not as a cause but an effect and manifestation" (Diyanet, 2016: 2-4). Nevertheless, Diyanet, like Azhar, extensively addresses and challenges numerous Islamic concepts and teachings employed by jihadist propaganda. This aims, it explains, "to expose how they exploit Islamic values" and to reveal the two basic epistemological problems it identifies with jihadist militancy: "*usulsüzlük*" as mentioned above, and "instrumentalising religion" (Diyanet, 2015: 8). Foreign contextual factors are hence dominantly emphasised over textual ones in Diyanet's discourse.

RMU equally addresses both types of factors. Its explanations are yet less contentious and more balanced with regard to "domestic" and "foreign" (Western) elements. It should, however, be noted that the Moroccan public documents and statements often point to Wahhabism and Shi'ism as "foreign" elements without explicitly naming a country. These two currents are usually discredited as threats to "Moroccan Islam" which defines Moroccan exceptionalism vis-à-vis other Arab/Muslim countries, as will be discussed later.

In explaining contextual factors, Ahmad 'Abbadi, the secretary-general of RMU, identifies "four dreams" that IS tried to realise and "ten grievances" it exploited. In his analysis ('Abbadi, 2016a, 2016b), jihadists aspire to realising four dreams to cure four modern failures. First, with the abolition of the Ottoman caliphate many Muslims felt themselves to be "orphans" and the subsequent Arab regimes failed to unite Muslims. This gave rise to a "dream of unity" under the banner of a caliph. Second, the Saudi-Wahhabi resurgence emerged in order to purify Islam, yet the promise failed because Saudi Arabia collaborated with the "enemy" for political gains in the region. Thus the "dream of purity" is yet to be achieved. Third, corruption and bad governance in most Arab societies failed to offer a decent life for their citizens, hence a "dream of dignity". Finally, IS aspires to realise an apocalyptical "dream of salvation" whose alternative is simply eternal damnation.

Likewise, ten grievances lie at the heart of the message and appeal of IS for 'Abbadi: 1) conspiracy theories still blame the Western powers for the turmoil in the region; 2) colonialism went away, but without reconciliation or damage repair; 3) the Israeli-Palestine conflict is still unresolved; 4) Muslims face double standards in international affairs; 5) Arab/Muslim governments are either unresponsive or ineffective to address the humiliation that believers undergo in international media and the entertainment industry; 6) the Muslim world is in conflict all around; it is like a "Molotov cocktail"; 7) Iran's influence is expanding at the expense of the Sunni world and Syria is in catastrophe; 8) the West has infiltrated the traditional value system and hence corrupted the true Islamic values; 9) Eurocentric readings falsify history and geography, thus ignoring Muslim contributions; 10) defamation of the Prophet and the Qur'an still remains ('Abbadi, 2016a, 2016b).

This analysis shows that for RMU IS's emergence and attraction are mainly an outcome of foreign and domestic political, ideological and geopolitical factors. This contextual approach is well reflected in its analyses of textual factors. RMU scholars identified more than 20 concepts which, they believe, are distorted by IS. They are principally those related to such Islamic concepts as sovereignty, governance, state, community, taxation, war and killing. It is worth mentioning here that a particular concern of RMU is to demonstrate that IS is neither Islamic nor a state. This explains why RMU focuses more on concepts that are about Islamic political theology, so to speak. The concepts, on the other hand, include more theological ones such as faith, unbelief and religion ('Abbadi, 2016c). They are yet explained in the framework of contextual factors mentioned above. RMU's Unit of Dismantling Extremist Discourse launched the aforementioned book series in order to give a more contextualised understanding of these concepts. Through this series, RMU aims to provide scholarly argumentative tools to expose the jihadist narrative.

In disclosing jihadist textual misinterpretations, RMU chiefly employs the *maqasid al-shari'a* approach. This has a particular significance in the Moroccan context. In pre-modern Islamic thought, the idea of *maqasid al-shari'a* was derived from the jurisprudential principles of *istislah* (seeking the good) or *maslaha* (seeking public good), which were initially introduced by the Maliki school of jurisprudence. This particular school has been, and is still, the official school of thought in Morocco. Therefore, the accusation that jihadists fail to consider the objectives of divine legislation is far more stressed in RMU's counter-theology.

When compared to other three, NU takes a quite different track in explaining textual and contextual justifications. Despite the fact that it recognises the role of "mass poverty" and "injustice" it asserts that the problem is much more exacerbated by textual factors. Following its International Summit of Moderate Islamic Leaders in 2016, NU issued a declaration (NUD, 2016) which identified "specific modes of interpreting Islam" as "the most significant factor causing the spread of religious extremism among Muslims" (4). NU openly blames "Middle Eastern countries" whose "supremacist" and "ultraconservative" teachings promote these specific modes. Saudi Arabia is at the top of the list. It even labels IS people as "Wahhabis" and its fighters as the "Wahhabi army" (Rahmat Islam Nusantara, 2016). Besides S. Arabia, Iran and Qatar are also held responsible. For NU, all three seek "political legitimacy" for their regional supremacy and "weaponise sectarian differences" to this end (NUD, 2016: 4). In 2017, this time *Gerakan Pemuda Ansor* (GP Ansor), the youth branch of NU, convened a conference in which NU ulama elaborated more on the textual factors. The meeting adopted the GP Ansor Declaration on Humanitarian Islam which provocatively suggested "it is false and counterproductive to claim that the actions of al-Qaeda, ISIS, Boko Haram and other such groups have nothing to do with Islam, or merely represent a perversion of Islamic teachings." They rather represent "obsolete tenets of classical Islamic law, which are premised upon perpetual conflict with those who do not embrace or submit to Islam" (GPADHI, 2017: 10). In their analysis, these tenets resulted from the Middle Eastern historical context of conflicts for power in the formative period of Islam. This has in time produced a worldview where "religious supremacy," "hatred," and "political domination" prevailed. In order to cure the "rapidly metastasising crisis," the declaration suggests Muslims reconciling the "problematic" Islamic teachings with the "ever-changing circumstances of time and place." The conditions, it reasons, where "orthodox Islam" and "contemporary civilization" emerged "differ significantly" (GPADHI, 2017: 3-6). NU, thus, calls for a comprehensive strategy to develop "an alternative Islamic new orthodoxy" through "re-contextualising the [traditional] Islamic teachings" that "authorise and explicitly enjoin such violence" (GPADHI, 2017: 5). Yahya Cholil Staquf, NU's secretary-general, who is the key figure behind the institution's recent push for new orthodoxy, markedly affirmed in an interview to a German newspaper (Staquf, 2017) that "there is a crystal clear relationship between fundamentalism, terror and the basic assumptions of Islamic orthodoxy. So long as we lack consensus regarding this matter, we cannot attain final victory over fundamentalist violence within Islam." In his view, there are particularly "three centres of concern" with regard to "traditional Islam," all related with Muslim demands about political governance, legislation and social interaction. He asserts "the [IS]'s goal of establishing the global caliphate stands squarely within the orthodox Islamic tradition" although the idea is no more realistic today. Muslims will keep clashing with contemporary politics, he thinks, as long as "the traditional norms of Islamic jurisprudence" are assumed to be "immutable" and "absolute" (Staquf, 2017). He also urges the West "not to force Muslims to adopt a moderate interpretation of Islam. But Western politicians should stop telling us that fundamentalism and violence have nothing to do with traditional Islam" (Staquf, 2017). Given that "[NU]'s battlefields are as much at home as they are in the larger Muslim world," whether these calls reflect a consensus within the institution and what long-term affects they would bring are yet to be seen (Dorsey, 2018).

Different Interests, Different Counter-Theologies

The synoptic analysis above illustrates that the four organisations address both textual and contextual factors in explaining the ascendancy of militant jihadism. They, however, differ in expounding how they interact with each. This difference is due to their distinct national and institutional contexts. Their respective counter-religious strategies, accordingly, converge and diverge.

In explaining contemporary jihadism, Azhar regards foreign political contextual elements as more decisive than textual ones. Yet, its counter-strategy is chiefly based upon rectifying extremist "misreading" and "misinterpretation" of the texts. Azhar has a clear institutional motivation for such a choice. It has recently been the target of harsh critiques from various social and political actors, including the secular, liberal and some Christian groups as well as the Egyptian president. It is stated to be ineffective in meeting the religious extremist challenge due to its inability to renew its religious discourse and to modernise its clumsy and out-dated curriculum which, some claim, includes extremist teachings on such issues as blasphemy, slavery and apostasy. Ibrahim Eissa, a prominent journalist and writer, even contends that the institution indeed provides "an environment that is conducive to extremism" (cited in 'Azzam, 2015). As a response, Azhar officials insist that such accusations downplay the role the institution has been playing in promoting authentic and moderate Islam. A spokesperson responded that Azhar's curriculum has been in effect for centuries whereas terrorism emerged recently and most terrorists were trained in non-Azhar institutions (cited in El Kholy, 2015). Moreover, as the most established Sunni academic organisation, Azhar views itself as "the highest scholarly authority for all Muslims... protecting [them] against deviated and extremist ideologies" (Azhar Brochure, 2017: 35). Its counter-strategy accordingly prioritises conceptual reclamation to restore true Islam. Such a strategy could vindicate Azhar's claim to be the internationally leading scholarly Sunni platform that functions as "the impregnable fortress working to spread the true religion and moderation" (Azhar webite). To put it differently, Azhar's counter-theology is designed to represent its institutional exceptionalism.

Like Azhar's, RMU's counter-theology rests upon conceptual reclamation. However, unlike Azhar's, it tends to interpret the textual factors in the light of contextual ones; hence it focuses more on a certain kind of textual distortion. Again unlike Azhar's *wasatiyya*, its religious orientation has a dominant theological motif, namely *maqasid al-sari'a*. Azhar's *wasatiyya* embraces various (Sunni) interpretations and subsequently employs different theological tools to substantiate its reclamation strategy. This indeed functions as a means to keep its autonomy vis-à-vis other religious actors and the state in Egypt. While enjoying royal support, RMU, on the other hand, sticks to the "teleological" approach to promote Moroccan exceptionalism. Its counter-theology is hence particularly framed by *maqasid*. We should also note that more emphasis on "foreign" Middle Eastern currents (i.e. Wahhabism and Shiʻism) rather than on Western political actors in pointing out contextual factors highlights the exceptional character of Moroccan Islam.

We see a similar approach in Indonesia's NU. Unlike many other Sunni criticisms, the inner dynamics of the Middle Eastern power struggle is much more emphasised in NU statements. But, unlike with RMU, not just today's Middle East but also its historical context is equally, even more, responsible for the textual distortions feeding jihadist narratives. In NU's analyses, hence, the textual and contextual factors appear as mutually conditioning, both today and in the past; yet the focus is more on the textual factors, unlike the other three. NU's difference can be attributed to the motivation to single out the Indonesian exceptionalism as a non-Arab and non-Middle Eastern Muslim-majority society which is believed to have successfully developed a plural, tolerant and inculturated Islam in the archipelago. NU's strategy thus differs substantially from the others. The problem, for NU, is not the Islamic concepts misread and abused today by the militants. It is instead yesterday's "problematic" and "obsolete" teachings (of the Middle East) that pave the way to jihadist distortion. Accordingly, rather than rectifying the misinterpreted concepts, NU proposes a wide-ranging and more ambitious theological strategy. NU thus appears to develop an "alternative" rather than a "counter" theology. In so doing, its leading theological motif is *rahma* or divine grace/mercy. Despite mentioning *maqasid al-shariʻa* (GPADHI, 2017: 3, 20), NU holds that *rahma* is the "primary message of Islam" and "the source of universal love and compassion." Referring to Qur'an 21:107, they suggest that even the Prophet Muhammad was sent exclusively to achieve *rahma* on earth. They say that the "true purpose of Islam" is "to promote the spiritual and material well-being of humanity" as well as "to establish social harmony and justice" (GPADHI, 2017; NUD, 2016). For NU, the nature of today's jihadist textual distortion is hence not conceptual. It is a distortion about the very purpose of religion.

In approaching textual and contextual factors, Diyanet stands in the opposite pole to NU. It exclusively blames the contextual factors and sees textual distortions simply as a result. In explaining jihadism, the emphasis is significantly on Western powers, their colonial struggles or their failures to include/integrate Muslims in Europe. It even claims that we would most probably be witnessing Hindu or Confucian justifications of violence if people in China or India experienced the same socio-political conditions that people now have in the

Middle East (Diyanet, 2016: 3). The solution, it infers, must be first and foremost political instead of religious. Notwithstanding, like Azhar and RMU, Diyanet lists several Islamic concepts and teachings that are, it thinks, exploited by the jihadists in responding to conditions they face. The emphasis in addressing them is yet more to expose the jihadists' "lack of methodological expertise", "eclectic pragmatism" and "instrumentalisation" rather than a conceptual reclamation (Diyanet, 2015; 2016). An explanation of why Diyanet allots considerable effort to correcting these distortions although it sees them essentially as an outcome of international political factors could be to highlight the peculiarity of the religious interpretation that Diyanet follows. As Turkey has Ottoman heritage as the last Muslim empire, Diyanet sees itself as the heir apparent of the Ottoman religious legacy and authority. It thus favours Turkish exceptionalism. In implying this exceptionalism, however, it resembles Azhar rather than RMU. Although Turkish Islam, like Moroccan Islam, represents a particular combination of Sunni elements, the tone and language Diyanet employs against IS's exploitation is akin to that of Azhar. Diyanet's increasing competition with Azhar to claim Sunni authority may explain this convergence. In line with the Turkish government's political ambitions, the last decade witnessed an unprecedented increase in Diyanet's visibility and outreach among Muslim societies and at several international Muslim platforms.

Despite such differences, they all agree, to differing extents, that the jihadist phenomenon has a theological aspect. A common strategy is thus to reveal their theological failures. These failures, they similarly identify, arise from their lack of comprehensive religious knowledge and lack of expertise in jurisprudential methodology. They argue that this paves the way to literalist, non-contextualised, exclusivist, selective and pragmatic readings that disregard the goals of divine message and teachings. As a solution, all, in a similar fashion, advocate for a balanced handling of three classical Islamic disciplines, namely *fiqh* (jurisprudence), *kalam* (doctrine) and *tasawwuf* (spirituality). Such a combination, they hold, is lacking in narrow textual expertise of Salafist/jihadist methodology. Yet their combinations differ. It is officially Maliki-Ash'arite-Sufism of al-Junayd in the Moroccan case, whereas it is practically Hanafi-Maturidite-Sufism of Ibn Arabi/Rumi in the Turkish case. NU and Azhar, on the other hand, both claim to harbour all four Sunni *madhahib*, two schools of Sunni doctrine and their respective branches of mainstream Sufism. Azhar, furthermore, gives space to Salafist and Islamist textual hermeneutics as well as sometimes entering into dialogue with Shi'ite authorities. This openness, they claim, reflects their *wasatiyya* or centrist approach, which forms Azhar's distinctive feature and is the basis of its global appeal as well as its main religious orientation against jihadist extremism (Bano, 2015).

It is clear that these various combinations represent diversity and vibrancy within the Sunni tradition. These institutions aim to take advantage of resting upon an established tradition to defeat contemporary challenges. Nevertheless, this often makes them more vulnerable. On the one hand, their specific understandings of Sunni tradition compete with each other in terms of authority and influence. The Salafi view, instead, pushes for a global, transnational, pure, certain and authentic Islam. The latter attracts more in time of crises and uncertainty. On the other hand, the Salafi methodology often appears more attractive because it offers a practical and simple hermeneutics whereby one's dependence on a religious authority is kept limited. Unlike demanding traditional Sunni scholarship, it gives the believer the chance of direct and freer engagement with the normative sources. In explaining the global influence of Saudi Salafism, Masooda Bano observes that along with generous Saudi sponsorship and the credibility it entertains as it emanates from the birthplace of Islam, a third factor is also crucial. It is this last point that many Sunni organisations miss about Salafist methodology: Salafist methodology "gives the individual greater autonomy" in religious issues by "arguing for a direct engagement with the foundational texts" and by "minimising reliance on the weighty cannon" of Sunni commentaries. (Bano, 2018a: 12) The Sunni tradition does not historically have a central body and various Sunni institutions significantly lost ground in the colonial and post-colonial periods. Moreover, the increasing globalisation, digitalisation and popular literacy have fractured their authority in contemporary times. The Salafists are filling this vacuum through their emphasis on authenticity and simplicity. Therefore, a counter theological strategy that heavily accentuates the advantages of having an established tradition will be less likely to be a wining strategy in fighting against militant jihadism.

An Evolving Counter-Theology?

The tone of Muslim critiques and responses to jihadists is often argumentative and apologetic. This is also true for the four cases examined here. This is understandable given that a great concern and motivation is to restore the image of Islam via exposing and correcting theological distortions. A noteworthy aspect is, however, that they sometimes refer to modern ideas and concepts in their counter-arguments and efforts. One can observe a tendency where they engage with modern/Western discourse and cover such issues as human rights, citizenship, minority rights, justice, democratic state, women rights, freedom, etc.

In June 2011, as an immediate response to the changing political landscape following the Arab uprisings, Azhar, for instance, issued a document on the future of Egypt. The document stated that Egypt should be a "modern" and "democratic" state based on a constitution that ensures full separation of powers and that guarantees equality for all citizens. It mentioned human rights to be supported and called for respecting freedom of thought; hence demanded the institutional independence of Azhar.[4] Nathan J. Brown (2011: 13) argues that the document "represents not only a laudable search for common ground [between conservative and liberal groups] but also a measure of a political bargain" whereby Azhar's "endorsement of liberal principles" is balanced with "a clear statement of support for its own independence." Although Azhar failed to assert the principles stated here in the later period of al-Sisi, it is worth mentioning that it showed its proclivity, even will, to make room for modern and liberal political discourse. More recently, in March 2017 Azhar convened a multi-faith international conference on "Freedom and Citizenship: Diversity and Integration." The conference particularly aimed to discuss citizenship in various aspects and followed by a declaration.[5] The declaration mentions the Prophet's Charter of Madina as an Islamic basis of the idea of citizenship. But reflecting the contemporary *Zeitgeist*, it also "reaffirm[s] the importance of equality between Muslims and Christians in terms of rights and responsibilities defined by the state. Indeed, both Muslims and Christians are considered one nation" (Azhar Conference, 2017: 10).

In a similar fashion, the 2016 Marrakesh Declaration, which came as a direct response to IS's abuse and massacre of non-Muslim minorities, called ulama to develop a jurisprudence of the concept of citizenship compatible with Islamic principles embodied in the Medina Charter. Hosted by the Moroccan king, the declaration highlighted that the objectives of this charter provide a suitable framework for constitutionally including modern international norms enshrined in the United Nations documents, particularly the Universal Declaration of Human Rights.[6] RMU's secretary-general 'Abbadi likewise talks about the importance of human rights, socio-economic development, the need to make the state accountable to its citizens in order effectively to face religious extremism

('Abbadi, 2016b). Moreover, in corollary with its mission, RMU interprets principles of *maqasid* in a broader and progressive manner ('Abbadi, 2016a; 2016b; al-Idrisi, 2016) to provide religious legitimacy to the governmental reform agenda in political, social and economic areas. NU, on the other hand, in 2017 convened the Global Unity Forum (GUF) with the participation of the representatives of various non-Muslim groups. The Forum stated that religions are supposed to "contribute to civilisation" not to "destroy" and "interfaith cooperation is needed to realise global peace" (GUF, 2017). In the Forum, NU also underlined that its proposed alternative theology should include non-Muslim contributions as well.

We can detect a similar tendency in Diyanet's statements. Although it does not explicitly refer to any international declaration or statement on human rights and freedoms, a liberal universal spirit is discernable. It, for instance, urges religious scholars "to accurately present Islam's view on 'human' regardless of their religion, language, and ethnicity" (Diyanet, 2016: 43). It affirms (Diyanet, 2015: 26) "Islam projects and promotes diversity." Diyanet, likewise, criticises the attitude that "prioritises only the rights of belief of those who are in the majority or who belong to one's own group." It warns that "the moral attitude should rather value and observe the right of belief for anyone and the right to practise their belief no matter that they constitute a small or big community" (Diyanet, 2015: 39).

These examples illustrate that Sunni counter-theology cannot be characterised only by an argumentative or dialectical approach when responding to militant jihadism. They rather show a tendency where it can engage with modern and/or liberal discourse on human rights, citizenship, diversity, democratic state and social justice. As a matter of fact, the insistence on contextual and purposive analysis of normative religious sources can be taken as a step forward for more engagement. Yasin Arnold Mol (2016) supports this observation. In his analyses of recent (English) fatwas denouncing terrorism, he explores:

> One of the interesting aspects of these counter responses against extremism is that they show how mainstream Sunni Islam, partially as a response to extremism, has incorporated modernist and reformist thought on reinterpretation of the Qur'an and the Islamic tradition, and on human rights, liberal governance, and religious pluralism … The globalisation of Islamic radicalism has forced mainstream Sunni Islam to globalise not only its discourse, but also its content (56-57).

We already have several progressive Muslim scholars and activists who call for more intellectual and hermeneutical engagement with modern or post-modern thought in facing puritanist Islamic hegemonic discourse (e.g. Duderija, 2017; Abou El Fadl, 2005; Moosa, 2005). The mainstream Sunni discourse has not yet responded to this call in a clear positive way. However, considering the tendency exemplified above, we can predict that it is more likely to interact in future with progressive and liberal Muslim discourse in responding to militant jihadism. Before that, another big challenge is yet to be met, however. The Sunni authorities seem to fall in a moral crisis in the upcoming period as their discourse and actions are becoming more associated with the "official Islam" of their respective countries where the political authority applies decisive pressure to design a particular version of acceptable Islam in order to counter terrorism.

"Official Islam" and Sunni Religious Authorities

Robbins and Rubin (2017) observe that as a response to "the new challenges in the regional environment following the Arab uprisings," four Arab countries (Egypt, Tunisia, Jordan and Morocco) opted to enhance the "official Islam" model where the religious space is controlled through allocating financial resources, political capital, and institutional power to elements of official Islam. Brown's analysis of "official Islam" in Egypt, Morocco, Oman and Lebanon brings similar conclusions (Brown, 2017). This is already valid for Turkey and Indonesia, even long before the "war on terror." Following their analyses as well as considering the Turkish and Indonesian examples, we can make the following observations: the official Islam model is essentially designed to promote state-sponsored and -controlled religious establishment in order to limit the impact and outreach of alternative and/or popular Islamist movements that may challenge the political establishment and to prevent the spread of religious extremism. Despite county-specific differences, practically speaking, the following initiatives are commonly observed while building "official Islam": the promotion of a particular religious identity attributed to the distinctive feature of Islamic understanding and practice in a given country and which often overlaps with national identity, bureaucratisation of religious institutions and actors, stricter observance of mosques and preachers, more control on or centralisation of fatwa bodies, attempts to standardise Friday sermons, providing modernised training to imams and other religious functionaries with proper acceptable doctrinal training.

Another common tendency is to advertise its own brand of official Islam abroad as best practice or an effective antidote to religious extremism, and accordingly to give more international visibility to the official religious establishment in question.

For their four cases, Robbins and Rubin (2017) note that although each recognises the clear value of official Islam controlling the religious space, their ability to do so depends on two factors: the country's inherited religious institutions and the country's regime type. Although not elaborated in their study, Turkey represents perhaps the most successful case of official Islam. In Turkey, religious and national identities are indispensably interconnected, and through Diyanet the state plays an unparalleled role in the religious field. Beginning with the introduction of the so-called "Turkish-Islamic Synthesis" in the aftermath of a *coup d'état* in 1980, Turkish "official Islam" has gradually gained importance (Eligür, 2010). Diyanet, as the religious state apparatus of Turkish Islam, today controls both the administration of mosques and imams as well as issuing fatwas which are operated separately in our other three cases. Similarly, Diyanet exerts certain influence on imam training programmes that are separately provided by the vocational *imam-hatip* high schools or universities' theology faculties. Being one of the biggest state-funded religious bureaucracies in the Islamic world, Diyanet's planned budget for 2019 exceeds that of several ministries including energy, transport, urban development, science and technology (BÜMKO, 2019). Since 2002, Diyanet has been enjoying generous political, financial and moral support by the Turkish governments under the AK Parti rule. Thanks to this support and despite it having lacked traditional authority in the eyes of both devout Muslims at home and the wider Sunni community abroad, Diyanet is recently taking centre stage as a leading Islamic scholarly platform, and perhaps potentially a globally influential leadership of Sunni Islam (Bano, 2018b). Diyanet has also expanded its base and reach abroad, particularly in Europe which hosts the largest Turkish diaspora (e.g. see Öktem, 2012; Öztürk, 2016, Öztürk and Sözeri, 2018).

Morocco seems to have emulated the Turkish example of official Islam. Following the 2003 Casablanca bombings, the royal establishment initiated sweeping reforms in the governing religious field to counter religious terrorism. Previous kings had opted to govern the religious sphere with a strategy of diversifying and co-opting non-state religious actors. King Muhammad VI, instead, implemented a strategy of developing more extensive religious institutions (Bruce, 2015: 183). This has led to a highly bureaucratised management of Islam in Morocco (Wainscott, 2017), very similar to what we are witnessing in Turkey. Nevertheless, rather than administering the religious field through a single institution, Morocco established or reorganised different institutions which operate under the king's leadership and coordination. RMU was indeed an outcome of these reforms. A critical point in these efforts was to promote "Moroccan Islam" as a particular national religious identity based on the specific elements of Sunni Islam that have been adopted in the long history of the country. Moroccan Islam provides an "optimum" combination of four elements embedded in Moroccan religious life: the Maliki school of jurisprudence, Ash'ari school of doctrine, certain branches of sober Sufism and the central role of the king as the "*amir al-mu'minin*" or Commander of the Faithful who embodies the other three elements (Honerkamp and Calabria, 2013). As such, it also represents an exceptional national-religious identity vis-à-vis other Arab/Muslim societies. RMU is assigned to intellectually support this objective. It functions as the leading scholarly platform within the reformed Moroccan religious bureaucracy and the "centrepiece of the monarchy's reforms to the religious field" (Wainscott, 2017: 48). It also advertises Morocco's official Islam abroad.

In Indonesia, official Islam is represented by two leading yet competing organisations, NU and Muhammadiyah. Thanks to their respective highly complex structures, the two organisations have long dominated the religious, social and political life in Indonesia and have reached "a degree of societal penetration that is unparalleled in the Muslim world" (Van Bruinessen, 2013: 21). NU is yet the bigger religious partner of Indonesian official Islam. In 2015, as a part of its fight against rising militant Islamism, NU introduced the idea of *Islam Nusantara*, or Islam of the East Indies. The idea contrasts Indonesia's Islamic experience with that of the Middle East. It emphasises that Indonesian Muslims have followed a different track in embracing Islam in the pre-modern period and embracing in the modern era the *Pancasila* (Staquf, 2015; 2018; Taylor, 2018). The *Pancasila* is the founding "Five Principles" that define modern Indonesia as a multi-religious, multi-ethnic, secular and constitutional nation-state. NU sees itself as a natural outcome of the former and a decisive actor that provided religious legitimacy for the latter. Through promoting *Islam Nusantara* both in Indonesia and abroad, NU tries to contradistinguish the Indonesian experience as an exceptional "local/national" alternative to the "transnational" and "purified" Islam, currently dominated by Arab Salafism. The concept is now widely circulating and many political leaders, including the president Widodo himself, give support to the idea. It must also be noted that the president appointed Yahya

C. Staquf, the secretary-general of NU, to the prestigious Presidential Advisory Council in May 2018. This exemplifies the cooperative relationship between NU and the Indonesian state, which characterises Indonesia's official Islam.

In Egypt, we have a similar but more complex situation. It is not cooperation but mutual interdependence that defines the relationship between Azhar and the political authority. Nasser's nationalisation reforms in the early 1960s were decisive for Azhar and the Egyptian religious sphere. These reforms put Azhar under the direct control of the Egyptian state. Its political and organisational autonomy was extensively challenged. Nasser and the succeeding presidents have consistently pursued coopting Azhar to justify their policies and political priorities, especially against the Muslim Brothers (MB). In facing the militant Islamist challenge, the political elite fears that undermining or ignoring Azhar's contribution may provide more space and attraction to extremists. While trying to keep its religious and intellectual autonomy, Azhar, on the other hand, pursues a policy that avoids a serious clash. It keeps benefiting state support to further its penetration and authority although this requires compromises in return. The institution, simultaneously, resists political demands that would, otherwise, give the image of total absorption. Therefore, in the case of Egyptian official Islam, the religious and political partners are often guarded and cautious, if not suspicious, of each other. The tension between the two has recently been becoming more apparent (El Taki, 2017, Meital, 2017) as the autocratic rule of al-Sisi presses for a substantial change in religious discourse and curricula to more effectively counter jihadist extremism, which jeopardises the already fragile social coexistence and national unity.

Some link the rise of contemporary appeal to Salafi methodology and the jihadist interpretations to the inability of traditional Sunni authorities whose nature and roles were remarkably altered by colonial and post-colonial policies. The official Islam model can be seen as an attempt to re-empower these authorities. Nevertheless, this empowerment comes with a notable cost. The religious establishments are now under more surveillance from the state and have few options but to cooperate with them. This in turn brings a credibility question which risks, in the long run, the effectiveness of their religious message. This will have implications for the relevance and ability of the "organised religion" in the Sunni world and it would affect the fight against religious extremism.

Zeghal (2007) explains the popularity and credibility of Azhar with its traditional role of being a "buffer zone between radical and/or political Islam on the one hand and state-defined Islam on the other." Bano (2018c), however, argues that this was seriously challenged in the post-Arab Spring period mainly due to the explicit support that Azhar leaders gave to al-Sisi's iron-fist rule. This was not the first time that Azhar backed controversial governmental policies. Nevertheless, "the intensity of violence associated with the al-Sisi regime makes [Azhar's] defence of state atrocities more questionable than in the past" and "some prominent Azhar scholars (former as well as current) have condemned the Brotherhood with such ferocity that they have severely compromised their moral authority" (Bano, 2018c: 58). Therefore, Azhar today witnesses an unprecedented moral and legitimacy crisis both inside and outside Egypt. Furthermore, Azhar is under continuous attack by the growing secular and liberal groups who question the institution's domineering initiatives with a religious agenda thanks to the governmental support it enjoys in the name of fight against religious extremism. The future ramifications of the competition in Egypt for the religious field and its implications for Islamist extremism are yet to be seen.

Turkish Diyanet is going through a similar credibility crisis although it is pointed to as a pretty effective case for official Islam. Diyanet is in fact a newcomer to the global Sunni agenda and asserts itself as the leading authority of moderate Sunni Islam. Turkey's democratisation and economic boom since 2002 that undermined the Kemalist bureaucratic and military tutelage was critical in Diyanet's ascendancy. Notwithstanding, Turkey has been witnessing a serious democratic and economic backlash for the last few years. Especially after the failed coup attempt in July 2016, the regime in Turkey turned into an authoritarian rule with a huge crackdown on dissidents and civil society that has never been witnessed in modern Turkish history. Furthermore, corruption has become so widespread and the pace of economic development slowed down sharply. Diyanet's unconditional support to many controversial and oppressive governmental policies and their justification on religious grounds as well as its total silence on corruption claims that also implicate senior Diyanet officials bring its credibility into question. Furthermore, its disregard of child abuse scandals because they happened in some religious boarding schools aroused suspicion about its credibility. Along with secular and liberal critiques similar to those in Egypt, some devout Muslims have also become critical of such condoning. A notable reaction to such failures of official Islam in Turkey is the recent rise of deism among young people. At several occasions, meetings and statements, Diyanet expresses concerns about increasing deist tendencies in society. It is possible that in future Diyanet may be losing its appeal and power of persuasion although it keeps reaching out to all walks of society. Relatively speaking, Islamic militancy has never been a key threat in modern Turkey. Nevertheless, the sharp political and social polarisation in the country and the discursive justification of violence on many accounts in recent years increase concerns about a possible rise of militancy. Furthermore, many already are suspicious about the Syrian policy comprising some sort of cooperation with certain jihadist groups against the Syrian regime and lack of cohesive and long-term integration policies about more than three million Syrian refugees in the country. Whether they will make Turkey more vulnerable to extremist violence is not clear. How the eroding religious credibility of Diyanet will affect the appeal of extremists in this context is yet to be seen.

NU does not have such an intense moral or credibility crisis. It still largely holds its appeal. However, the political discourse has recently become more conservative and intolerant in Indonesia. In the liberal post-Suharto era, Islamic activism has both increased and diversified and religious activism has been marked by the rise of not only political Islamists but also various Salafi groups, including the militant ones. It is no coincidence that Indonesia has witnessed several deadly jihadist attacks in recent years. Security authorities fear that Indonesia would be a future breeding ground for Islamist militancy in South Asia (see, e.g., Lloyd and Dredge 2014). Likewise, Martin van Bruinessen, a leading Dutch expert on Indonesia, observes (2013) a "conservative turn" in the country that resulted from the "Arabisation" trends among Indonesian Muslims. The religious and political attraction of "transnational Islamic puritanism" threatens the multi-ethnic and multi-religious character of Indonesian society. It in turn "undermines the established nation-wide Muslim organisations (Muhammadiyah and NU) that had been providing religious guidance for most of the 20th century" (Van Bruinessen, 2018: ii). In late 2016 in Jakarta, huge public demonstrations were held under the banner of "Islam Defence Action" (*Aksi Bela Islam*). These were the largest mass Muslim mobilisations in Indonesia's modern history. Although they were organised by various fundamentalist and conservative factions the majority of the participants belonged to the mainstream and non-violent Muslim body (see Herdiansahi *et al.*, 2017 more on these demonstrations). Although NU officially discredited these demonstrations and even organised a counter one in cooperation with non-Muslim organisations, they already signalled that NU is at least losing ground. The recent diversification of the religious sphere in Indonesia seems to provoke more competition about religious authority. Moreover, the emphasis of Salafi groups on simplicity, authenticity, universality and purity directly challenge NU's religious rhetoric on inculturation and the exceptional local character of Indonesian Islam. In future, we will be observing more theological clashes between the two visions of Islam in Indonesia. Furthermore, the conservative and Salafi groups will most probably harshly react to NU's recent proposal to re-contextualise previous Islamic teachings.

It is difficult to foresee whether we see similar authority or credibility crises in Morocco. Morocco is the youngest among the other three in terms of adopting a clear "official Islam" model. The bureaucratisation of the Moroccan religious field bears fruit only recently. Its fate is yet to be seen. Assessing our four cases, it would be possible to make the following observation with regard to official Islam and militant jihadism. The credibility question that is more likely to arise in various official Islam models where religious establishments are urged to cooperate or negotiate with political authority would trigger more debate on organised religion, local Islam and religious education. This in turn would bring more questions about the nature and role of Sunni authorities and about their capacity of resilience against the Salafist claims.

Conclusion

Militant jihadism is more than a religious phenomenon but triggered heated debate and controversies on several Islamic teachings and practice both among Muslims and between Muslims and the wider world. In most cases, jihadist organisations have a Sunni provenance. Therefore, Sunni responses and counter-arguments have become of particular attention and significance. According to the synoptic analysis of the discourses of the four leading Sunni institutions carried out in this chapter, the following appear to be the common elements in their critiques: Jihadists have extensively impaired the image of Islam worldwide. Their violent strategy and actions inflict the most harm on Muslims. Islam does not justify terrorism even though defensive war could be justified on certain grounds. Jihadists promote a literal, simplistic, selective and excommunicatory approach. It essentially lacks a comprehensive and balanced treatment of intellectual, practical and spiritual aspects of Islamic teachings and praxis which has been the hallmark of Muslim orthodoxy. They are religiously heretic groups, and their heresy is often manipulated in line with political, sectarian and economic interests.

The counter-theologies of these four institutions differ due to their differences in explaining the emergence and appeal of militant jihadism. Although they all show a general tendency that understands the jihadist phenomenon primarily as a result of the socio-political context in the Middle East, they have dissimilar views on what has really gone wrong with this context and how it has affected the jihadist textual distortion. Moreover, their explanations are usually framed by their varying interests ensuing from their distinct institutional and national contexts in which they operate. The counter-theology of each organisation is designed to reflect the "exceptional" character of its respective institutional and national context. Therefore, while they seem to converge in employing a similar counter-religious strategy, namely exposing and/or correcting the jihadist distortion, what is to be rectified and how it is implemented differs in each case.

Furthermore, their counter strategies reveal several challenges. An important one is about religious authority and authenticity. In the globalised world where religious knowledge is unprecedentedly popularised, the Salafist emphasis on more direct and individualised engagement with the foundational texts becomes more attractive and reachable. In addition, the Salafist claim on authenticity, purity and universality provides a stronger anchor for the believers who seek straightforward responses in an already perplexing world. The reactionary, revolutionary and venturesome jihadist propaganda surely takes advantage of this Salafist worldview. In response, Sunni authorities dialectically defend their religious authority and authenticity with reference to their expertise in complex, accumulated and pretty technical traditional canons. They base their legitimacy upon this established tradition, which is at the very target of the Salafist/jihadist struggle. Therefore, the dialectical Sunni counter-theologies aiming at undoing jihadist "distortion" with reference to authenticity and authority is less likely to be an affective strategy to face militant jihadism in the long run. The theological fight should rather be given in a different field, namely challenging the Salafist/Jihadist claim on simplicity and certainty whereby direct and exclusive access to the divine truth is presupposed. To succeed in this latter fight, an effective way could be to demonstrate and centralise, in an Islamic framework, the diverse and complex nature of divine involvements with creation. This is perhaps the most viable option to challenge the exclusivist jihadist vision. Invoking the rich legacy of Islamic tradition may help in such an attempt. In this case, Sunni religious strategy is more likely to be successful only if it views tradition not as a warehouse of the established ideas or methods but as a repository for further creative hermeneutical engagements. This necessitates approaching the Islamic legacy not in a regressive and retrospective but a progressive and prospective way. This leads us to the suggestion that the theological advance against militant jihadism rests paradoxically on more engagement with the progressive and liberal Muslim discourse rather than on the Salafist or conservative one. NU's attempt to develop a new Islamic orthodoxy seems to be more promising as a counter-strategy to defy Islamic extremism, in this sense. Besides, the ability of Sunni authorities for discursive and methodological flexibility in adapting to social change can also be helpful in addressing the Salafist/jihadist claim on simplicity and certainty. That we see some indications of Islamic discourses evolving in dialogue with modern, reformist or liberal discourse, as illustrated above, is of particular importance. Whether and how Sunni authorities continue this engagement and whether and how they will be able to convince their followers in this enterprise will be critical for the fate of Sunni religious strategy over militant jihadism.

An arduous challenge waiting here is whether these institutions keep their moral authority within the limits of the trendy official Islam models of which they are compelled to be a part. On the one hand, the global fight against Islamic violent extremism has opened up new political space and legitimacy for the religious establishments both at home and abroad. On the other hand, it has provided political authorities more legitimacy to exert influence in the religious field. In a field where both religious and political authority claim legitimacy, the former is required to compromise if it decides not to totally submit to or clash with the latter. Depending on the type of political actors' way of governing, this compromise may seriously risk religious credibility as exemplified in the case of Azhar and Diyanet. Despite often being depicted as an effective way to counter extremism, the official Islam model may be counter-productive in the long run, given the anti-establishment ethos of jihadist revolutionaries and their dexterity in translating individual or collective discontents into violent activism. Whether the Sunni authorities can retain their moral credibility will hence matter in effectively countering the jihadist challenge.

Notes

1 These books are available online in Arabic at http://www.arrabita.ma/Article.aspx?C=107195 [accessed 25 October 2018].
2 For contemporary Salafism see, among others, Meijer, 2009; Lauzière, 2016; Rougier, 2008 and Wiktorowicz, 2006.
3 For more on this distinction and Muslim conceptions of jihad and holy war from past to present see Cook, 2015; Bonner, 2006; Habeck, 2006; Gerges, 2005, Firestone, 2002.
4 For an evaluation of this document see Maged 2012.

5   The declaration is available at http://www.azhar.eg/observer-en/al-azhar-declaration-on-citizenship-and-coexistence-issued-by-his-eminence-the-grand-imam-of-al-azhar [accessed 12 October 2018].
6   For an evaluation of this document see Hayward, 2016.

References

'Abbadi, Ahmad. (2016a). *Fi tafkik al-khitab al-mutatarrifa*. Rabat: RMU, [online]. Available at: http://www.arrabita.ma/Article.aspx?C=107197 [accessed 6 November 2018].

'Abbadi, Ahmad. (2016b). *Deconstructing Daesh*. Hudson Institute [online]. Available at: https://www.hudson.org/research/13331-deconstructing-daesh [accessed 6 November 2018].

'Abbadi, Ahmad. (2016c) *Fi tafkik al-mafhum al-jihad*. Rabat: RMU, [online]. Available at: http://www.arrabita.ma/Article.aspx?C=107198 [accessed 6 November 2018].

Abou El Fadl, K. (2005). *The Great Theft: Wrestling Islam from the Extremists*. New York: Harper Collins.

al-Idrisi, K.M. (2016). *Al-davlat al-islamiyya: qira'at fi shurut wa bayan al-tahafut al-khitab al-mutatarrifa*. Rabat: RMU, [online]. Available at: http://www.arrabita.ma/dossiers/akhbar/images/attachments_2010_05_28(2)/jadidnew.pdf [accessed 6 November 2018].

al-Tayyib, A. (2014a) 'Danger of Takfir'. *Azhar Website* [online], 1 June 2015. Available at: http://www.azhar.eg/observer-en/danger-of-takfir [accessed 10 October 2018].

al-Tayyib, A. (2014b). "Forward", in *Al-Azhar Stands Against Misconceptions: Selections from al-Azhar Intrenational Conference on Confronting Extremism and Terrorism December 2014*, Cairo: Dar al-Quds al-'Arabiyya, pp.7-12.

al-Tayyib, Ahmad. (2015a). "Opening Speech" at *The Muslim World League International Conference on Islam and Counter Terrorism*, Makka, February 22-25.

al-Tayyib, Ahmad. (2015b). 'Grand Imam's Opening Address', in *Statements of the Muslim Coouncil of Elders* (MCE). Abu Dhabi: MCE pp. 55-56.

al-Tayyib, A. (2016a). 'Opening Speech', in *Geneva Meeting: The Role of Religions in Promoting Peace and Countering Violence, Hatred*. Abu Dhabi: MCE, pp. 3-13.

Azhar Brochure. (2017). *Al-Azhar International Peace Conference Programme*. Cairo: al-Azhar.

Azhar Conference. (2017). Proceedings of *Freedom and Citizenship: Diversity and Integration*. Abu Dhabi: MCE.

'Azzam, S. (2015). '*Ibrahim 'Issa: al-Azhar yufir al-bayiat al-hadina li-l-irhab fi masr*.' Masrawy, [online], 15.April.2015. Available at: http://www.masrawy.com/News/News_Egypt/details/2015/4/15/530790/ [accessed 12 October 2018].

Bano, M. (2015). 'Protector of the "al-Wasatiyya" Islam: Cairo's al-Azhar University', in M. Bano and K. Sakurai (eds), *Shaping Global Islamic Discourses: The Role of al-Azhar, al-Medina and al-Mustafa*. Edinburgh: Edinburgh University Press, 2015, pp. 73–92.

Bano, M. (2018a). 'Introduction', in M. Bano (ed) *Modern Islamic Authority and Social Change Vol.1*. Edinburgh: Edinburgh University Press, pp.1-51.

Bano, M. (2018b). 'Diyanet: Taking Centre Stage', in M. Bano (ed) *Modern Islamic Authority and Social Change Vol.1*. Edinburgh: Edinburgh University Press, pp. 271-292.

Bano, M. (2018c). 'Al-Azhar University: A Crisis of Authority', in M. Bano (ed) *Modern Islamic Authority and Social Change Vol.1*. Edinburgh: Edinburgh University Press, pp. 55-78.

Bonner, M. (2006). *Jihad in Islamic History*. Princeton: Princeton University Press.

Bruce, B. (2015). *Governing Islam Abroad: The Turkish and Moroccan Muslim Fields in France and Germany*. PhD Thesis. Sciences Po.

BÜMKO (Bütçe ve Mali Kontrol Genel Müdürlüğü). (2019). *2019 Yılı Merkezi Yönetim Bütçe Kanunu Teklifi*. [Online]. Available at: http://www.bumko.gov.tr/Eklenti/11291,2019mybkteklificctvcllerpdf.pdf?0 [accessed 20 October 2018].

Cochrane, J. (2015). 'From Indonesia, a Muslim Challenge to the Ideology of the Islamic State'. *The New York Times* [online] 26 November 2015. Available at: https://www.nytimes.com/2015/11/27/world/asia/indonesia-islam-nahdlatul-ulama.html [accessed on 28 October 2018].

Cook, D. (2005). *Understanding Jihad*. Berkeley: University of California Press.

Diyanet. (2015). *DAİŞ'in Temel Felsefesi ve Dini Referansları Raporu*. Ankara: Diyanet Din İşleri Yüksek Kurulu Başkanlığı.

Diyanet. (2016). *Dini İstismar ve Tedhiş Hareketi: DEAŞ*. Ankara: Diyanet Din İşleri Yüksek Kurulu Başkanlığı.

Dorsey. J. M. (2018). Reforming the Faith: Indonesia's Battle for the Soul of Islam. *Modern Diplomacy* [online], 30 October 2018. Available at: https://moderndiplomacy.eu/2018/10/30/reforming-the-faith-indonesias-battle-for-the-soul-of-islam/ [accessed 12 November 2018].

Duderija, A. (2017). *The Imperatives of Progressive Islam*. New York: Routledge.

Eligür, B. (2010). *The Mobilization of Political Islam in Turkey*. Cambridge: Cambridge University Press.

El Kholy, I. (2015). 'Al-Azhar Controversy Leads to Curriculum Updates'. Al-Monitor [online] 5 June 2015. Available at: http://www.al-monitor.com/pulse/originals/2015/06/egypt-azhar-university-curriculum-updates-extremist-sisi.html#ixzz5SyBJ1Q48 [accessed 5 October 2018].

El Taki, K. (2017). 'Rivalry for Religious Dominance in Egypt', Carnegie Endowment for Peace [online], 21 December 2017. Available at: http://carnegieendowment.org/sada/75093 [accessed 5 October 2018].

Firestone, R. (2002). *Jihad: The Origin of Holy War in Islam*, Oxford: Oxford Univ. Press.

Fouad, A. (2015). 'Al-Azhar Refuses to Consider the Islamic State an Apostate'. Al-Monitor [online], February 12, 2015. Available at: http://www.al-monitor.com/pulse/originals/2015/02/azhar-egypt-radicals-islamic-state apostates.html#ixzz5VHNTpt50 [accessed 25 September 2018].

Gerges F. (2005). *The Far Enemy: Why Jihad Went Global*. New York: Cambridge University Press.

GPADHI. (2017). *Gerakan Pemuda Ansor Declertaion on Humanitarian Islam*. Jakarta: Gerakan Pemuda Ansor. Online. Available at: http://www.baytarrahmah.org/media/2017/Gerakan-Pemuda-Ansor_Declaration-on-Humanitarian-Islam.pdf [accessed 5 November 2018].

GUF. (2017). *Global Unity Forum*. Jakarta: Pimpinan Pusat *Gerakan Pemuda Ansor*. Online. Available at: http://www.baytarrahmah.org/media/political-communiques/2016/201605 12_Ansor-Global-Unity-Forum/20160512_Appendix-1_Declaration-of-Global-Unity-Forum_English.pdf [accessed 5 November 2018].

Habeck, M. (2006). *Knowing the Enemy: Jihadist Ideology and the War on Terror*. New Haven: Yale University Press.

Haywrad, S. (2016). *Understanding and Extending the Marrakesh Declaration in Policy and Practice*. Special Report. Washington D.C.: United States Institute of Peace.

Hegghammer, T. (2010). *Jihad in Saudia Arabia: Violence and Pan-Islamism since 1979*. Cambridge: Cambridge University Press.

Herdiansahi, A.G., Putri, D. A., Ashari, L., and Maduratmi, R. (2017). 'The Islam Defence Action: A Challenge of Islamic Movement to Democratic Transition in the Post 2014 Indonesia'. *Wacana*, 20(2), 57-67.

Honerkamp, K. and Calabria, M. D. (2013). *Moroccan Islam: A Unique and Welcome Spirit of Moderation and Tolerance*. Washington D.C.: Georgetown University's Center for Contemporary Arab Studies.

Lauzière, Henri. (2016). *The Making of Salafism: Islamic Reform in the Twentieth Century*. New York: Columbia University Press.

Lloyd, P. and Dredge, S. (2014). 'ISIS Recruitment Video Join the Ranks Urges Indonesian Muslims to Migrate to the Islamic State'. *ABC* [online], 28 Jul 2014. Available at: https://www.abc.net.au/news/2014-07-28/isis-releases-recruitment-video-target-indonesian-muslims/5629960 [accessed 15 October 2018].

Maged, A. J. (2012) 'Commentary on the Al-Azhar Declaration in Support of the Arab Revolutions.' *Amsterdam Law Forum* 40(3), 69-76.

Meijer, R. (2009) *Global Salafism: Islam's New Religious Movement.* London: Hurst and Company.

Meital, C. (2017). 'In Egypt, Clashes Between the Institution of the Presidency and The Institution of al-Azhar'. MEMRI [online], 21 August 2017. Available at: https://www.memri.org/reports/egypt-clashes-between-institution-presidency-and-institution-al-azhar [accessed 20 October 2018].

Mol, Y. A. (2016). "Denouncing Terrorism in the West: English Publications of Anti-terrorism Fatwa's as Western Islamic Discourse'". [Online]. Available at: [accessed 15 November 2018].

Moosa, E. (2005). *Ghazali and Poetics of Imagination.* Chapel Hill, NC: Univ. of North Carolina Press.

Mustafa, M. (2014). '*Wakil "al-azhar": li hadha al-asbab lam nukaffir da'ish'*. *Vetogate* [online], 12 December 2014. Available at: https://www.vetogate.com/1374000 [accessed 2 October 2018].

Brown, N. J. (2011). *Post-Revolutionary al-Azhar*. Washington D.C.: Carnegie Endowment for International Peace.

Brown, N. J. (2017). *Official Islam in the Arab World: The Contest for Religious Authority*. Washington D.C.: Carnegie Endowment for International Peace.

NUD. (2016). *International Summit of Moderate Islamic Leaders Nahdatul Ulama Decleration*. Jakarta: Nahdatul Ulama Central Board. Available at: http://www.baytarrahmah.org/media/political-communiques/2016/20160510_ISOMIL-NU-Declaration/20160510_Appendix-2_Nahdlatul-Ulama-Declaration_05-10-16.pdf [accessed 5 November 2018].

Öktem, K. (2012). 'Global Diyanet and Multiple Networks: Turkey's New Presence in the Balkans.' *Journal of Muslims in Europe* 1, 27-58.

Öztürk, A. E. (2016). 'Turkey's Diyanet under AKP Rule: From Protector to Imposer of State Ideology?' *Southeast European and Black Sea Studies* 16, 619–635.

Öztürk, A. E. and Sözeri, S. (2018). 'Diyanet as a Turkish Foreign Policy Tool: Evidence from the Netherlands and Bulgaria.' *Politics and Religion*, 11(3), 624-648.

Rahmat Islam Nusantara. (2016). Film by IIQS & ANSOR. Online. Available at: https://www.youtube.com/watch?v=GLqaJlTjA5Y [accessed 5 November 2018].

Robbins, M. and Rubin, L. (2017). 'The Ascendance of Official Islams'. Democracy and Security, 13(4), pp. 363-391.

Rougier, B. (ed) (2008). *Qu'est-ce que le salafisme?* Paris: PUF.

MCE (Muslim Council of Elders) Statement. (2017). *Statements of the Muslim Council of Elders*. Abu Dhabi: MCE.

Saker, T. (2017). "Why does Egypt's Largest Muslim Beacon, Al-Azhar, Refuse to Declare IS "apostate"?'. *Egypt Independent* [online], 14 April 2017. Available at: https://ww.egyptindependent.com/why-does-egypt-s-largest-muslim-beacon-al-azhar-refuse-declare-apostate/ [accessed 12 October 2018].

Spannaus, N. (2018). 'History and Continuity: Al-Azhar and Egypt', in M. Bano (ed) *Modern Islamic Authority and Social Change Vol.1.* Edinburgh: Edinburgh University Press, pp. 79-101.

Staquf, Y. C. (2015). 'How Islam Learned to Adapt in "Nusantara"'. *Strategic Review: The Indonesian Journal of Leadership, Policy, and World Affairs*, 5(2), pp. 18-28.

Staquf, Y. C. (2017). '*Terrorismus und Islam Hängen Zusammen*'. Interview by Marco Stahlhut. *Frankfurter Allgemeine Zeitung* [online], 19 August 2017. Available at: http://www.faz.net/aktuell/feuilleton/debatten/islamgelehrter-terrorismus-und-islam-haengen-zusammen-15157757.html. English translation is available at: http://www.baytarrahmah.org/media/2017/FAZ_A-Conversation-with-Kyai-Haji-Yahya-Cholil-Staquf_08-19-17.pdf [accessed 10 October 2018].

Staquf, Y. C. (2018). 'The Enduring Threat of Islamist Politics in 'Reformasi' (post-Soeharto) Indonesia and Its Global Ramifications'. *The Jakarta Post* [online], 22 May 2018. Available at: http://www.libforall.org/lfa/media/2018/jakarta-post_enduring-threat-of-Islamist-politics-in-reformasi-Indonesia-and-its-global-ramifications_05-22-18.pdf [accessed 10 Octobero 2018].

Taylor, C. H. (2018). 'Maneuver in the Narrative Space: Lessons from Islam Nusantara'. *Strategic Review: The Indonesian Journal of Leadership, Policy, and World Affairs*, 8(1), pp. 36-51.

Van Bruinessen, M. (2013). *Contemporary Developments in Indonesian Islam: Explaining the "Conservative Turn"*. Singapoure: ISEAS.

Van Bruinessen. M. (2018). *Indonesian Muslims in a Global World: Westernisation, Arabisation, and Indigenous Responses. The RSIS Working Paper.* Singapore: S. Rajaratnam School of International Studies.

Wainscott, A.M. (2017). *Bureaucratizing Islam: Morocco and the War on Terror.* Cambridge: Cambridge University Press.

Wiktorowicz, Q. (2006). 'The Anatomy of the Salafi Movement'. *Studies in Conflict & Terrorism*, 29, pp. 207–239.

Zeghal, M. (2007) 'The "Recentering" of Religious Knowledge and Discourse: The Case of al-Azhar in Twentieth-Century Egypt', in R. Hefner and M. Q. Zaman (eds), *Schooling Islam: The Culture and Politics of Modern Muslim Education.* Princeton, NJ: Princeton Univ. Press, 2007), pp.105–130.

Concluding Considerations

Johan Leman and Serafettin Pektas

The chapters in this volume have attempted to give a picture of the various aspects of militant jihadism as of today and have discussed its probable future in and around Europe. We are still far from suggesting clear projections. There are some critical unknown factors that may have a huge impact on future developments. We do not know, for instance, whether IS and al-Qaeda will cooperate one day in the future, or even will become one organisation. Today this seems unlikely, given that there are strategic differences between the two movements and that there are also personal aversions between their respective leaders. Nevertheless, leaderships may change and may transform the organisations. Whatever happens, militant jihadism will not disappear in the foreseeable future and we still cannot confidently predict in which direction it will transform. Following the analyses provided by our contributors, let us put some elements together of what we know so far.

Instant Jihadism

Those who have analysed the jihadisation process since the official emergence of IS's territorial Caliphate in July 2014 have very often used step by step models to explain the process. These models attempted to explain how young people between 14 and 25 years old have ended up with militant jihadism as a gradual process: how they adhered to a minority branch in Salafism, namely the *al-salafiyya al-jihadiyya*, why its *takfiri* perspective was so attractive to them, how they have been moved by tailor-made, intense propaganda, how this has led to radicalisation and finally turned them into jihadist fighters. While studying the case of 20 youngsters from the first generation of Muslims who left Belgium for Syria between 2012 and 2015, Leman (2016), for instance, mostly referred to gradual conversion theories to explain how these young people decided to reconstruct the rest of their lives in such a dramatically different way from their peers. In the event of suicide attacks, one could similarly explain how these people have gradually decided to create a clean *umma* free from *jahiliyya* (moral savagery), and how this decision has step by step led them to further their expectation to survive with such a clean identity in the perception of co-Muslims in the physical world as well as in Paradise (Asad, 2018:77-79).

Such a gradual process is, however, no longer present among current "lone wolves" and other people who have recently become jihadists. The profiles of recent lone wolves tell that they no longer follow this step by step ideological path in adopting their new identity. It is "instant jihadisation" which seems to be on the horizon. The frustration and aversion against Western society is determinant and one or two simple jihadist references to the Quran or *hadith* are sometimes enough to give it an empowering content in a minimum of time.

Global Yet Fragmented Jihadism

Global militant jihadism started with the Afghan war in the 1980s and later with the Kashmir crisis. It subsequently advanced with the creation of al-Qaeda. In Europe, it started in 1995 with metro bombings in Paris organised by Algerian-French militant Khalid Kelkal and developed further since then. The Syria crisis and emergence of IS brought unprecedented global popularity. At the beginning of the Syrian crisis, the jihadist call stimulated many young Muslims to leave their country for humanitarian reasons to support suffering Muslims in their fight against Bashar al-Assad. At the same time, an iconic apocalyptic dimension came to the scene: some *hadith* already prophesied that Sham (the Levant) would trigger events that would finally bring about the end of time. This added a significant apocalyptic glamour to the global jihad.

The Sham-caliphate turned out to be a deceiving and cruelly inhumane experience, and many Muslims will surely not engage in such a new experiment in the next few years. However, what one may learn from the recent past is that if a Muslim country feels itself to be under attack, there are surely young Muslims worldwide who are disposed to show their loyalty by fighting for it with the locals. If the situation has something iconic, such as the Sham's supposedly apocalyptic role in the last case, the pull factor will become even stronger.

In the meantime, we will most likely witness a fragmented process where Islamist cells will be militantly active in various countries, spread over the Caucasus, Central Asia (possibly due to the Uyghurs' persecution by the "atheist" China), South-East Asia, Central and North-West Africa, or again in the Near East (since in Iraq the situation is not very promising). Some pull factors for jihadist engagement outside Europe will continue to exist in the coming decades. Meanwhile, Libya, as analysed in this volume, will remain for some time a highly important country for the future of militant jihadism. As a "failing state" and a highly convenient door to Europe, Libya provides a lot of potential for future jihadist engagement.

The Unreturned from the Levant

The number of IS militants or sympathisers detained in Iraq or in Kurdish and Turkish prisons in Syria is estimated to be still quite high. The numbers vary according to different sources. But there are still a minimum of some 20,000 fighters, detained or not, believed to be in Syria and Iraq. What will happen to them? Will they seek revenge if they manage to be released? Will these people opt for normal life or will they opt to continue their crimes there? It is plausible to predict that many of them will keep their ideology. But how will this happen? Will they adhere to local jihadist cells or will they look for new jihadist opportunities once the jihadist leadership proposes some alternatives? How about those who will disengage? Will their disengagement mean total abandonment or will they just give up active militancy in the field but continue to inspire others as veteran jihadists? What about the children of the unreturned? Will they continue the job that their parents were unable to finish or will they be able to create a different and brighter future from that of their parents.[1] These are questions to be answered to give a realist picture of future militant jihadism.

Cyber and Digital Opportunities

Digital technologies, the Internet and social media are developing at an unprecedented pace. They have already challenged the conventional borders, be they territorial, political, social or cultural. More importantly they have created a cyber space where an unbridled exchange of virtual content has been made possible. Jihadist terrorists are among the most interested beneficiaries of this huge virtual opportunity. Many observers agree that the worldwide appeal of IS brand jihadism among younger generation was closely related to its professional use of digital technologies and cyber space. Bin Ladin occasionally recorded VHS videos to disseminate his message and expected them to be broadcast by a TV channel. Al-Baghdadi, instead, favoured creating aggressive social media teams, issuing online magazines in several languages, creating highly professional audio-visual jihadist contents and investing in other cyber outreach opportunities. There has been a clear decline in IS online content since it lost Raqqa in Summer 2017. Many analysts, however, today talk of a possible "virtual caliphate" after the demise of IS's territorial caliphate. Furthermore, dark web and encrypted online platforms may secure jihadist militant activity besides wider outreach. Alkhouri already gave us a picture of such cyber opportunities. Cyber jihadism will thus remain a critical concern in the future. We can identify at least two important fields where militant jihadism will be employing new digital and online technology the most: the incitement of lone actor attacks in the West, mainly in Europe, including Russia, and promoting attacks with drones or with simple, improvised yet damaging weapons.

The most recent "post-Caliphate" jihadist terrorist attacks were carried out by the "lone wolves." Cyber space is a good source of these terrorists not only for inspiration but also in organising an attack and in preparing the weapons. This trend seems to be continuing into the foreseeable future. Moreover, it is possible that the terrorists may learn or buy more know-how from non-jihadist cyber criminals and take over their *modus operandi*. In considering the future harm of militant jihadism, security authorities should try better to understand the tactics, techniques and procedures that these online terror actors are more likely to employ.

At this point, we should think of the possible role that *Emni*, the IS's former intelligence apparatus, may play for the jihadist use of cyber techniques; and for encouraging and backing lone wolf attacks. It is already known that some *Emni* people managed to escape from Raqqa before it was liberated. Intelligence sources suspect that some of its units are reorganising themselves in Europe. Whether these units will be able to function effectively and if so to what extent they will prioritise use of cyber space and technology is currently unpredictable. This should urge European intelligence and security services to become better informed about the functioning of the possible *Emni* cells and their priorities in the continent.

Jihadist militants are adaptive, smart and creative people. New digital technology brings further imagination and flexibility. It would then be reasonable to predict that they would be thinking of attacking with unconventional weapons enabled by this new technology. Weaponised drones are such an option. They can cause a lot of damage and casualties to such targets as outdoor events or critical energy facilities. Explosive drones make these targets physically more vulnerable. Similarly, terrorists may continue to attack with different types of IED (improvised explosive devices). They had used mass shooting weapons in the suicide attacks in the Bataclan Theatre in Paris in November 2015. It was during the heydays of IS. The Manchester Arena suicide attacker, rather, detonated an improvised home-made bomb in May 2017, a few months before the fall of Raqqa. It is highly probable that the jihadist terrorists will prefer IEDs in future attacks instead of conventional shooting weapons, given the increasing surveillance of weapon use and trafficking after the attacks shocked Europe in recent years. The al-Qaeda *mujahidin* were trained to hijack planes or to skilfully attack a US military base. The post-Caliphate IS *mujahidin* will most probably be trained in designing, developing and using small-scale weaponised drones or simple yet destructive weapons with the support of new technology.

Women and Children in Future Jihad

The place of women in future developments of jihadism merits reflection. One may expect feminisation of jihadism not only in attacks or in inspiration for them but perhaps more importantly in the socialisation of future generations. As illustrated in Chapter 5, women may have both passive and active roles in Islamist jihadism. For ideological reasons, most investment will probably go to passive roles for women. However, it is clear that there is still more potential among women as "critical mass" to be engaged for jihadist actions. Recent trends verify this possibility. In 2016, women already represented 25% of the arrested jihadists in the European Union. In 2017, 23% of the total terrorist plots in the European Union involved women.

Education is often regarded as a passive role that jihadist women are expected to be (or already were) mostly involved in. Nevertheless, we would be misled if we continue to consider it as a mere passive role. Education is an efficient and sustainable way of indoctrination and it will become an important new priority for future militant jihadism. It is so even today when compared to the case in the past (e.g. Ingram, 2018).

This brings us to what jihadism may try to do with children. As well illustrated in Perešin's analysis, jihadists will not disregard the future potential that children and teenagers could bring to future jihadism. We can expect that they will try to lower the age for candidate jihadists and to achieve that, they will invest in education, in the internet and if possible also in some places outside the schools where they hope to create new "sanctuaries" in the future to reach out, indoctrinate and recruit. Policy makers should thus clearly understand that working with children and youngsters in urban neighbourhoods merits much more care than is currently the case. In reflecting upon the future, we should not, on the other hand, miss the opportunity that women could significantly contribute to the fight against and to the prevention of radicalisation.

Returnees

There is a widespread assumption that returned foreign fighters will seek to carry out terrorist attacks at any condition and in a more determined way. Many experts, however, think that there are different options available for them. There will certainly be those who wish to stay as hardliners. Nonetheless, there will also be those who will choose to disengage or simply stay passive because of advancing age or disillusionment or because they will change their minds. Some will, instead, be wishing to turn back and keep fighting again against the concrete "oppressors." Some may also think of a career move. Therefore, we will be seeing different scenarios with regard to the future decisions of "returnees." Considering this fact, Teun van Dongen predicts a low probability / high impact scenario about future terrorist attacks by the returnees. We will see whether his prediction comes true. If his projection is realised and the attacks are quite rare, when they do occur, as he foresees, they may cause many casualties. This may again paralyse politicians to develop proactive policies. In such a scenario, not only the focus of the debate will shift but also the determination to take effective yet long-term measures will be risked. The recent rise of anti-immigrant populist policies and right-wing extremism in Europe already confirms this possibility. Such a scenario will not, however, hinder but most probably will be conducive to the existence of the breeding ground.

Western Prisons

Closer observation reveals that criminal behaviours among young people already comprise an implicit form of radicalisation. What happens in prison is that, if prison life is not immediately oriented to reintegration into society, this implicit form of radicalisation may become confirmed and supported by jihadisation. The seemingly "noble" content of jihadism can activate an instant or gradual jihadism and this may feed and justify aggressive feelings vis-à-vis the society. A high risk in prisons is also that the prisoners may find opportunities to socialise into a normalisation process of criminal behaviour and criminal networking. How to cope with it will be an important challenge for an effective prevention policy in the future.

Terrorist Blind Spots

Safe havens have always played an important role in the organisation of criminal groups such as mafias. That they may also exist in democratic and liberal countries is proven. The role of the small but very dangerous "Molenbeek network" in the Paris and Brussels attacks is perhaps the most impressive example of this possibility. Molenbeek is just ten minutes away by metro from the headquarters of the European Union. May it happen again? If jihadists in the future again have a chance to do it, why should they not try to organise it again?

The Molenbeek case hopefully teaches us two critical lessons. First jihadism in an urban setting functions more like a mafia rather than a conventional terrorist organisation. Hence, past achievements against mafia can inform counter strategies against future urban jihadist threats. Secondly, jihadist recruiters start to collect their poisonous fruits after an incubation period of approximately seven or even more years before their "terrorist urban sanctuary" comes to the surface. A retrospective analysis of the Molenbeek case, for instance, tells us today that Ayaachi Bassam, an important jihadi preacher, installed himself in the district in 1992 and created its jihadist mosque only five years later, in 1997. His activities became visible only in 1999. He guided the marriage of Dahmane 'Abd al-Sattar who on 9 September 2001 killed Ahmad Shah Mas'ud, the leader of the Northern Alliance and the only remaining opposition commander against the Taliban in Afghanistan. Similarly, Khaled Zerkani, the most efficient recruiter in Molenbeek, arrived in 2002, remained invisible for about 9 years, and began recruiting youngsters for Somalia and Syria only from 2011 onwards. Henceforth, the authorities in democratic societies should obviously invest in positive social networking and positive social control among their citizens and in efficient intelligence infiltration where there are signs of the possible creation of "blind spots" or where they know that there are dysfunctional institutions.

Financing Jihadist Terrorism

Money is important for any terrorist activity and jihadist terrorists will be seeking new financial sources in the future. They will most probably approach to financial reserves in the bank sector deposited so far, to some charity organisations, to trade of stolen pieces of art, and some other criminal activities. Some Belgian judicial files, as discussed in Chapter 9, demonstrate that human trafficking and migrant smuggling already permit creation of financial capital, networking, communication and transfer of jihadists in the past. This clearly suggests that in the future jihadists will try to localise such criminal money, earned by smuggling, in local cells in a country of destination or in transit countries as well as in the centre, wherever it may be in future. Financing terrorism is certainly not the main objective of migrant smuggling; but unfortunately this criminal business may create new opportunities for some jihadist financing. Along with other difficulties and challenges brought by migrant smuggling, the authorities should consider this aspect when tackling militant jihadism.

Efficiency of Counter Theologies

The debate among Muslims about the religious credentials of Islamist jihadism will continue and this will have consequences. It is, however, not the debate itself alone that will have an impact on future jihadist transformation. Who frame the counter-theologies and how they frame will perhaps be more decisive. Today, the counter-religious arguments and strategy are strongly nationally tailored. They reflect the political and institutional concerns of the religious authority in question. No doubt there is much more care and cooperation than before among religious and political leaders in Muslim countries to prevent violent jihadism and religious extremism. In practice, this usually manifests itself as a particular collaboration between political and religious authorities. However, this collaboration in reality takes place as a negotiation, competition or sometimes a clash over the meaning of Islamic (Sunni) authority and the governance of the religious field. Furthermore, it has the potential to bring a credibility challenge to the religious institutions. If not managed properly, this challenge may in future cause (more) disillusionment about their moral authority, which will undermine, in turn, the effectiveness of their counter-theologies no matter how superbly they are designed. The success of the (Sunni) religious strategy against militant jihadism, on the other hand, will depend less on its ability for argumentative and conservative engagement with the jihadist discourse on authenticity and purity. It will, rather, depend more on its ability for a critical and creative engagement with modern, progressive and/or reformist discourse on such issues as democracy, social and gender justice, pluralism and citizenship.

A Systemic Analysis

When we put together the dynamics discussed above in a systemic approach, we can identify two fundamental axes that will support the survival of violent jihadism. First, the existence of a "pull country" in the Islamic world that can attract some Muslims from outside who feel ready to go there in order to defend Islamic interests (for humanitarian or other reasons) and to ease the suffering of this part of the "Islamic body." Secondly, the persistence of simplistic, exclusivist and pragmatic Salafist interpretations that legitimise such violent jihadist militancy, expressed in one liner form or in more complex arguments, online or offline, in prisons or in urban blind spots, by veteran jihadist recruiters or by jihadist women indoctrinating their children with anti-Westernism. In the meantime, we will be seeing the lone wolf attacks from time to time. They may exist for a long period but they are more likely to be only functional in the sense that they feed Islamophobia, inter-ethnic, inter-religious and inter-sectarian tensions in a society. Possible actions of *Emni* cells, which probably still exist, are an unknown factor.

On 29 April 2019, *al-Furqan,* one of IS's media outlets, released a video in which al-Baghdadi is viewed alive and speaking to his aides. The video came shortly after the fall of Baghouz, the IS's last siginifcant territory in Syria. This was also the first visual appearance of al-Baghdadi since he first publicly appeared at Mosul's Grand Mosque al-Nuri where he declared his "Caliphate" in 2014. In the video, he encourages his followers to keep fighting, to "harm the enemy" through a long "battle of attrition" and to seek revenge for the group's losses. Previously, on 22 August 2018, al-Furqan had released an audio message where al-Baghdadi reportedly gave a long speech on the occasion of the Muslim celebration of *'id al-adha*. In this record, he addresses the "allies of the caliphate" anywhere and invites them to continue the fight against "seculars, liberals, godless people and unfaithful ones." He advises them to use explosives and cars in attacks. His call found an immediate echo. The day after its release, a jihadist sympathiser killed two people and injured a third one with a knife in Paris. *Amaq*, the IS's news agency, claimed the attack. With such appearances, the jihadist leader, on the one hand, gives the message that he wants to keep taking the stage. The sporadic attacks by lone wolves carried out with less complex instruments that may kill only a few people will provide this visibility. On the other hand, he gives a second and more important message: until IS finds a suitable place for the new "caliphate" in future – probably in the Caucasus, in Northern, Western or Central Africa or in East Asia – IS will continue a fragmented and glocalised jihadism.

To what extent Europe and the West will be affected by these messages will depend on the extent of the Western military engagement in these non-Western regions, on the extent of their ability to get young Muslims to feel that they are included and accepted in the West and on the extent of how the jihadist ideas, messages and images keep flowing at both cyber and real social space. It will be geopolitics, the presence or absence of successful social inclusion and intra-Islamic debate that will determine if violent jihadism has a future or not in the West.

Notes

1 For a recent analysis of this question see Renard and Coolsaet, 2018.

References

Asad, T. (2018). *Attentats-suicide: Questions anthropologiques*. Brussels: Zones Sensibles.

Ingram, K. (2018). *IS's Appeal to Western Women: Policy Implications*. The Hague: International Centre for Counter-Terrorism.

Leman, J. (2016). 'L'évolution vers un djihadisme militant, militaire', in *Justice & Sécurité / Justitie & Veiligheid*, 4:1-15.

Renard, T. and Coolsaet. R. (2018). *Children in the Levant: Insights from Belgium on the Dilemmas of Repatriation and the Challenges of Reintegration*. Security Policy Brief No.98. Brussels: Egmont Institute.

About the Authors

Mohamed-Ali Adraoui is currently a Marie Sklodowska Curie Fellow at the Georgetown University School of Foreign Service and a Visiting Scholar at the Harvard Weatherhead Center for International Affairs in the US. He is also a member of the Paris-based IPEV – The International Panel on Exiting Violence. He holds a PhD degree in Political Science from the Paris Institute of Political Studies (Science Po). He was Max Weber Fellow at the European University Institute in Italy and a Senior Fellow at the National University of Singapore. His research deals with contemporary international relations, the Islamic world, political Islam, Salafism, sectarianism and the US foreign policy towards Islamism.

Laith Alkhouri is the Co-founder and the Senior Director of Advanced Intelligence Solutions at Flashpoint, a business risk intelligence company based in New York. He heads the company's advanced and customised intelligence solutions for a range of government and commercial clients. He holds an MS degree in International Affairs at The New School University with a concentration on International Conflict and Security and a BA degree in Political Science from Manhattanville College. He has conducted primary source research into terrorist groups and their supporters, focusing on their cyber footprints. He has presented his findings to audiences at many US governmental and security institutions, including the US State Department, Department of Justice, and the Council on Foreign Relations. As an expert on terrorist groups' operational capabilities and counter extremism, he is also a frequent commentator for national and international media. He is a member of the New York Analyst Roundtable (NYAR) – a private network of security analysts – and an executive advisor for The MPOWER Project – an NGO focused on preventing violent extremism.

Nadim Houry is the Executive Director of the Arab Reform Initiative (ARI). Prior to joining the ARI, he was Human Rights Watch's director of its Terrorism and Counterterrorism Program and oversaw the organisation's response to violations committed by extremist groups as well as abuses committed in the name of counter-terrorism. He worked for over a decade in the Middle East where he was the Director of Human Rights Watch's Beirut office and the deputy director of its Middle East programme. He previously served as deputy counsel for the Volcker Commission, where he spent more than a year conducting fact-finding missions in the Middle East as part of the United Nations' corruption inquiry into the Oil-for-Food Programme. An attorney by training, Nadim previously worked as a lawyer in New York.

Adolfo Gatti is a Senior Intelligence Analyst at Lumina Analytics in Florida where he leverages Artificial Intelligence and machine learning processes to analyse terrorism, international security, as well as physical and political risk. He obtained his MA in Law and Diplomacy at The Fletcher School at Tufts University in Massachusetts, where he specialised in international security and Europe. Prior to his graduate school, he worked at the Harvard Kennedy School's Belfer Center as a researcher for Senior Fellow Mr. Kevin Rudd, the former Prime Minister and Foreign Minister of Australia. He holds a BA degree in Economics and International Relations from Boston University in 2013.

Stef Janssens is an analyst on human trafficking and migrant smuggling at MYRIA, the Belgian Federal Migration Centre. He is also an associate member of the Leuven Institute of Criminology, KU Leuven, Belgium. He has acted as an advisor to Belgian parliamentary commissions on organised crime and trafficking and to the US Embassy in Belgium. With Prof. Leman, Janssens co-authored several articles in specialised journals and a book on migrant smuggling and human trafficking in Europe.

Johan Leman is an Emeritus Professor in Social and Cultural Anthropology at KU Leuven. He holds a PhD degree in Social and Cultural Anthropology, an MA in Eastern Philology and History, Doctorates in Philosophy and in Theology, all at KU Leuven. He is the President of FOYER, a regional minorities centre in Brussels. He is the former Chief of Cabinet of the Royal Commissioner for Migrant Policy in Belgium and the former Director of the Federal Centre for Equal Opportunities and Opposition Against Racism. He is also the former and first chair holder of KU Leuven's Gülen Chair for Intercultural Studies. His fields of research include religion in migration, migration and integration policies, human trafficking and migrant smuggling, and Sicily.

ABOUT THE AUTHORS

Serafettin Pektas holds a PhD degree in Arabic and Islamic Studies from KU Leuven and was a Post-doctorate Fellow at the Research Institute for Religions, Spirituality, Culture and Society at UC Louvain, Belgium. He studied theology and interfaith dialogue at the Pontifical Gregorian University in Rome. He also holds an MA degree in Sociology from Boğaziçi University, Istanbul. He has been involved in various NGO work on intercultural and interfaith dialogue in and around Brussels. His research interests include Islamic extremism, contemporary Muslim thought, comparative theology and interfaith engagement.

Anita Perešin holds a PhD degree from the University of Zagreb with a dissertation on the transformation of al-Qaeda and the consequent security sector reform after 9/11. She got her MS degree with a thesis on modern mass media and the new terrorism paradigm. She is currently Senior Adviser in the Office of the National Security Council of the Republic of Croatia. She has had many duties related to national security and countering terrorism within the Croatian security sector. She has extensively published on national and global security. She is a visiting lecturer at different universities and international schools abroad on national security and countering terrorism. Her current research interests focus on the role of Western women in IS and the use of children for IS external operations.

Teun van Dongen is an independent national and international security expert. He holds a PhD degree from Leiden University, which he gained by writing a doctoral dissertation on counter-terrorism effectiveness. He worked as a policy analyst at The Hague Centre for Strategic Studies (HCSS), a think tank in the Netherlands, and he has been a lecturer in Comprehensive Security at the Inholland University of Applied Sciences. During his period at HCSS, he has been seconded to the Dutch National Coordinator for Security and Counterterrorism. Teun regularly writes for academic journals, newspapers and international affairs magazines.

Arturo Varvelli is Senior Research Fellow at ISPI-Italian Institute for International Political Studies and Co-Head of ISPI's MENA Centre. He is also a lecturer at IULM University in Milan and Visiting Fellow at the European Foundation for Democracy (EFD) in Brussels. He holds a PhD degree in International History at the University of Milan, where he worked as a lecturer. He has served on research projects commissioned by the research office of the

Italian Chamber of Representatives and Senate, the Italian Ministry of Foreign Affairs as well as by the European Parliament and Commission. His research interests include Libya, Italian foreign policy in the MENA region and jihadist groups in North Africa.

www.ingramcontent.com/pod-product-compliance
Ingram Content Group UK Ltd.
Pitfield, Milton Keynes, MK11 3LW, UK
UKHW021835140426
5217IPUK00021B/1461